Intonation in the Grammar of English

Equinox Textbooks and Surveys in Linguistics
Series Editor: Robin Fawcett, Cardiff University

Published titles in the series:

Analysing Casual Conversation
Suzanne Eggins & Diana Slade

Multimodal Transcription and Text Analysis
Anthony Baldry & Paul J. Thibault

Meaning-Centered Grammar: An Introductory Text
Craig Hancock

Genre Relations: Mapping Culture
J.R. Martin and David Rose

Language in Psychiatry: A Handbook of Clinical Practice
Jonathan Fine

The Power of Language: How Discourse Influences Society
Lynne Young and Brigid Fitzgerald

The Western Classical Tradition in Linguistics
Keith Allan

Intonation in the Grammar of English
M.A.K. Halliday & William S. Greaves

Forthcoming:

An Introduction to English Sentence Structure: Clauses, Markers, Missing Elements
Jon Jonz

Text Linguistics: The How and Why of Meaning
Jonathan Webster

Teaching Multimodal Literacy in English as a Foreign Language
Len Unsworth, Viviane Heberle and Robyn Louise Bush

Learning to Write/Reading to Learn: Scaffolding Democracy in Literacy Classrooms
J. R. Martin and David Rose

Multimodal Corpus-Based Approaches to Website Analysis
Anthony Baldry and Kay O'Halloran

Intonation in the Grammar of English

by

M. A. K. Halliday and William S. Greaves

equinox

LONDON   OAKVILLE

Published by

Equinox Publishing Ltd

UK: Unit 6, The Village, 101 Amies St, London, SW11 2JW
USA: DBBC, 28 Main Street, Oakville, CT 06779

www.equinoxpub.com

Intonation in the Grammar of English
First published 2008

British Library Cataloguing-in-Publication Data
A catalogue record for this book is available from the British Library.

ISBN-13: 978-1-904768-14-2   (hardback)
ISBN-13: 978-1-904768-15-9   (paperback)

Library of Congress Cataloging-in-Publication Data
Halliday, M. A. K. (Michael Alexander Kirkwood), 1925-
  Intonation in the grammar of English / M.A.K. Halliday and William S. Greaves.
      p. cm. -- (Equinox textbooks and surveys in linguistics)
  Includes bibliographical references and index.
  ISBN-13: 978-1-904768-14-2
  ISBN-10: 1-904768-14-8
  ISBN-13: 978-1-904768-15-9 (pbk.)
  ISBN-10: 1-904768-15-6 (pbk.)
  1. English language--Intonation. 2. English language--Grammar. 3. English language--Accents and accentuation. 4. Oral communication. I. Greaves, William S. II. Title. III. Series.
  PE1139.5.H25 2006
  421'.5--dc22
                       2006010518

Typeset by Catchline, Milton Keynes (www.catchline.com)
Printed and bound in Great Britain by CPI Antony Rowe, Chippenham, Wiltshire

Contents

PART II: INTONATION AND MEANING

PART III: ANALYSIS GUIDE WITH DETAILED COMMENTARY

Acknowledgements

This book has been a long time in the making, and we owe much to the many colleagues and others who have encouraged us along the way. In particular, we would like to thank all those who have made available to us the texts that we have used to present and illustrate our analysis:

Dr Hilary Nesi for the 'Pipeline' dialogue;

Mary Lou Finlay and the Canadian Broadcasting Company for the 'Prince Lazarus' interview;

Anne Thwaite and Edith Cowan University for permission to reproduce video and other material from *Language in Contexts*;

Ruqaiya Hasan for 'Sit up straight!', an extract from her data collected for the analysis of semantic variation;

Christian Matthiessen for 'The Wallace Line' from *Hailstorm*;

Elizabeth Cooper-Kuhlen for 'You've got to have a system';

Melissa Groo and *The Elephant Listening Project* at Cornell University for an example of a forest elephant (loxodonta cyclotis).

We also wish to express our gratitude to David Benson, for help with technical details of acoustic analysis, and to Ashley Watkins, for help with the manuscript, especially preparation of the figures. To others that we have failed to acknowledge here we offer our sincere apologies. Our thanks also to our publishers, and to all those who have enquired after the progress of the book, for their patience and continued support.

Using the CD

The CD which accompanies this book contains a digital version of the text, which you can open on your computer, together with the sound files used in the book and some additional material which you can analyse yourself.

System requirements

The materials on this CD should work on any computer platform – Windows, Macintosh or Linux – which is capable of playing sound, either through headphones or via a loudspeaker (most newer computers are suitable) and which has a multimedia-capable PDF viewer installed (see below for suitable sources of software if this is not already installed).

CD Contents

- Halliday-Greaves (a PDF file)
- Page 6 Quiz (a PDF file)
- Links (a folder of soundfiles)
- Thwaite (A folder of videos, soundfiles and transcripts)

Using the digital version of the book

The file called 'Halliday-Greaves' contains the entire book in PDF format. There is a crucial difference between the digital version and the paper version. Both versions contain numerous sound icons (the word PLAY plus a small image of a speaker). In the book these are just ink on paper, but in the CD version you can click on the icons to hear the sounds we are writing about (and if your cursor hovers over the icon you will see the name of the actual soundfile which is in the *Links* folder on this CD)

We would strongly recommend that you have the CD running in your computer at the same time that you are reading the text, and that you play the sounds whenever you come to a sound icon.

If you are like most people — certainly including the authors of this book — you will require a certain amount of time to set things up so that you can view the book on the screen as you want, and can play the sounds. If you avoid going through this process, you will skip one of the most important features of the book — and will be completely unaware of what you are missing.

So we suggest that you try it now. With good luck it will be a simple matter – you may even find that your computer is already suitably equipped and everything will work when you first open the file and click on a sound icon. Here are the basic steps:

1) You will need a PDF viewer software installed on your computer which can play multimedia. The free *Adobe Reader* is suitable and can be downloaded for

all computer platforms from http://www.adobe.com. For windows only, the free *Foxit Reader*, which is a much smaller program than *Adobe Reader*, can be downloaded from http://www.foxitsoftware.com.

2) Load the CD ROM into your computer and navigate to it.

3) Double-click on the Halliday-Greaves PDF file to launch and view it.

4) Close the paper version of your book and start reading from the CD — right here in 'Using the CD'.

5) Here is a sound icon to try out: PLAY◀. Click on it. If you hear a sentence, all is well. Your computer will work the same way with the other 280 or so icons in the book.

6) If you hear nothing, consult an expert. Someone with experience in working with sound will be able to sort such problems out quickly, and after that's done all you will have to do is click.

7) You can set the viewing preferences in your PDF reader to adjust how the book looks on the screen. For example, if your screen is large enough, you might want to set the preferences to show two pages side by side – so each double-page spread is visible. If so, make sure you also set the option to 'display cover page', which will ensure that the right and left pages on the screen are as you see them in the printed book.

8) You can also use your PDF reader to zoom in on particular figures, or to jump to different parts of the book, or (using it like an index) to search the contents of the book.

9) On most computers, the PDF will open automatically displaying two pages at a time. It should also display 'bookmarks' on the left-hand side which you can click to go straight to any part of the book. You can change these settings, if they do not suit your own situation, within your PDF reader after the PDF has opened.

Note

When you first click on a sound icon, your PDF Reader will probably alert you to the fact that the program is trying to play a sound file, and will ask your permission to do so. If you are given an option to 'Use current settings', or to 'Add document to trusted list' or similar, you should click 'yes'. This should stop the program from asking the question in future when it tries to play the files on this CD.

The *Links* folder

In addition to the 'live' version of *Intonation in the Grammar of English*, the CD contains *Links*, a folder containing the soundfiles themselves. Pausing the cursor above any of the sound icons in the book reveals the precise name of the sound in the *Links* folder.

This should allow you to identify the source file, should you want to explore it further in Praat (see below).

The *Thwaite* folder

The CD also contains the video files, soundfiles and transcripts from Thwaite, A. (1997) *Language in Contexts*. These will allow you to explore a range of different registers of English. If you want to view the movies on a PC, you may find you need to install QuickTime software. This is free, and can be downloaded from

http://www.apple.com/quicktime/download/.

Praat

Praat is the computer program we used to analyse the sounds used in this book. It is free, and widely used by linguists and phoneticians to analyse speech sounds (its name means 'talk' in Dutch). If you want to explore the sound files further yourself (and we recommend that you do so), then download and install Praat from

http://www.fon.hum.uva.nl/praat/.

If you need help in installing Praat there is a great deal available on the web. A Google search for 'install praat', for example, turns up: 'This handout tells you how to download and install Praat on your own computer'.

Any of the sound files contained in the *Links* folder can be viewed and analysed using Praat.

Part I

The study of speech sound

1 Locating and thinking about speech sound

1.1 Speech sound: locating the phenomenon

Sound, the medium that makes human speech transmission possible, impinges on us from birth onwards — and probably from before that. Brain scientists like Gerald Edelman and Merlin Donald have recently explored the response each unique individual brain has to such stimulation during the explosive, jungle like formation of new neurons and the virtually countless synaptic connections that network them into the system we call human intelligence. Both authors are particularly interested in the interplay between cultural context — in particular culturally transmitted semiotic systems — and the evolution of the individual brain configuration and consequent mental processing capacity which each of us develops. For Edelman, a central concept is the more or less random overproduction of connections during this phase, and the 'pruning' of these through a process of natural selection: particular connections which work as the brain organizes itself are exercised and strengthened; those which do not happen to provide a useful link in the interplay between external stimulation and internal processing perish for lack of exercise.

Sound participates in this process in two ways: first as a 'low level' input — pure sensory data, which must be distinguished from other perceptions such as sight, touch and smell, and which must be qualitatively and quantitatively distinguished in terms of uniqueness (for example Mother's voice as opposed to Sister's), of loudness, of temporal organization, and so forth. Many of the neuronal connections selected in or selected out because of the degree to which they prove useful in the development of such processing will be located in the hippocampus, and in lobes which evolve particularly to process these aspects of sound; but the same selective process will take place as information dealt with in these areas is successfully transmitted to other areas of the brain which make use of this information.

Sound also participates as 'high level' input. In a human social environment, a crucial factor in 'pruning' in the higher regions of the brain is that the sound impinging on the infant and developing child is in one respect quite unnatural: it is coded sound, carrying the signals of human language, a system external to the biological organism, which has co-evolved with the human brain during the incredibly brief (in evolutionary terms) period between prelinguistic hominids and articulate modern homo sapiens.

Linguistically coded sound and the human brain which processes it are entirely distinct phenomena: language is communal — a behaviour which exists between human beings; brains are unique: a configuration of neural 'wiring'. Language is transmitted over the whole existence of a culture, through the historical continuity of human interaction. The brain, on the other hand, is a physical phenomenon uniquely created by each individual in response to stimulation, including, importantly, culturally patterned stimulation. Its overall structure is, to be sure, determined by the gene pool of the species, but this genetic coding determines only that the physical structures of our brains are roughly similar. The actual neural networking in which our intelligence is constituted is not laid down through genetic determination, but rather evolves dynamically: as synaptic connections are established by chance and are then 'selected' through use, the process of 'Neural Darwinism' described in, for example, Edelman and Tononi (2000) or Ellis and Toronchuk (2005). And in the higher regions of the brain one of the most important such uses is response to the stimulus of socially coded input signals — human speech sound in particular.

But although our individual brains and our social codes of communication are of different orders of reality, they are intertwined in the closest of symbiotic relationships both in homo sapiens' evolution as a species and in the unique development of every individual neural network.

Social interaction is clearly as beneficial to human survival as any physical trait: the group that hunts better, makes war more effectively, combats disease more efficiently — this is the group that will survive. Semiosis, the tool that enables humankind to gain intellectual, and therefore material, control of nature, is what has allowed a rather weak and defenceless kind of animal to reach a state of evolutionary dominance in which it is, arguably, driving other species off the planet at a rate equalled only by the greatest periods of mass extinction.

And the dialectical relationship between language and social evolution is clear: as patterns of human interpersonal interaction and the development of fields of coopera- tive productivity become more complex, pressure is put upon the communal language system to expand to accommodate such development — and each expansion of a group's language provides the group with increased symbolic power with which it can expand the richness of its interpersonal relationships and material productivity, and hence of its ability to survive.

Clearly a similar dialectic takes place in the process of biological evolution. Complex neural networking is what makes language processing possible. The social and linguistic activity of an individual's human environment is certainly a contributing factor in personal survival in difficult times, and someone who can manipulate the common symbolic medium more effectively is at an advantage. Given two individuals in the same social environment, the one genetically disposed to make the greater number of neural connections, and to prune them more sensitively in terms of the coded stimuli the organism receives, is the one who is the more likely to survive. The social evolution of mankind and the physical evolution of homo sapiens are inextricably bound together.

Any language is a single seamless system: it is one thing, which can best be thought about, however, in four different ways — meanings the language system can create, lexicogrammatical patterns which give form to those meanings, phonological patterns which enable the communication of those forms, and phonetic substance through which the phonological patterns are uttered and perceived. For the newborn, sound can not yet be perceived as a coded signal: the neural networks are not yet in place, and the requisite social experience is totally lacking. The infant is assaulted on all sides by sound, but a great deal of social and neural development will have to take place before the organism can turn the coded sound which surrounds it into a component of symbolic exchange. This book is concerned with one language — English — at all four strata; but our particular aim is to show the place that one particular kind of patterning, the intonation system in the phonology, has within the whole indivisible language system. This is not unrelated to the question of the role of melody and rhythm in the field of music. Aniruddh Patel (2008) *Music, Language and the Brain* locates speech sound in terms of music in a book with a map not unlike our own, covering 'Sound Elements: Pitch and Timbre', 'Rhythm', 'Melody', 'Syntax', 'Meaning' and 'Evolution'. And Patel, too, focuses his book on 'ordinary speech', while recognizing that 'no comparison of rhythm in language and music is complete without a discussion of poetry and song' (2008: 154). Patel finds the link between musical and vocal cues particularly strong in terms of affect (2008:344) but where he explores these in terms of the musical and vocal cues themselves, we are more concerned with the way the English language system has evolved to express anger, fear, happiness, sadness and tenderness – through all its resources but, in this book, particularly those resources most directly relatable to music. We begin, however, with a question more particularly directed towards phonetics: just how is it that a person interested in language should think about sound?

A first step is just listening. Scroll down a few lines on your computer to find 1.1.2 Nine sound icons. We are deliberately not naming these sounds, because we would like you to begin this first engagement with the main subject matter of the book by coming at it from your own conceptual background. Paying attention to an 'unknown' sound will help you to develop the habit of listening along a number of dimensions. To start you doing this, we offer a number of questions to bring to each sound. Your answers at this stage will be impressionistic, intuitive, and, almost certainly, not the same answers you will come up with after working through the balance of the book. But they are, nevertheless, very important answers: they will give you a reference point for measuring changes you make in the way you think about phonic substance. You will, in fact, experience this in the course of dealing with the nine sound icons immediately below. As you listen to them a number of times in the process of answering the questions, you will find that the way you listen is changing, and so is what you hear.

This is important in the light of the considerable amount of 'laboratory' work the book will make use of. Instrumental analysis is a wonderful — and quite delightful — way to 'get at' sound: one wonders how the science of phonology progressed so far without it. But it is only one 'window' into a process that begins in the brain of a speaker, proceeds through the medium of air, and is processed in the brain of the hearer. The 'view' provided by heightened awareness of what you can perceive as you concentrate on your own perception of the sensation of hearing sound is equally important.

In 1.1.2 Nine sound icons (overleaf) click on Button A. Through your earphones or the computer speakers you will hear a sound. Tick the appropriate answer in each of the six sections. The various questions help you think about the sounds in different ways. You'll be intrigued with what you hear. Write down your answers to the questions and keep them handy to refer to and to refine as you progress through the book.

1.1.1 Initial impressions of a variety of sounds

These questions relate to sound icons:

A☐   B☐   C☐   D☐   E☐   F☐   G☐   H☐   I☐

1   Is it human voice sound or something else?
   - ☐ Human
   - ☐ Non human animal
   - ☐ Mechanical
   - ☐ No idea

2   Does it carry some kind of message?
   - ☐ No message
   - ☐ Message, but I have no idea what it means
   - ☐ Message. I think it means...

3   Does it awaken some kind of emotional response in you?
   - ☐ Strong Describe it:...
   - ☐ Weak Describe it:...
   - ☐ No response

4   Do you recognize a quality in the sound? Something you can describe with an adjective, like *rough*?
   - ☐ No recognizable quality
   - ☐ An adjective which describes it is:...

5   How much can you say about the sound's rhythm?
   - ☐ It has no particular rhythm
   - ☐ It seems to be rhythmic, but I can't tap it
   - ☐ I think there is a clear rhythm. It goes:......................................

6   Does the sound seem to carry a melody of some kind?
   - ☐ I don't hear any particular melody
   - ☐ I think there is a melody there, but I can't hum it.
   - ☐ I was able to hum the melody
   - ☐ I would describe the melody this way:..

Note: A PDF file of this page is available on the CD which accompanies this book and may be printed and distributed without violation of copyright.

1.1.2 Nine sound icons

A PLAY ◀   D PLAY ◀   G PLAY ◀
B PLAY ◀   E PLAY ◀   H PLAY ◀
C PLAY ◀   F PLAY ◀   I PLAY ◀

1.2   How speech sound can be thought about

1.2.1 Thinking about speech sound in physical terms

From one point of view the sound of language is just that: sound. It is just one of many kinds of noise that are accessible to the human ear, like the sounds of birds and frogs and insects, the sounds of traffic on land and in the air, the sound of waves breaking, of thunder clapping and of objects impacting on each other and on the ground. Since these are physical phenomena, the sounds of language can be studied in the branch of physics known as acoustics.

Sound requires a medium such as air, in which each molecule is in continuous movement, in effect bumping into other molecules and thus exchanging energy. The air pressure at any one place is a kind of average of billions of billions of such movements. Local changes in air pressure, whatever the cause, are transmitted through the air in waves, perhaps traveling a long distance as individual molecules vibrate and pass on energy without themselves moving.

The simplest kind of wave that exists is called a sine wave, or 'sinusoid'. Though a perfect sinusoid is an idealization that would never occur in a natural speech waveform, sinusoids are important to understand because any of the complex waves found in nature can be decomposed into a set of sinusoids through a process called Fourier analysis, the basis for the images used in this book. Any sinusoid can be described by three parameters, namely amplitude and frequency (both of which relate to intonation) and phase.

Amplitude relates to the amount of change in air pressure from its equilibrium position. Frequency is the rate at which air pressure moves through cycles — increases above equilibrium, returns to equilibrium, drops below equilibrium and returns again to equilibrium. (Superimposed on this 'fundamental' frequency are 'harmonic' frequencies, waves occurring at shorter intervals which are integral subdivisions of the fundamental.) The voiced sounds we hear in nature are thus the combination of several waves. Phase is the temporal mapping of the different waves onto one another; it determines the exact shape of the waveform, but is not normally relevant to the perception of speech sounds.

In addition to these two parameters, amplitude and frequency, there are two other factors which enter into the production of voiced sound, namely duration and timbre. Duration means the length of time that any particular sound wave persists in a relatively unchanged form. Timbre is the distinctive quality or colouring of the sound wave, which enables us to distinguish one musical instrument from another, even when they are playing the identical phrase at the same pitch and volume. But timbre is not a separate physical property; rather, it is the particular combination of features, and especially the mode of transition from one state to the next, that makes a wind instrument sound different from a string instrument, and both sound different from percussion. But it is not possible to represent timbre as a single parameter capable of being described in quantitative terms.

1.2.2 Thinking about speech sound in biological terms

The sound wave is propagated from some generating source; in the case of speech sounds, from a human speaker or some instrument that is designed to simulate a human speaker. (There may be some intermediary device, such as a telephone or a recording tape.) It may, or may not, reach one or more human hearers before its energy dissipates below the threshold of human hearing. But the wave itself lies between speaker and hearer, and the physicist thinks of it as a single undifferentiated phenomenon.

In this respect, the thinking of a biologist is quite different. The biologist thinks in terms of a source (the point of production), and of a target (the points of reception). In other words, while the physical aspect of speech sound, the sound wave, is external (and hence neutral) to the speaker and the hearer, the biological aspect of speech sound resides in the human body, in the neurophysiology of speech production (brain to diaphragm, larynx and the organs of articulation) and of speech reception (outer, middle and inner ears to brain). Of course, like all biological processes, these processes are subject to the laws of physics, even if these are not fully understood at the neurobiological level. But they themselves are processes of life; and, more specifically, of higher-order human consciousness.

In speech production, a stream of air is set in train by an airstream mechanism within the body: typically the diaphragm ('pulmonic airstream') but sometimes the larynx ('glottalic airstream'). This is then moulded and coloured by the vocal cords and the pharyngeal and buccal-nasal tracts (the pharynx and the mouth and nose, with the tongue and lips as the most energetic and formative agency). Some stages of this process can be quantified in physical terms, such as the variation in air pressure as the airstream emerges from the mouth and nose; but the main parameters — tongue and lip movements, and the resulting postural configurations — are described in terms of relative values and movements.

In speech reception, the sound is transmitted through the ear and construed by the brain as (variation in) loudness, pitch, length, colouring (sound quality, consonantal and vocalic) and voice quality. Clearly these properties relate non-randomly to the physical properties of the sound wave; but the relation between the two is extremely complex. In the first place, the brain attends to transitions rather than to steady states, and it attends to the whole rather than to the component parts. And there is much in the signal which the brain neglects. In the second place, the brain is not, as it were, waiting around to receive a stimulus; rather, it is itself engendering mappings of an elastic perceptual space (which in turn embody the ongoing mappings of transitional probabilities), and those then resonate with, or selectively recognize, the inner ear's electrochemical 'translations' of the physical properties of the sound wave.

Thus both the biologist and the physicist, from their complementary standpoints, construe the sound of language in their own disciplinary terms, even if it is the linguistic significance of the phenomenon of speech sound that provides the motivation for studying it. And the linguist will always attend to the physical and biological basis of speech sound, even while seeking to increase our understanding of the functioning of sound in language.

1.2.3 Thinking about speech sound in engineering terms

The most immediate context in which the physical and biological models come to be applied is to be found in the work of a third group of specialists, namely engineers. Sound engineering typically involves (in part, or even exclusively) recording, transmitting and reproducing the sound of speech, whether the engineer is working in telecommunications or in a specialized field such as audiology, or in a research laboratory in phonetics or speech science where they are engaged in speech synthesis and speech recognition. The engineer is likely to be operationalizing both the physical and (some aspect of) the biological properties of speech sounds, and the experience of sound engineers has played an important part in helping us to understand the way speech sounds are produced, transmitted and received.

1.2.4 Thinking about the sound of language as expression of meaning

By many people, however, the sound of language will always be heard as meaning-full — simply because it is the sound of language. They would not construe it as an independent phenomenon, but always as (in some sense) the 'carrier' of meaning.

For a philosopher of language, or a semiotician (in the original sense of this term as 'one who studies meaning — the meaning that is inherent in systems of any kind'), the significant consideration is that linguistic meaning has to be expressed in some medium or other. It does not greatly matter which. Sound is one among a number of possible media, or 'modalities'. It may be in some sense the primary one (a fetus hears before seeing), but it has no particular significance other than its role as a carrier.

There are other specialists for whom the sounds of speech convey meaning of some particular kind — meaning which they would think of as being extrinsic to language proper. For a social dialectologist the sounds of language, in the way they vary systematically within a population, are the symptoms of linguistic change; and in this guise they reveal aspects of the social structure of the speech community, since both the sounds that people produce, and, even more perhaps, the attitudes that people hold towards the sounds that others produce, vary significantly and systematically according to their social class.

For sociologists and psychologists interested in questions such as crisis management and conflict resolution, the sound of language is a critical source of evidence for domination and submissiveness, and for the emotional states and attitudes of the interactants. Here the speech sounds serve as indices of recognizable forms of human social behaviour, and typically correlate with other, non-linguistic behavioural traits.

For clinicians in various specialties the sounds of language provide information about the kind and degree of disorder in subjects afflicted with a wide range of different pathological conditions: developmental delays and disorders in children, language loss in aphasic patients following a stroke or other insult to the brain, psychiatric maladies of various kinds, and so on.

In these contexts it is the sound of language not just as a generalized phenomenon (as a medium) but in its specific properties and manifestations — either the internal relations within the sound system itself, or the relations between certain sounds (or types of sound) and certain meanings (or types of meaning) — that determine the way that the sound of language is heard.

There are two groups of specialists that are further distinguished in that, while they are also concerned clinically with sounds as bearers of meaning, they are not using the sounds as evidence for something else (as a diagnostic instrument); they are intervening in people's production or reception of the sounds themselves. One is the speech therapists. They think of the sounds of language as potentially deviating from some definable norm; their task is to enable subjects to modify their production of deviant sounds so that they approximate more closely to some recognizable model. In the past, this task was sometimes confused with that of inducing the subjects to approximate more closely to a model that was socially acceptable — that of a standard dialect or accent. In other words, speech therapy was confused with elocution (or what used to be called 'orthoepy'). We should perhaps include elocution teachers here as another group of specialists whose professional responsibility is to intervene in the way people produce their speech sounds.

The other group is the audiologists. Their task is to intervene at the other biological pole, in the way speech sounds are received: that is, to improve the hearing of subjects afflicted with hearing loss. This involves diagnosing and measuring the extent and the type of deafness. The audiologist considers the sound of language in a very special way, as needing to be made accessible to the human ear — or rather, to the human brain — with a degree of redundancy sufficient to make listening (i.e. understanding of spoken language) possible. This may be facilitated by software such as the NOAH programs.

1.2.5 Thinking about the sound of language as construction of meaning

How then does a linguist think about the sound of language? A short answer might be: professionally — in a specific sense, namely that a linguist is defined as someone for whom language is the object under attention. For all the various specialists mentioned in the last section language is not object but instrument: that is, they are studying language in order to throw light on something else. The linguist, by contrast, studies language (and also other things) in order to throw light on language. Of course, the boundary between these two stances, translated into kinds of scholarly activity, is nothing like an absolute one; there are plenty of mixed categories and borderline cases. But the difference between the two perspectives is clear enough.

At the same time, the category of 'linguist' itself is by no means homogeneous. Like most sciences, linguistics has been specializing out into numerous different branches. Among the various parameters that define these specializations, like time depth (synchronic / diachronic) and geographical language group (Chinese / Pacific / Balkan etc.), perhaps the parameter that is most pervasive (and most significant methodologically) is that of stratification: which stratum, or level, in the overall architecture of language is the one that is under attention. In the broadest terms, the answer will be one of three: the sounds, the wordings, or the meanings — hence the division of linguists into phoneticians, grammarians & lexicologists, and semanticists. (The level of wording, or lexicogrammar, is methodologically complex: traditionally it demanded two distinct approaches according to whether the focus was on the more general categories, those of grammar, or the more specific categories, those of lexis.) Here, then, there would seem to be a further variation in the way the sound of language may be thought about: for the phonetician, sound is object, whereas for the others — grammarian, lexicologist, semanticist — sound is presumably an instrument, providing an entry to the other aspects of language which they have in focus of attention.

In fact, however, the situation is not quite like that. It is true that a grammarian (that is, someone who is engaged in theorizing about and describing grammar) is not at the same time attempting to investigate speech sounds. But neither is it the case that speech sounds are off the grammarian's agenda. The reason is that there can be no wordings, and no meanings, in language except as these are constructed out of some medium of expression; and the only medium of expression that co-evolved along with wordings and meanings is that of sound (it would be nice to be able to talk in this context about 'soundings', but that would perhaps be too remote from the established usage of the term).

Thus whether they are phoneticians or not, all linguists tend to think of the sound of language in much the same way: as the resource with which the meanings of language are constructed. Sounds are thought of not as the expression of something else which exists independently of them, but as an integral part of a single complex phenomenon — a language, and the elements of varying extent that go to make up a language. They are concerned with different facets of the same phenomenon.

This still leaves room, of course, for many different emphases and alignments. If we consider some of the groups currently working in phonetics (or 'speech science', as they now prefer to call it), we will find important differences in their special interests and approaches.

1.3   Some specific ways of thinking about the sound of language

1.3.1   The Institute for Perception Research IPO, a joint venture of Philips Electronics and Eindhoven University of Technology

The IPO approach, which originally started from the study of Dutch intonation, classifies types of pitch movement in terms of phonetic features which are relevant to perception by native speakers. The technique that characterizes this approach is called 'analysis-through- resynthesis' (de Pijper 1983: 5). This involves the reconstruction of an intonation type with different values of its physical properties such as amplitude and fundamental frequency. The experimental interest is on the points at which the constructed sound is perceived as different from the original sound.

In this approach a pitch contour is considered to consist of one or more segmental pitch movements. The pitch movement at each segment is represented by the smallest number of straight lines which are perceptually equivalent to the actual pitch movements; and the combination of those segments, termed a pitch contour, is shown by a single continuous line. Therefore, a pitch contour is phonetic: a constructed sound which is judged equivalent to a natural one. The number of pitch contours is unlimited.

However, the infinite number of pitch contours can be categorized into the finite number of intonation patterns. Defining intonation as 'the ensemble of pitch variations in the course of an utterance' ('t Hart, et al. 1990: 10), the IPO approach proposes six intonation patterns in English (ibid: 87). They contrast with each other phonetically and perceptually: 'The six different types of ... configurations are the phonetic manifestation of an equal number of basic intonation patterns' ('t Hart, et al. 1990: 87).

The phonological categorization of intonation in the IPO approach is phonetics-based, starting its analysis from 'the acoustic signal, with as few linguistic preconceptions as possible' (de Pijper 1983: 4). The IPO approach admits the relations between intonation and grammar, but they are 'neither obligatory nor unique' ('t Hart, et al. 1990: 100). We would agree that there is no one-to-one relationship between intonation and grammar; however, we consider grammar to be as important as phonetic features in theorizing a set of phonological categories. The IPO approach has been particularly helpful to us by providing insights into the acoustic properties of sound which affect the perception of melody.

1.3.2 ToBI

ToBI, *Tone and Break Indices*, was proposed by Silverman et al. (1992) as an agreed system for transcribing prosodic structures which could be used consistently by researchers in various fields.

ToBI provides tiers in which different linguistic phenomena are analysed. As the most basic components of ToBI, Beckman and Elam (1997) proposed four tiers: tone, orthographic, break index, and miscellaneous. The tone and break index tiers, which deal with the phonological and lexical phenomena, are the center of the linguistic analyses.

The tone tier mainly concerns the phonological events. Abstracting various pitch movements into H (high) and L (low), this approach describes three kinds of pitch movements: pitch accents, phrase accents, and boundary tones. There are six types of pitch accents, which refer to the pitch movement of stressed syllables: H*, L*, L+H*, L*+H, H+L*, and H*+L (the asterisk * indicates the central part of the pitch accent). The boundary tone is the last component of a tune and is represented by either H% or L%. The phrase accent is the component between the last pitch accent and the boundary tone, and it is represented by H- or L- without any diacritic. Here is an example that Beckman and Elam (1997: 10) use:

Marianna made the marmalade.
  H*   H*   L-L%

In this utterance, 'there are two syllables that are relatively more prominent than any other, the accented syllables in the words *Marianna* and *marmalade*' (Beckman and Elam 1997: 10). This approach does not require indication of the placement of the nuclear syllable, 'since the word with nuclear stress is defined positionally; it is the last accented word, or the accented word (if there is only one in the phrase)' (Beckman and Elam 1997: 11). From the nuclear syllable to the end, the pitch falls from a relatively high position, and it keeps falling toward the end.

The break index tier is related to the prosodic events as well, but in an indirect way: 'Break indices represent a rating [on a scale from 0 to 4] for the degree of juncture perceived between each pair of words and between the final word and the silence at the end of the utterance.' (Beckman and Elam 1997: 31).

The tone tier and the break index tier are responsible for different linguistic phenomena, lexis, phonology and / or phonetics. In the tone tier, the boundary of the prosodic unit (tune) never separates a word. In the break index tier, the grammatical unit word again determines boundaries: break indices, which are based on evaluating the sound, are assigned between every grammatical word.

1.3.3 Metrical phonology; autosegmental phonology

Metrical phonology recognizes a hierarchy of sound patterns based on the word considered as a phonological unit: words consist of metric feet, feet consist of syllables and syllables consist of elements, typically onset plus rhyme. These structures are displayed as binary branching trees, with each pair characterized as strong plus weak; these represent degrees of stress or of sonorance, depending on position in the tree. In autosegmental phonology the units are established specifically on a phonological basis, each one being the location of some particular sound pattern in the language. See in particular Goldsmith 1990 and Ladd 1996.

In Systemic Functional Linguistics phonology and grammar are represented as distinct strata, each with its own hierarchy of units (known as the 'rank scale'); the units may vary among different languages, and there may be coincidence between a pair of units on the two strata, for example morpheme and syllable. In English the phonological rank scale is made up of tone unit (also referred to as 'tone group'), foot, syllable and phoneme, with (for some purposes) introduction of a hemisyllable consisting of onset plus rhyme; that of grammar is made up of clause, phrase/group, word and morpheme. We shall see below that there is an 'unmarked' association between the tone unit and the clause (Chapter 4 and Chapter 5).

1.3.4 Optimality Theory

Optimality Theory (OT) was first developed by Prince and Smolensky (1993) as an alternative theory to Metrical phonology. It is based on Generative Grammar, which (unlike Systemic Functional Linguistics) starts from an assumption of language universals. In particular, OT proposes a universal set of violable constraints, with variations among languages derived from differences in the ranking of those constraints.

OT's main contribution is the descriptions of syllable and foot structures. The syllabification of English is described in terms of the following constraints with this particular order:

PEAK, LICENSING, SONORITY >> FAITHFULNESS >> ONSET, NOCODA, *COMPLEX[1]

(Hammond 1997: 41)

This ranking means that PEAK, LICENSING, and SONORITY are not violable in English, and that FAITHFULNESS is less violable than ONSET, NoCODA, and *COMPLEX. For example, *cat* is phonologically described by three phonemes as /kæt/, so there are four candidates for the optimality in terms of the syllabification: /kæt/, /k/+/æt/, /kæ/+/t/, and /k/+/æ/+/t/; however, because of the inviolable constraints, all the candidates except the first one are eliminated from the list.

Characterized as trochaic, the stress pattern of English is described by four constraints with the basic pattern *foot*:

ROOTING >> TROCHEE >> PARSE-SYLLABLE >> BINARITY[2]

(Hammond 1997: 44–45)

A foot in OT is the basic unit of rhythm, and must begin with a stressed syllable. The OT foot finds its rhythm in the pronunciation of a word, generally a word as isolate in its citation form; this is structured as a stressed syllable followed by no more than one unstressed syllable. Not all syllables are included in the feet which make up OT phonological words.

An SFL foot finds its rhythm not in a word but in a stretch of discourse — one or more tone units. As in OT, an SFL foot begins with a stressed syllable, but in SFL all syllables in a tone unit must be accounted for in foot segmentation. This difference may be more apparent than real, as SFL structures a foot not as strong syllable followed by weak syllable(s), but rather as the functions Ictus optionally followed by Remiss. The syllable at Ictus stands out in terms of length, amplitude, pitch change and place in the unfolding rhythm, and the Remiss (if present) includes any syllables that are not salient. (See below, section 1.4.) Honeybone (2004) describes a set of relationships between Optimality Theory and the work of J. R. Firth, who was seminal to the development of our approach.

1.4   Some characteristics of our own approach in this book

Our own approach here falls clearly within what we have characterized as the linguist's perspective: we are thinking of the sound of language as a resource for the construction of meaning. We are not attempting to be iconoclastic or revolutionary. Nevertheless there are certain respects in which our theory and our methodology are distinctive. Let us enumerate these in outline here.

The general model we are using is that of systemic functional theory (SFL). In this model, language is interpreted as a semiotic system (that is, as a system of meaning); human beings have other semiotic systems besides, but language is, taken all in all, the primary one. In particular, language is a semogenic, or meaning-*creating*, system; and it achieves this place in human life by virtue of a number of specific features. We will summarize the most important of these here; they will reappear in greater detail as they become relevant to the discussion.

Language is able to create meaning because in between the meaning and the sound there has evolved another level of organization, that of 'wording' (i.e. grammar and lexis). This is an abstract level of semiosis which probably evolved fairly late in human history — and which develops fairly late in human children, typically in the age span 1;4 to 2 years. It deconstructs the bond between the meaning and the sound (which is a feature of the 'languages' of other species, and also of the protolanguage developed first by human infants), and so enables the two — meaning and sound — to be recombined in indefinitely many ways; the effect of this is that a language system is entirely openended. We refer to these levels as 'strata', and to the phenomenon as a whole as 'stratification'. Stratification makes it possible for language to mean in more than one way at once; and this leads on to the second of the features we need to refer to here — modes of meaning.

Language 'means' in three different ways simultaneously. In the first place, it enables us to make sense of our experience. It does this by transforming experience into meaning — creating categories, and relations between categories, with which we can understand what goes on around us and inside us. We shall refer to this way of meaning as 'construing': thus, language construes human experience. In the second place, it enables us to act on other people. It does this by setting up systems of interaction and control, whereby speakers put their assertions and their desires across, and of appraisal, whereby they pass judgment and evaluate. We shall refer to this way of meaning as 'enacting': thus, language enacts human relationships. In the third place, as the way of managing this complexity, it enables us to construct text, a flow of discourse that 'hangs together' and provides the authenticating context for the first two. We shall refer to this way of meaning as 'engendering': thus, language engenders human discourse.

How does language then keep pace with the changing conditions of knowledge and of society? Essentially, language is a metastable system, which persists by constantly evolving in interaction with its environment. What we call the 'system' of language is the potential that is shared among the members of a speech community (one can think of it as stored within each individual's brain, always of course with minor differences between one individual and another). This meaning potential consists of sets of options, at every stratum; and these sets of options have varying probability profiles. For example, in English there is a set of options in the grammar which we could describe by saying 'each clause is either positive or negative in polarity; positive is more probable than negative by about one order of magnitude'. Every instance of a clause spoken or written in English perturbs the probabilities, ever so slightly — the cumulative effect being that the potential steadily changes over time: sometimes very gradually, sometimes at a relatively startling speed.

In modelling such a system, we treat a language as a resource: that is, we describe the sets of options and show how they are all related to each other, beginning with the most general and proceeding into ever-increasing detail (this vector of increasing detail is referred to as 'delicacy'). Each set of options is referred to as one system; and a set of related systems is referred to as a system network. Modelling language as resource, therefore, means that a language as a whole is being said to consist of a number of interrelated sets of choices. Any particular instance is modelled as a pass through these various networks — rather as we might model a particular instance of a journey as a pass through a number a networks of options showing all possible times, speeds, modes of transport, departure points and destinations, routes, deviations and the like.

Thus the basic axis of the description is paradigmatic: a category is located according to its value in the system — what it means — rather than according to how it is expressed or recognized. To use an analogy from lexicology, the model is like a thesaurus (where a word appears according to its place in the meaning potential), not like a dictionary (where a word appears according to how it is spelt). Of course, the description then goes on to make explicit how the category is to be recognized: with each option there is a statement of its realization. Thus, if an English speaker opts for negative polarity there is likely to be a negative word in the clause, typically *not*. Notice, however, that until we take account of the more delicate options (the subcategories of negative), we cannot say if it will be *not* (or *n't*) or *never* or *no* or ... .When we get to the final stage of delicacy in a system (or when we decide we have gone far enough), the next step in realization is to move to a phonological representation — for example a sequence of phonemes such as /nɐt/ or /nt/ or /nevəʳ / or /noᵘ/.

It is thus through realization that we relate one stratum to the next. In the most general formulation, we can say that meanings are realized in wordings, and wordings are realized in sounds. Ultimately, if we want to tell the full story of any option in lexicogrammar or semantics, we have to be able to move above the level of meaning — the semantic stratum — and recognize a still higher stratum of context. This means the cultural context of the language as a whole (the knowledge systems, social practices and discourse formations that constitute the culture), and the situational contexts of each particular instance. The context also is modelled in linguistic terms, in order to show that language and context form a single eco-social system.

From this point of view, the semantic stratum — the resources of a language considered as a system of meanings — appears as an interface between the lexicogrammatical system and its material and social environment. And this notion of interface takes us back to the consideration of sound. At the other end of language, so to speak, is the interface with a different facet of the material environment — the human body, and in particular its resources for producing and receiving speech; and the surrounding air. We have spoken so far of just a single stratum of sound, calling it 'phonetic'. But we need to distinguish, within this concept, between the physical and biological resources and the way these are deployed in any particular language. In other words, we need to distinguish between a level of phonetics and a level of phonology. When we talk about the sound system of English, the significance of any category we refer to (whether a prosodic category, such as pitch movement, or an articulatory one, such as the shape and position of the tongue) will be its semogenic value — its function in the total meaning potential of the English language. This is a phonological consideration. With this distinction in mind we can specify the goals of the present work.

This book is about a particular portion of the phonetic resources of language: the prosodic resources of intonation and rhythm. These are discussed within a particular context, that of the phonological resources of one language, namely English. We shall try to show how intonation contributes to the making of meaning in English, and how this topic may be investigated using modern computer-based techniques of analysis and representation. These techniques provide a much richer and more elaborate treasury of information than was available a generation or even a decade ago. They do not replace the human investigator; they do make the human investigator's work more complex — but also more thorough and more revealing. For an account of other work involving intonation seen from an SFL perspective, see 'Intonation in Systemic Functional Linguistics' in *Continuing Discourse on Language: A Functional Perspective*, ed. Webster et al, vol. 2.

There are three writers on English intonation whose work we would mark out as compatible with and in particular respects complementary with our own. One is Martin Davies, who has paid special attention to intonation in poetry and to the prosodic features inherent in written text. One is Paul Tench, who has stressed the multifunctional nature of intonation and extended the scope of intonation studies to encompass patterns in discourse. (Tench 1992 provides a selection of systemic papers on different aspects of phonology.) The third is John Wells, whose book *English Intonation: an introduction* appeared after our manuscript had been completed; this is a major contribution from a leading phonetician taking account of the needs of students of English, both as first and as second language. All these scholars share our view of the place of intonation in language, and the place of intonation studies in linguistic science. And we take this occasion to pay tribute to the work of the late Afaf Elmenoufy, an outstanding worker in the field of English intonation who we had at first hoped would join us as a third author of this book. We hope these few remarks will help to locate our enterprise in the context of contemporary prosodic studies. In the next three chapters we will outline the various components of our approach.

Notes

1   These constraints are defined in the following terms (Hammond 1997): PEAK — syllables have one vowel; LICENSING (syllabic licensing) — all words are composed of syllables; SONORITY: onsets must increase and codas must decrease in sonority; FAITHFULNESS: input and output are identical; ONSET: syllables begin with a consonant; NoCODA: syllables end with a vowel; COMPLEX: syllables have at most one consonant at an edge.

2   ROOTING — words must be stressed; TROCHEE — feet are trochaic; PARSE-SYLLABLE — two unfooted syllables cannot be adjacent; BINARITY — a monosyllabic foot cannot occur before an unfooted syllable.

2 Representation of sound

2.1 Two dimensional representation: air pressure and time (wave form)

A wave form graph plots time on the horizontal X axis and air pressure on the vertical Y axis. This form of graph is closely analogous to the physical data, and can be used to understand both frequency and intensity of sound.

From the physical point of view, the task in analysing sound is to look at it in material terms: to measure it from different physical perspectives. The physicist concentrates on transmitted sound, that is, the alternating states of compression and rarefaction in the medium, air, which constitute the wave passing the sound from speaker to hearer. These changes in air pressure can be measured at any point between the sound source and the sound target using a microphone, which contains a diaphragm through which an electric current can flow. When the diaphragm is distorted in one direction because the air at the microphone is compressed, the flow is positive. When the diaphram is distorted in the opposite direction because the air at the microphone is rarefied, the flow is negative. In either case the greater the distortion of the film the greater the flow of the current.

This varying electrical current is fed into a device such as a sound card, which interprets it in digital terms. A computer program then produces a pictorial image analogous to the changes in pressure at the microphone. The raw data the phonetician usually begins with, then, is a graphic image, separated, by a series of conversions, from the minute changes in air pressure which it represents. The line in the image represents these changes in terms of the dimensions 'air pressure' (upward movement of the line represents increase in air pressure and downward movement represents decrease in air pressure) and 'time' (distance from left to right represents unfolding time). Time is generally scaled in units of 1/10, 1/100 or 1/1000 of a second, while the amplitude of the air pressure may be scaled in units such as pounds per square inch, or Pascals. Praat represents air pressure in Pascals, represented as points between +1 and -1. This is fine for understanding the relative ranges of air pressure variation, but should not be taken as literal indication of air pressure without calibrating Praat. And even with calibration, the values are arbitrary in the sense that they depend on the particular make of microphone, the distance between the speaker's mouth and the microphone, the presence of other objects (such as a soft chair or other people), the particular sound card processing the voltage changes produced by the microphone, and so forth. We have therefore labelled them 'nominal'.

Figure 2.1.1 represents time and air pressure changes when the word *pig* followed by a period of silence.

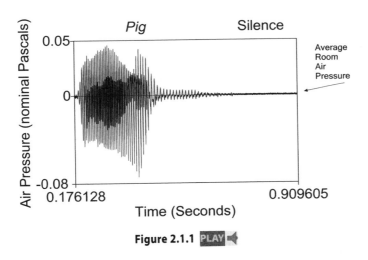

Figure 2.1.1 PLAY ◀

Time is directly represented horizontally. The picture covers 0.733477 seconds, beginning at 0.176128 seconds into the recording, and ending at 0.909605 seconds. The
intensity of air pressure is represented vertically, ranging from 0.05 Pascals above average
to -0.08 Pascals below average.

Figure 2.1a is a detail of the silence. In a theoretical room with no sound at all such a
picture would be an absolutely straight line: time would flow, but the air pressure would
remain constant. In a real recording however there is always noise, some of which will
be added by the microphone and the computer during the conversion from sound wave
to computer representation. To reveal the noise, we have reduced the Air Pressure scale,
which now ranges from -0.01 to 0.01 nominal Pascals.

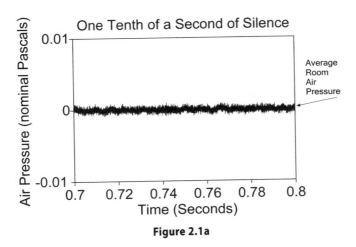

Figure 2.1a

'Reading' the picture is straightforward. In the horizontal dimension we can 'see' the
time moving along in 0.02 intervals. In the vertical dimension the line moves slightly,

but always close to the 0.0 point. The air at the microphone during this silence remained at average room pressure.

When someone is speaking, air pressure does not remain average. Figure 2.1b shows air pressure change in a very short interval during the word *pig*.

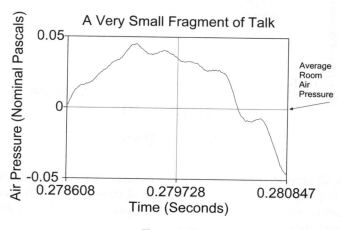

Figure 2.1b

The time axis tells us that the picture begins at 0.278608 seconds into the recording and ends at 0.280847 seconds: just over two milliseconds At the beginning of that period the air pressure was average, it rose gradually and evenly, then fell evenly but with small bumps, and finally fell rapidly but with one clear bump. The change from the highest air pressure to the lowest is just under one tenth of a Pascal.

Once the physicist can 'see' air pressure in terms of air pressure changes over time, he or she can look at the picture to find the particular patterns of intensity and duration and their frequency of repetition, which relate to what we hear as 'loudness', 'quality', and 'pitch'.

Computer programs have been developed to do this work. Some of these are quite expensive. But WinCECIL and Speech Analyser (http://www.sil.org/computing/speech-tools/) and Praat (http://www.fon.hum.uva.nl/praat/), all of which we use, are available to scholars at minimal or no cost. (We are providing fairly detailed descriptions of how WinCECIL and Praat work because the general principles of using such programs will apply to others.)

Listen to the sound. It is much easier to understand wave forms, to comprehend the segmentation referred to above, for example, if you listen to the sounds the wave forms represent.

2.1.1 Periodic and non-periodic sound

Wave form patterns which repeat themselves are called periodic. Those which do not are non-periodic.

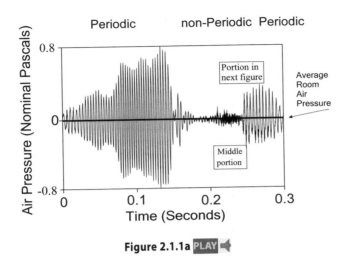

Figure 2.1.1a PLAY

The middle portion of the wave form in figure 2.1.1a, which sounds so different, also looks very different. The initial and final sections are open and regular; much of the middle section is black and irregular. Figure 2.1.1b (noise + 7 cycles), which takes a portion running from the middle of the black area in Figure 2.1.1a into a corresponding amount of the final more open section and stretches it out, will help to make clear what is going on in the air to cause such a difference in the sound quality:

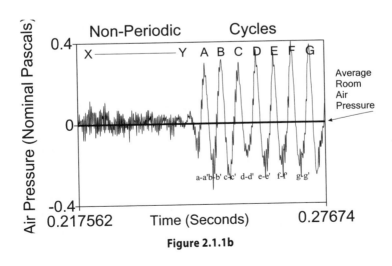

Figure 2.1.1b

The first half of the frame, X-Y, shows very rapid and irregular changes from compression to rarefaction: the distances up and down seem to vary randomly, and the way they are spread out on the horizontal time axis also seems very irregular. The second half, A-G, is very regular: the distances A-B, B-C, C-D and so on are almost equal; moreover, the small up and down movements in the segments a-a', b-b', c-c', d-d' and so on are also regular. In both respects the second half is distinctly different from the first half. It is hard to hear this from the whole sound, X through G: PLAY ◄ Sound 2.1.1.1b But listen now to X through Y only: PLAY ◄ Sound 2.1.1.1b1, and then the second half, A through G only: PLAY ◄ Sound 2.1.1.1b2, and finally X through G but with a silence separating the two parts: PLAY ◄ Sound 2.1.1.1c.

2.1.2 Periodic sound:

2.1.2.1 Cycles and frequency

Periodic sound is more clearly seen in an expanded wave form. Figure 2.1.2.1 is a detail from Figure 2.1.1 above, showing only the two cycles at A and B. Cycles can be shown beginning and ending at any point which is easy to recognize. A and B are shown beginning (and ending) at the point where air pressure crosses the average room pressure line and continues upward towards the maximum pressure reached in the cycle.

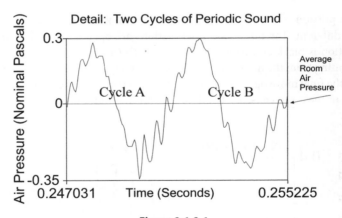

Figure 2.1.2.1

Frequency refers to the rate at which cycles repeat. Fundamental frequency in speech sound, generally referred to by the abbreviation F0, corresponds to the rate at which individual bursts of air escape through the space between the vocal cords.

An anatomist can say a great deal about the physical causes of fundamental frequency: a certain pressure in the lungs forcing air through a narrow gap between the vocal cords (the glottis), and the way a certain tension in the vocal bands causes them to vibrate chopping the air stream into individual puffs, each of which sets in motion the air vibration eventually recorded as one cycle in the wave form. For adult women F0 is roughly in the range from 200 Hz to 400 Hz; for adult men F0 ranges from 60 Hz to 200 Hz, and for adult male elephants F0 can be a lot lower than that — so low that we can barely discern it as a rumble. In fact we cannot hear at all some rumbles that adult male elephants make (though we may *feel* them if standing near), as some of their calls are below 20 Hz, that is, infrasonic, or below the lower limit of human hearing; one call was recorded at 5 Hz. Here is an example of a forest elephant (loxodonta cyclotis) courtesy of Melissa Groo at The Elephant Listening Project at Cornell University.

PLAY ◀ Sound 2.1.2.1

Cycles A and B in Figure 2.1.2.1 would have been set in motion by two such bursts. The air at the microphone in Cycle A begins at average pressure, becomes compressed to about a third of a Pascal, then becomes rarefied to about a third of a Pascal below average room pressure, and expands again to average room pressure to end the cycle. This whole process is repeated in Cycle B.

Each cycle in Figure 2.1.2.1 takes roughly the same amount of time, .004 seconds, and this is known as the period of the waveform. Frequency (cycles per second) is simply the reciprocal of period. So 1 divided by .004 gives 250; there would be two hundred fifty repetitions of the pattern if the sound continued unchanged for one second. The sound represented by Figure 2.1.2.1 has an F0 of 250 Hertz.

This regularity of bursts, fundamental frequency, is particularly important in the study of intonation.

2.1.2.2 Fundamental and higher frequencies

There are also smaller and much more frequent changes of pressure within each cycle. These are part of what we hear as the quality of sound. Figure 2.1.2.2a (five cycles) presents cycles A through E. An anatomist would be interested in the details of Figure 2.1.2.2a because of the way the sound results from features in the body of the speaker, in particular the size and shape of the nasal and oral cavities.

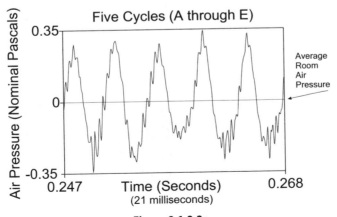

Figure 2.1.2.2a

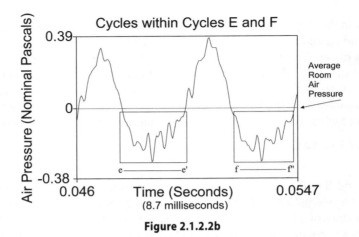

Figure 2.1.2.2b

Figure 2.1.2.2b shows the fully vocal sound [i] in Figure 2.1.2.2a in even greater detail. The portions within rectangles E (e-e′) and F (f-f′) each cover about two milliseconds, and each contains about five small compression peaks. Again there is regularity, but this included pattern has a frequency in the order of thousands, rather than the order of hundreds, of cycles per second. The vocal bands produce many such included patterns. The way in which some of these are enhanced and some suppressed as the vocal tract changes shape is of great interest in the study of accent, but in considering these very high frequencies, we have really pushed beyond the ability of a two dimensional wave to represent air pressure changes accurately. Spectrograms (see below) offer a better way to examine the patterns involved.

2.1.3 Non-periodic sound

Figure 2.1.3a and Sound 2.1.3a below show the French word *merci*. The non-periodic segment stands out clearly because the irregular changes in pressure occur so rapidly that the computer screen can't draw them properly. Because there are more swings in the waveform than pixels on the screen, the non-periodic portion appears almost solid black.

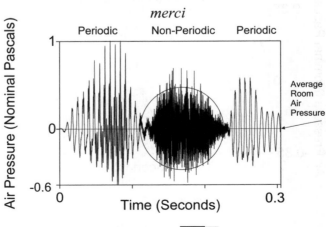

Figure 2.1.3a PLAY

Figure 2.1.3b, expanding a portion of the non-periodic sound, allows us to see the rapid irregular changes in detail. There are no clearly repeating patterns

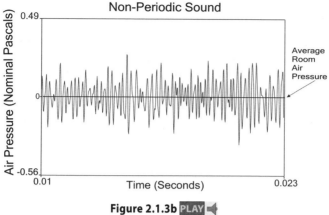

Figure 2.1.3b PLAY ◀

2.1.4 Combined periodic and non-periodic sound

The English word *measure* and the French word *aujourd'hui* both offer examples of a combination of periodic and non-periodic sound: the fricative [ʒ]. Figure 2.1.4 illustrates this combination. It begins with a periodic cycle. The next eight cycles maintain the fundamental frequency as the lungs continue to force air through the glottis in regular bursts, but the tongue moves to the top of the mouth, causing turbulence as the airstream is accelerated between the tongue and the hard palate. The resulting rapid irregular changes in pressure show up as black. In the final cycle the tongue has moved away and the wave returns to purely periodic sound. The periodicity has been maintained throughout, with non-periodic sound added for a while and withdrawn.

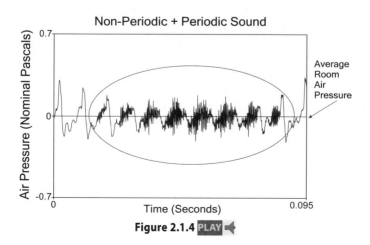

Figure 2.1.4 PLAY ◀

2.2 Two-dimensional representation: fundamental frequency and time (frequency line)

2.2.1 Representation of frequency

An F0 graph plots time on the horizontal X axis and fundamental frequency on the vertical Y axis. Wherever there is periodic sound there will be a line. Where there is no sound, or where the sound is non-periodic, there will be no frequency line.

The frequency line will go up as the frequency increases, and down as it decreases. Figure 2.2.1a shows a frequency line which is continuous because it represents a stretch of sound which is entirely periodic, and slopes downward because each cycle is slightly longer than the previous one.

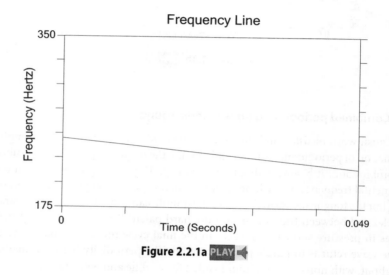

Figure 2.2.1a PLAY

The vertical scale at the left extends from 175 Hz at the bottom of the frame up to 350 Hz at the top of the frame. The units marked off by the small lines in the scale are 25 Hz each. The frequency line begins just below the 250 Hz marker (at about 240 Hz) and falls gradually to a little below 225 Hz. If you click sound 2.2.1a, you will probably hear the fall, even though the segment is very short.

The next figure, 2.2.1b, displays the same sound as a wave form (air pressure line) and frequency line together, and this makes it possible to compare the gradual increase in the time taken by each cycle with the gradual fall in the frequency line. A look at the wave form lets you know that the frequency is falling. The frequency line lets you know where the fall begins and ends on the Hertz scale.

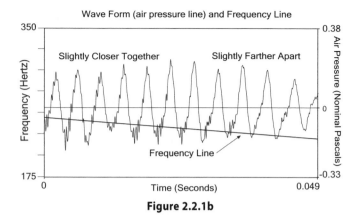

Figure 2.2.1b

Figure 2.2.1c again shows a frequency line imposed on an air pressure line (wave form). The program has produced a frequency line only where the sound is periodic; there is nothing above the central non-periodic portion.

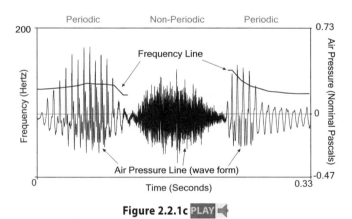

Figure 2.2.1c PLAY ◀

Figure 2.2.1d shows the program producing a frequency line for sound which is both non-periodic and periodic. The wave form clearly shows the F0 cycles taking up about .01 seconds and continuing across the frame, and also clearly shows the added turbulent non-periodic sound in the central eight cycles. It is less obvious that the central cycles are slightly longer than the outer ones, but this is very clearly shown by the frequency line, which begins at 110 Hz and drops to 102 Hz before rising to 113 Hz.

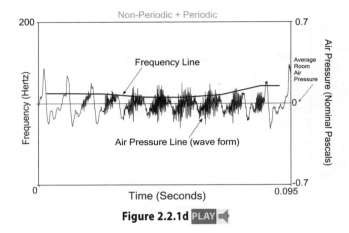

Figure 2.2.1d PLAY 🔊

2.2.2 Hertz or semitone

The Hertz scale represents frequency; it is oriented towards the physicist, as it gives information directly representing the movement of matter. The semitone scale represents pitch; it is oriented towards the musician, who is concerned with perception, the way sound is heard. (Figure 2.2.2 will satisfy both: it has a Hertz scale on the left side and a semitone scale on the right side.)

The basic perceptual unit is the octave, the point in increasing frequency at which a sound seems to repeat itself at a higher pitch — the 'Middle C', 'High C' and so forth which will be familiar to many from childhood music lessons. An octave is not a fixed number of cycles per second, but rather a certain ratio between frequencies. Specifically, if two frequencies have a 2:1 ratio, they will sound one octave apart. The range from 10 to 20 Hertz is one octave, with a difference of ten cycles per second between the bottom end and the top end. But the range from 440 (the A above middle C) to 880 Hertz is also an octave — with, in this case, a difference of four hundred and forty cycles per second between the bottom end and the top end.

Semitone representation divides each octave into twelve units, and so, mathematically, divides the octave's 2:1 ratio into twelve equal parts. A semitone can thus be defined as a frequency ratio of 1.059:1, where we can notice that $(1.059)^{12} = 2$ — twelve semitones make one octave.

Because a semitone relationship is a ratio between two numbers, there is a greater frequency range between notes at the top of an octave than between notes at the bottom. Table 2.2.2 shows one octave, starting at 440 Hz and ending at 880 Hz. Semitone 57 at the bottom of the octave begins at 440 Hz and ends at 465 Hz. It has a range 26 Hz. Semitone 68 at the top begins at 831 Hz and ends at 879 Hz. It has a range of 49 Hz. When played on a piano, however, the progression will sound even and any note played an octave higher will sound 'the same but different'.

Table 2.2.2

Semitone	57	58	59	60	61	62	63	64	65	66	67	68	69
Hertz	440	466	494	523	554	587	622	659	698	740	784	831	880
Range	26	28	29	31	33	35	37	39	42	44	47	49	

Figure 2.2.2 shows the cursor set about half way through the word *juice* spoken by a woman whose voice is rising. The circled information at the bottom of the screen tells us that the cursor has intersected the frequency line at 440.7 Hz, and that this is within the range of semitone 57.

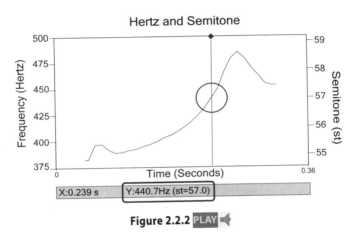

Figure 2.2.2 PLAY 🔊

A physicist might describe the rise on *juice* as being about 100 Hz, while a musician might say it was just over four semitones.

2.2.3 Frequency and pitch

'Frequency' and 'pitch' are closely related terms dealing with the same phenomenon, the transmission of sound in air, but analyzing it in different frameworks: 'frequency', as we have seen, deals with the physical side of the phenomenon, and 'pitch' refers to the way it is perceived by humans and (we assume) other sentient beings.

In considering speech sound we are, of course, interested in both frequency and pitch. When we talk about the sound of intonation contours, we speak of 'pitch changes', 'loudness', 'tone', 'quality', 'length' and we might even bring in terms like 'staccato rhythm', 'octave', 'beat', 'rest', and so forth. But because much of the work on intonation is done with the help of instrumental analysis of sound waves, we also use terms such as 'frequency', 'amplitude', 'duration' and 'Hertz'.

One way of dealing with the difference between frequency measurement in Hz and pitch measurement in semitones is to plot frequency on a logarithmic, rather than a linear scale. The frequency line then corresponds quite closely to the sound we hear.

At about 500 Hz human perception of sound changes. The MEL scale, based on perception, was developed by Stevens, Volkmann and Newmann in 1937. In this scale the relationship between Hertz and MEL is fairly direct up to about 500 Hz, and logarithmic above that. Since intonation is concerned with F0, generally in the range from 50 Hz to 500 Hz, we will not use the MEL scale in this book.

2.3 Two-dimensional representation: energy and time (intensity line)

The term 'loudness' deals with a human (or at least animal) phenomenon, a response to a stimulus. But the stimulus is the movement of matter, and so to understand that stimulus the linguist has to put on the physicist's hat. In this case, we find that the perceptual attribute of loudness is closely correlated with a physical measurement called intensity.

Intensity is properly defined as the amount of sound energy that passes through a given area over a certain amount of time. If the given area happens to be an ear drum, we can think of intensity as measuring the rate at which sound energy arrives at our ears. Generally speaking, the more energy transmitted by a wave, the louder it will sound.

But how can the energy in a wave be measured? A picture of a tiny bit of the 'o' sound in the middle of the syllable 'con' shows that this is somewhat difficult to abstract:

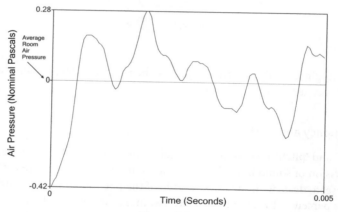

Figure 2.3a

There is clearly energy at work here: the air is at a state of considerable rarefaction at the beginning; less than 1/1000 of a second later it has been compressed; another 5/10000 of a second later it has been expanded to a pressure just below average room pressure. Another 5/10000 of a second later it has been compressed again; then it becomes slightly more rarefied, and then it becomes very slightly compressed; then it becomes rarefied to about average room pressure again, and so forth. Getting hold of this is complicated. It is not enough just to measure the distance from the state of greatest rarefaction to the state of greatest compression (in this case the distance from the low point at the beginning up to the top of the first peak). Every one of the vertical changes in the frame reveals energy, and so they all have to be taken account of. This can, in fact, be done very accurately, and there is an area of study involving audiology, acoustic phonetics, and psychology devoted to measuring the energy in the way most suitable for studying its physical effect on the ear and the psychological processing of the resulting electrochemical changes in the brain.

Here is the word 'paradise' with the wave and intensity of energy represented by Praat. 'Eyeballing' the wave for intensity we can see four chunks: the 'p' sound at the beginning, the 'ara', the 'di', and the 'se'.

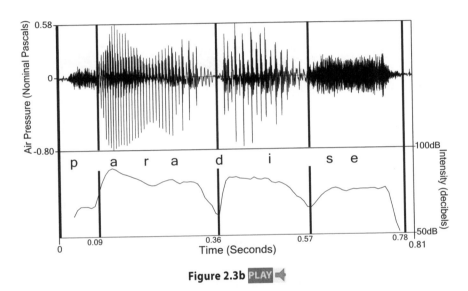

Figure 2.3b PLAY

Looking at the image we can get an impression of the energy in two ways: wave form in the top half, intensity in dB in the bottom half.

1) From the wave form. Here the vertical line indicates the degree of air pressure: compression and rarefaction. The wave form shows relatively small swings from compression to rarefaction at 'p' part. These swings increase greatly in size in the second section (although they decrease toward the end). In the third part the swings are roughly as great as in the second. At the last section, they become small again but they are not as small as they are in the first section.

If we pay attention only to the high and low points, for instance by drawing a line touching the top of the wave from, we get a distorted impression of the energy. See Figure 2.3c.

2) From the intensity line. This is more abstract than the wave form, in the sense that it shows neither rarefaction nor compression. Rather, to calculate intensity, the computer program uses a special kind of average known as the root mean square, or RMS, pressure. Complicated as it sounds, the RMS pressure is simply an average calculated over a short period of time, after any negative pressure values have been converted into positive ones. The time span over which this averaging occurs can be adjusted in most software packages, since the ideal time span varies with the fundamental frequency of the sound being analysed. The intensity line, calculated from RMS pressure, is then plotted on a decibel scale, which looks closer to the way we hear the sounds in terms of loudness.

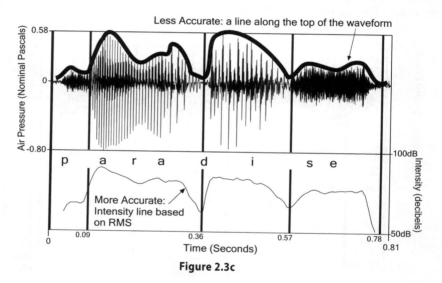

Figure 2.3c

The intensity line in the final 'se' section is almost as high as it is in the preceding 'i' section. The extra height of the final section corresponds to the darkness of the waveform above: there are so many changes from compression to rarefaction that the line drawing them runs into itself, giving a solid black effect, and the intensity line reflects the energy in these numerous smaller swings.

2.4 Three dimensional representation: spectrograms

Spectrograms represent time on the horizontal X axis, frequency on the vertical Y axis, and energy by the shade of colour or grey. Some spectrograms give a three dimensional topographical map image in which energy is represented in terms of mountains and valleys. The frequency range is much greater than the 50 Hz to 500 Hz F0 range typical of a fundamental frequency line. Typical ranges for a spectrogram are 0 Hz to 5,000 Hz, or to 10,000 Hz, or for some purposes to 20,000 Hz. The spectrogram represents the distribution of energy across different ranges of frequency as time unfolds.

Spectrograms can be divided into two types, narrow band and wide band, which differ in their time and frequency resolutions. The time resolution of a spectrogram refers to its ability to show rapid changes in the frequency content of a vocalization, while its frequency resolution refers to its ability to accurately show the frequencies present in a sound. Unfortunately, the mathematics used to calculate spectrograms dictates that, in general, time resolution can only be increased by decreasing the frequency resolution and vice versa. Whether a spectrogram is narrow band or wide band depends on the time length of its analysis window.

A wide band spectrogram uses a very short analysis window, and will have good time resolution but poor frequency resolution. This can be seen in Figure 2.4a, where the spectrogram is very clear in the horizontal dimension (along the time axis) but somewhat blurry in the vertical dimension (along the frequency axis). This means that, when displaying a voiced segment, a wide band spectrogram will reveal pulses of glottalic energy clearly as vertical bands, but will not be able to capture harmonics sharply. While it does not reveal individual harmonics, however, it does show formants — energy distributed across several harmonics reflecting the size and shape of the oral cavity.

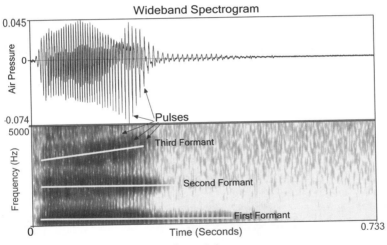

Figure 2.4a

Narrow band spectrograms, by contrast, use longer analysis windows and hence show more frequency resolution at the expense of time resolution. Narrow band spectrograms do not show the energy of individual glottalic pulses at all clearly, but they do sharply present the distribution of energy along the frequency axis, thus giving us a clear picture of harmonics. Notice that, unlike the wideband spectrogram, Figure 2.4b is blurry along the time axis (poor time resolution) and clear along the frequency axis (good frequency resolution):

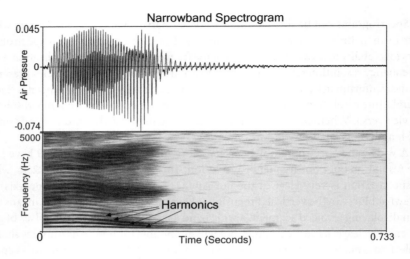

Figure 2.4b

Harmonics, which are shown on a narrow band spectrogram, are always multiples of F0. A waveform of voiced sound is made up of a number of harmonics.

F0 frequency can thus be judged three ways: from the distance between pulses in a waveform, by F0 analysis on the computer, and by the distance between the harmonics shown in the spectrogram. The lowest harmonic represents F0. Higher harmonics exaggerate the shape of changes in the lowest harmonic, as in Figure 2.4c.

Figure 2.4c

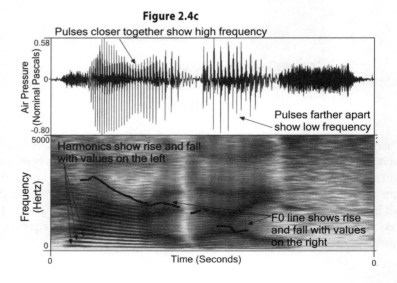

Formants are frequency ranges which are emphasized by the resonating chamber; they can be recognized in either type of spectrogram. In a broadband spectrogram the formants appear as rather thick somewhat fuzzy bands. In a narrowband spectrogram they appear as a darkening of several adjacent harmonics. The use of one or other type of spectrogram is a matter of what is being investigated. Most sound analysis programs will also calculate formants and represent them as lines or rows of dots.

Considerable information about vowels can be gained from the first two formants: F1 and F2. The basic shape is easy to remember. Here are the typical dimensions for an adult male speaker:

F1. If the tongue is high, F1 is low (around 280 Hz). If the tongue is low, F1 is high (around 860 Hz).

F2. If the tongue is front, F2 is high (about 2100 Hz.). If the tongue is back, F2 is low (about 820 Hz).

If the two formant ranges are plotted in this way, the results produce a shape very similar to the familiar vowel triangle, as found in any standard textbook of phonetics. See Figure 2.4d.

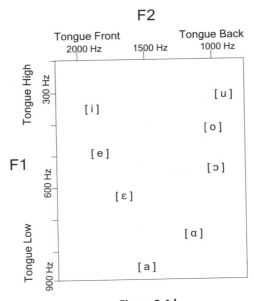

Figure 2.4d

2.5   Setting spectrogram and pitch for intonation analysis

The following figure shows the word *paradise* as a waveform (top), spectrogram (bottom) and pitch line (bottom).

The spectrogram is narrow band, so it shows more than twenty harmonics. As it stands, the ranges for spectrogram and pitch are quite different. Pitch, on the right, runs from 50 Hz to 400 Hz while the spectrogram range on the left runs from 50 Hz to 6000 Hz.

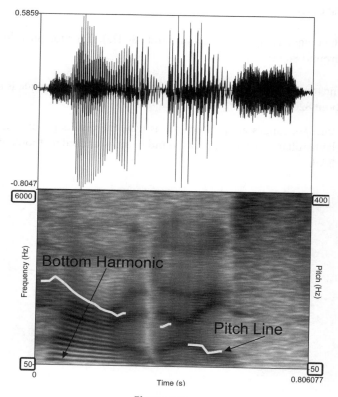

Figure 2.5a

The pitch line is less robust than the spectrogram – a small error is settings can cause a very inaccurate display. To check that all is well, impose the pitch line on the bottom harmonic by making the settings identical.

The first step is to get a rough idea of the range by clicking just above and just below the first harmonic and reading the values on the left:

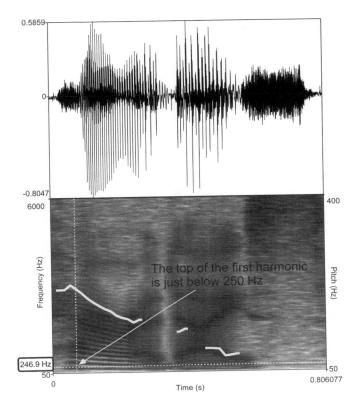

Figure 2.5b

The bottom turns out to be around 75 Hz. The second step is to change the pitch settings:

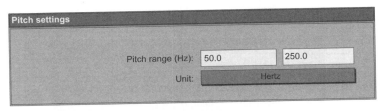

Figure 2.5c

The third step is to change the pitch display using advanced pitch settings:

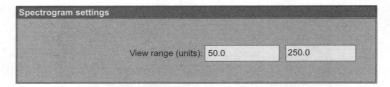

Figure 2.5d

And finally, change the spectrogram settings:

Figure 2.5e

Here is the result: It shows that the 'fine tuning' for pitch settings is reasonably good but not yet perfect, because the pitch line is not continuous where the harmonic indicates that it should be.

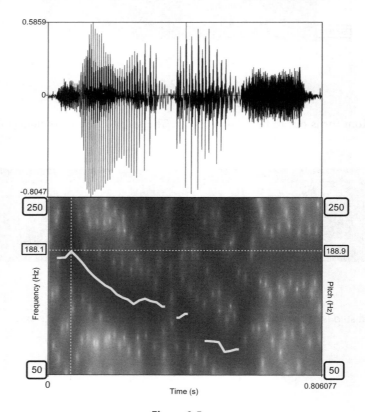

Figure 2.5e

Note that if some settings with the pitch are wrong the mistake shows up clearly because the pitch line departs from the center of the first harmonic:

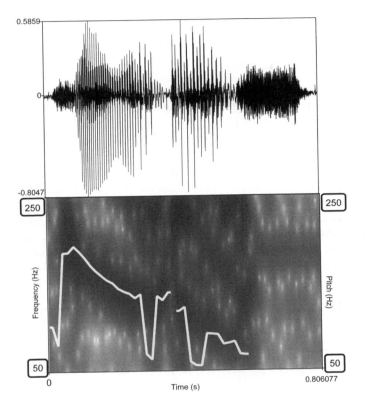

Figure 2.5e

3 Interpretation of sound

3.1 Phonology and lexicogrammar

3.1.1 Articulation and prosody

From the phonological point of view, the task in analyzing sound is to describe the features which make it meaningful as language; this means investigating how sound is organized systematically in each particular language, such as English. One important part of this task is the segmentation of sound in the individual bits which we recognize as the components of words.

Given a particular stretch of sound [kæt], an English speaker will recognize three segments in temporal sequence, /k/+/æ/+/t/ (or, as represented in standard orthography, c + a + t). These stand for the **word cat**, which in turn construes the (**experiential**) **meaning** 'cat'; and this meaning makes contextual reference to a species of domestic pet, or, in a more scientific register, to a sub-genus within the order of mammals. The wave form and spectrogram in Figure 3.1.1 show the acoustic/physical pattern that underlies this segmental organization.

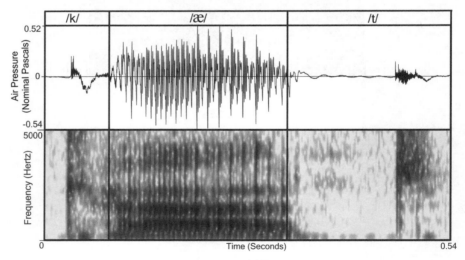

Figure 3.1.1 PLAY 🔊

These patterns are constructed in the articulation of the consonants and vowels that go to make up English syllables. This aspect of phonology, and the underlying phonetic processes, those of **articulatory phonetics**, are explained in many available textbooks of linguistics.

In this book we are concerned not with articulation but with the other aspect of phonology, namely *prosody*. Prosodic patterns are those involved in the construction of the higher phonological units, the *foot* and the *tone unit*; these are patterns of *rhythm* and *intonation*. More specifically, we are concerned with intonation, which is the property of the tone unit; but in the course of the discussion we will also deal with matters of rhythm (more explicitly, rhythm and stress), whose domain of operation is the foot. Where syllables, with their articulatory structure, typically construe experiential meaning, the meanings construed by intonation are typically of other kinds: *interpersonal*, *textual* and at times also *logical*. For explanation of these different kinds of meaning, called *metafunctions*, see Chapter 5 below.

3.1.2 Levels of analysis (strata)

We refer to the levels of analysis in language as *strata.* We recognize four strata: *semantics, lexicogrammar, phonology* and *phonetics.*

The four strata are related by *realization.* The term 'realize' is reasonably transparent: each step in the chain of realization brings one closer to the output in speech sound. But it is important to note that this means 'closer' only in analytical terms; it is the whole speech event which unfolds as an integrated process in time.

Patterns at each stratum are realized by other patterns at the stratum below. When we describe a given stretch of language, we may analyse it many times over; if we do this, then at each stratum the analysis is carried out within a different descriptive framework.

The units at one stratum do not generally match the units at other strata; for example, there is no unit of English grammar that matches the syllable or the foot of the phonology. But the higher phonological unit, the tone unit, does match a distinct unit in the grammar, that we call the *information unit.* One tone unit functions as the realization of one information unit.

Then why two names? Partly because, as we said, the units *do not* normally correspond across strata, so we cannot conflate other terms in this same way; but more importantly because it would give the wrong message. The information unit is a unit of the lexicogrammar; so it functions in the construction of meaning — it faces the semantics, so to speak. The tone unit, on the other hand, is a unit of the phonology; it functions in the organization of speech sound. It can be described in terms of the parameters we have been talking about: perceptual features of pitch, loudness and length — and, ultimately, in terms of the physical properties of fundamental frequency, amplitude and duration.

What then is the relation between the stratum of phonology and the stratum of phonetics? This is rather analogous to the relation between the grammar and the semantics. Semantics is where language interfaces with the outside world, the physical and social environment which we experience as being around us and inside us; the grammar organizes this experience into systematic networks of meaning. Analogously, phonetics is where language interfaces with the human body, the organs involved in the production and reception of speech; the phonology organizes this physiological resource into systematic networks of speech sound. Of course, both the internal organization of language and its interfacing with the eco-social and physiological environments take place in the human brain.

The organization at the 'inner' strata, those of lexicogrammar and phonology, is specific to each language. But since we all live on the same planet, and we all share the same brain and bodily structure, there is much in common both to the sounds we can produce and hear and to the meanings we can express and understand. This is not to say that all semantic and phonetic features are 'universal'; they are not. But when we learn a language other than our own, we start with (usually unconscious) expectations of what is likely and what is possible; so we assume that the same resources will be used for making speech sounds, even if they may be deployed in very different ways.

3.2 Information unit and tone unit

At each of the two inner strata, we find smaller and larger 'chunks', constituent units which carry the patterns operating at that stratum. Each unit plays its own specific part: in the lexicogrammar, for example, the **clause** carries (among others) the patterns of **transitivity**, construing the various types of process we experience in the world (processes of doing and happening, sensing and saying, being and having), and the various roles that go with each (who does or says what, to whom; who or what exists, and so on); the **verbal group** carries (among others) the patterns of **polarity** and **tense** (whether happening or not, and when) [see Halliday ed. Matthiessen 2004 for a detailed account of the grammar of English as interpreted in SFL]. In the phonology the foot organizes the timing of speech and the relative salience and duration of the syllables, while the syllable organizes the sequencing of consonants and vowels.

The two strata come to coincide most closely in the pairing of the information unit with the tone unit: the boundaries do not coincide exactly, but there is always a one to one correspondence. The information unit organizes the flow of discourse at the grammatical level, in terms of its news value: what parts are earmarked to be attended to and what parts to be 'taken as read'. Connected speech unfolds as an unbroken sequence of 'messages', in which the speaker is alternating between elements of Given and elements of New; these map into the structures of the other grammatical units, most powerfully into those of the clause.

The tone unit organizes the flow of discourse at the phonological level, in terms of its melodic shape: what parts carry the primary pitch movement and what parts are providing the accompaniment. Here the functioning elements are the Tonic and the Pretonic; these supply the framework within which the speaker's variations in pitch and loudness are perceived and interpreted by the listener. In the rest of this chapter we shall explore the nature of the tone unit.

3.2.1 Nature of the tone unit

The tone unit is characterized by various types of pitch contour. One example of this would be a falling contour, known as 'fall' or 'tone 1', such as we might expect to hear in the command *Run!*

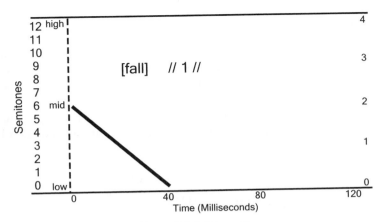

Figure 3.2.1 // 1 run //

This particular example shows a drop from the midpoint of a speaker's normal range of pitch movement. The drawing itself is not phonetically exact. It does not show the actual shape of the pitch change, but only the aspect that we are interested in — the fact that it drops, over the course of its run, from about the mid point of the speaker's average range to near the bottom. This is symbolized in words by 'fall' and in numeric coding by '1'. The drawing also suggests a nominal range of one octave (12 semitones) and a duration potential of 120 ms. 'high', 'mid' and 'low' represent the three reference points we use for frequency range, but the numbers at the right allow for a more delicate classification scheme, i.e. high, mid high, mid, mid low and low.

Much of the work of expressing grammatical meaning by intonation in English is done by choosing among a small set of such distinctive contours, covering the whole or one particular part of the tone unit. Before discussing these in greater detail, however, we need to specify how the tone unit is internally structured.

3.2.2 Structure of a tone unit

The tone unit consists of one obligatory element, the Tonic, together with one optional element, the Pretonic. The defining movement of the pitch contour is that associated with the Tonic element. The Pretonic contour patterns are tied to those of the Tonic, in the sense that the range of possible patterns of Pretonic depends on which Tonic is chosen. Each type of Tonic has a different set of Pretonic possibilities.

The tone unit is therefore defined in terms of these two patterns. A tone unit is the stretch of language having in its structure an obligatory Tonic, optionally preceded by an associated Pretonic as in Table 3.2.2.

Table 3.2.2

		Tonic
Pretonic	+	Tonic

3.3 The TONE system

We referred in the last section to the small set of distinctive pitch contours which carry grammatical meaning in English, and showed that these were a property of the tone unit; specifically, of that part of the tone unit which is obligatorily present — the Tonic. These distinctive pitch contours are referred to as tones.

The set of possible tones constitutes a system: an exhaustive paradigm of mutually exclusive options. (System names are in small capitals. See further section 4.1 below.) The primary system consists of five distinct tones:

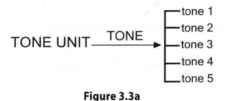

Figure 3.3a

These are realized by movements in pitch as follows [the symbol ↘ means 'realized as']:

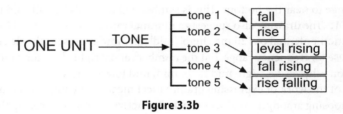

Figure 3.3b

If the numerical labels are found to be difficult to work with, it is always possible to refer to the tones by their phonetic realizations.

3.3.1 Simple and compound tone units

There are, in addition, two further types of contour which enter into the system of TONE: these are realized as 'fall + level rising' and 'rise falling + level rising'. It would be possible to label them 'tone 6' and 'tone 7'; but, as can be seen from their realization statements, this would obscure an important generalization that can be made about them — namely, that they are in fact composite tones made up, respectively, of tone 1 + tone 3 and tone 5 + tone 3. We can therefore introduce them into the system in two steps, as follows:

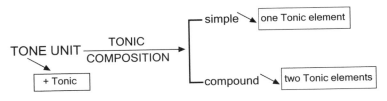

Figure 3.3.1a

This tells us that a tone unit may contain either one or two pitch contours. We shall refer to this as a difference in the number of points of *focus*: the tone unit contains either a single focus (simple tone unit) or a dual focus (compound tone unit). A dual focus always means one major plus one minor focus, in that order. The set of possibilities for dual focus is very restricted; this is explained in section 3.4.2 below.

// 1 ∧ I'm /taking the */**train** // is a simple tone unit, with the focus on *train*. You can hear this clearly. PLAY◄ Sound 3.3.1a With the addition of a secondary bit of new information, say the occasion of the trip, a minor focus may be added in the tone unit: // 13 ∧ I'm /taking the */**train** this */**time** // PLAY◄ Sound 3.3.1b Representing this as a system shows that there is meaningful choice available: the second utterance could very well have been simple rather than compound: // 1∧I'm /taking the */**train** this / time // PLAY◄ Sound 3.3.1c As you can hear, quite different meanings are produced by choosing the features 'simple' or 'compound'.

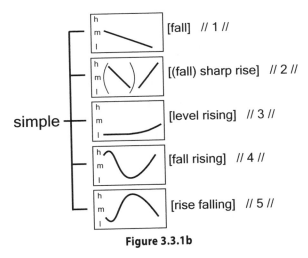

Figure 3.3.1b

The simple tones form a set of five shapes: that is, if a tone unit has only one focus, it will always assume a phonetic shape interpretable as one of these five tones.

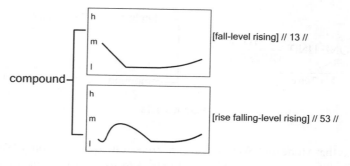

Figure 3.3.1c

The compound tones form a smaller set. There are two: fusions of tones 1 and 3 and of tones 5 and 3. (The number symbols are thus read as 'one three' and 'five three', not 'thirteen' and 'fifteen'.)

3.3.2 Pretonic element

We now need to consider the optional element in the tone unit, the Pretonic element.

Any tone unit, whether simple or compound, and whatever the tone selected, may have a further structural element preceding the Tonic. The possible structures of the tone unit were summarized in 3.2.2 above. These can be represented as a system showing structures as realization :

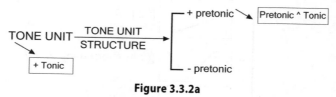

Figure 3.3.2a

Putting this together with the system network for TONIC COMPOSITION and TONE, we get:

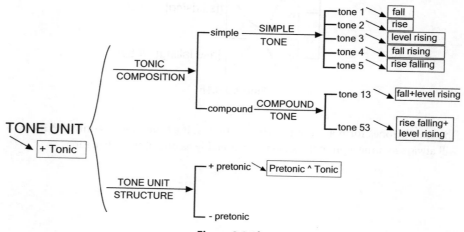

Figure 3.3.2b

3.4   Intonation systems in the establishment of meaning

Three systems are involved in making meaning through intonation: TONE, TONALITY and TONICITY. These are phonological systems; but they function directly as the realization of systems in the grammar. In this respect intonation systems differ from systems of articulation (consonants and vowels). Thus, while (say) the vowels /a/ /i/ /u/ are systemically distinct in the phonology, they have no direct lexicogrammatical function — there is no general meaning realized by the contrast between them. With intonation systems, on the other hand, there is; the contrast between rising tone and falling tone, for example, always realizes a contrast between terms in some grammatical system. Typically an intonational system will have more than one function in the grammar, depending on the lexicogrammatical environment; but in all cases their meanings are proportional. We shall exemplify this in the next three subsections.

3.4.1   TONE

A choice in tone can realize both *interpersonal* and *logical* meanings. We will illustrate from the logical first.

3.4.1.1   Tone expressing logical meaning

The grammatical relationship of coordination is signalled through the choice of a tone 3 ^ tone 1 sequence at the phonological level, as in the utterance:

> // 3 you buy the tickets // 1 and I'll pay for the dinner //
> PLAY ◀ Sound 3.4.1.1a

By contrast, the grammatical relationship of subordination is signalled through the choice of a tone 4 ^ tone 1 sequence, as in the utterance

> // 4 if you buy the tickets // 1 I'll pay for the dinner //
> PLAY ◀ Sound 3.4.1.1b

However, we can see that there is redundancy here, because the contrast between coordination and subordination is also being realized in the grammatical structure: (coordination) a and b, (subordination) if x [then] y. Clearly it is possible for the two forms of realization to vary independently; and this adds to the total meaning potential. For example we can have

> // 3 if you buy the tickets // 1 I'll pay for the dinner //
> PLAY ◀ Sound 3.4.1.1c

Here the grammatical structure sets this up as a condition, but the tone sequence masks its conditionality and assigns equal status to the two parts. Similarly we can have

> // 4 you buy the tickets // 1 and I'll pay for the dinner //
> PLAY ◀ Sound 3.4.1.1d

Here we can clearly recognize the opposite effect: the first clause, although grammatically coordinated with the second one, sounds as if it is to be interpreted as a condition. This in fact is the origin of the familiar type of utterance which is structured as a coordination but is actually meant as a threat:

> // 4 you try doing that again // 1 and I'll get really angry //
> PLAY ◀ Sound 3.4.1.1e

In the first pair of examples the clause structure and the intonational realization were working in parallel: the coordinator 'and' gave the same meaning as the tone 3 ^ tone 1 sequence, and the subordinator 'if' gave the same meaning as the tone 4 ^ tone 1 sequence. In the second pair of examples the two features were recombined, giving an effect that is 'marked' because it contrasts with the 'unmarked' association that we illustrated first. What is happening here is that there is an interplay between two systems, both a part of the grammar; one is realized in the grammatical structure, the other is realized in the intonation system, and the meanings are closely related, but they are not identical. This means that the unmarked combinations are not in fact redundant, and the marked ones are not self contradictory.

3.4.1.2 Tone expressing interpersonal meaning

Secondly, tone choice can also realize different interpersonal relationships between the speaker and the listener(s). Let us first set up the primary interpersonal system of SPEECH FUNCTION at the semantic stratum.

At the semantic stratum one of the units of meaning is the ***move***.

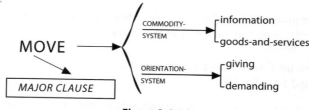

Figure 3.4.1.2a

This unit is the entry condition for two simultaneous two-feature systems dealing (1) with the COMMODITY being negotiated (goods and services versus information) and (2) with the negotiating ORIENTATION of the speaker (giving or demanding).

The four possible combinations specified by this network are important elements in our everyday talk about language, with the familiar names of statement, question, offer and command.

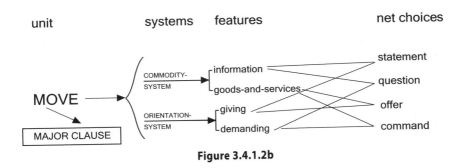

Figure 3.4.1.2b

Three of these have lexicogrammatical realizations which at first seem almost inviolable: a question realized by an interrogative clause: *Where's the sugar? Is it here?*, a statement by a declarative: *No, it's in the cupboard*, and a command by an imperative: *Put it on the counter*. (The offer is less predictable: *Would you like a coffee? Have a coffee. Here's a coffee*, and so forth).

It turns out, however, that questions, commands and statements are not as restricted in their grammatical form as it might seem. Take, for example, the interpersonal meaning 'statement'. The commodity 'information' can be 'given' in a number of ways. The second clause in the sequence 'You stole that blind man's money. Wasn't that kind.' is in the interrogative mood, but it clearly is not a question. The speaker here is not demanding information about the kindness of stealing — he or she is giving information: the message that such an action was not kind. Putting it as an ironic interrogative rather than a straightforward declarative gives it a sharp interpersonal meaning. The force of the speaker's attitude is conveyed along with the representational message.

Here we see the effect of the same kind of redundancy as we found with the logical meanings above. If we were showing the typical realizations of the four basic speech functions, we would also need to specify the tone, as in Table 3.4.1.2

Table 3.4.1.2

statement	declarative	neutral	tone 1
yes/no question	interrogative: polar	neutral	tone 2
wh- question	interrogative: non-polar (lexical)	neutral	tone 1
command	imperative	neutral	tone 1

But, on the same principle as before, the two parts of the realization can be de-combined and new meanings created by recombining them: e.g. declarative / tone 2 'You stole the blind man's money? (I can't believe it.)'

In this case, however, the TONE system allows for considerably greater possibilities. Consider the following utterances all containing the wording *I like it*, spoken in reference to a painting seen at an art gallery:

Awestruck art critic:
// 5 I like it //   (strong: 'I really like it');
PLAY ◀ Sound 3.4.1.2a

Budget conscious buyer:
// 4 I like it //   (reserved: 'I do like it, but...');
PLAY ◀ Sound 3.4.1.2b

Indecisive viewer:
// 3 I like it //   (non-committal: 'I don't object to it');
PLAY ◀ Sound 3.4.1.2c

Defensive viewer, when just accused of not appreciating the painting:
// 2 I like it //   (challenging: 'what makes you think I don't?');
PLAY ◀ Sound 3.4.1.2d

Viewer responding casually to question:
// 1 I like it //   (neutral.)
PLAY ◀ Sound 3.4.1.2e

Provided we use a declarative clause, the differences in meaning are proportional, expressing the attitudes of the speaker towards the listener and towards the content of his or her own message. We refer to this as the system of KEY and we can represent this set of systemic options as follows:

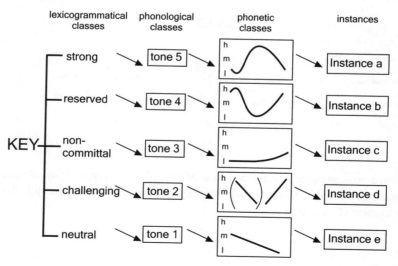

Figure 3.4.1.2c

For purposes of illustration here we have presented the five phonological alternants of simple tones as forming a single lexicogrammatical system. In fact from the lexicogrammatical point of view what we have here is really an interrelated set of smaller systems; these will be presented and explained in Part II below.

The question might be raised at this point: why do we show 'key' as a grammatical system rather than as a semantic system whose features are realised directly in the phonology — bypassing the lexicogrammar, so to speak? This would seem, on the face of it, to be a simpler solution, since it would avoid one level in the overall representation.

There are two parts to the answer. One is theoretical: the lexicogrammar is the theoretical construct that enables us to explain the semogenic (meaning-making) power of language as a whole — provided that we present it in a comprehensive account. The second is descriptive: systems realised by intonation intersect with grammatical systems of the more familiar kind (those realized in wording) in precisely the same way that these intersect with each other. Thus what might be locally a simpler solution turns out to be globally much more complex.

Let us illustrate this second point, coming back to the system of KEY. We said that the entry condition to this system was declarative clause (which is a term in the grammatical system of MOOD). Supposing the clause had been interrogative: *Do you like it?* It would still have been possible to vary the tone; but the meanings of the various tone choices would have been different. There is no proportionality such that

// 1 she likes it //   is to   // 2 she likes it //

as

// 1 does she like it //   is to   // 2 does she like it //

There is a different set of choices with interrogative mood, which we therefore represent as a different system. And this is comparable to the interaction between mood and modality, where both are systems realised in the wording. For example, the distinction between *must* and *may* in a declarative clause, as in *she must be tired* and *she may be tired*, is not the same as that in interrogative e.g. between *must she be tired?* and *may she be tired?* (which are also much less likely to occur).

Note that it is the grammatical categories of declarative / interrogative (mood) which are critical, not the semantic categories of statement / question (speech function). Thus even if *she's tired?* is a question, it follows the declarative pattern when combined with modality:

// 2 she must be tired //

versus

// 2 she may be tired //

We could gloss the meanings as follows:

// 1 she must be tired // 'I think it certain she is tired'
// 1 she may be tired // 'I think it possible she is tired'
// 2 she must be tired // 'I think it certain she's tired — do you agree?'
// 2 she may be tired // 'I think it possible she's tired — do you agree?'
// 2 must she be tired // 'do you think it certain she's tired?'
// 2 may she be tired // 'do you think it possible she's tired?

Let us pursue this illustration one stage farther, since it raises an issue which frequently arises in the intonational systems.[1]

Suppose we note that (as here) the contrast in meaning between *must* and *may* depends on the mood of the clause: it is one thing in declarative, another thing in interrogative. Two possibilities arise.

(1) The two may still be proportional; to choose a more likely example — if the phone rings:

(declarative)	that will be Tony	'I think it likely....'
	that might be Tony	'I think it possible....'

(interrogative)	will that be Tony?	'do you think it likely....?'
	might that be Tony?	'do you think it possible ?'

Here the two pairs are proportional. The difference is that in the declarative the speaker is giving his own opinion in the matter, while in the interrogative he is asking to be given the opinion of the listener. We would show these as two simultaneous (independent) systems, on the grounds that the meaning of the feature combination is predictable from the meanings of the individual features.

(2) In the intonational example, on the other hand, the meanings are not proportional:

// 1 I like it //	neutral, e.g. in answer to a question
// 2 I like it //	combative 'why do you assume otherwise?'
// 1 do you like it //	demanding 'I need to know'
// 2 do you like it //	neutral question

Although these might be explained, in terms of high level general notions about the meaning of falling and rising tones, they are not predictable from the potential feature combinations.

These two situations will be represented as different system networks, as in (1) and (2) below. Note that these are only fragments; the actual systems are of course much more complex.

(1)

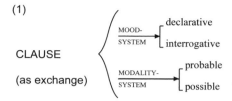

(2)

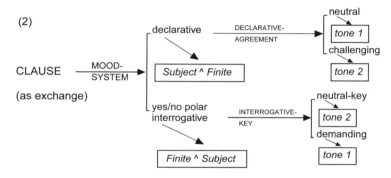

Figure 3.4.1.2d

To sum up this subsection: TONE is a system of the phonological stratum, located at the tone unit and made up of choices: first between simple and compound tone, then among five simple tones and two compound tones, making seven possibilities in all. The choices in the tone system function, in turn, as the realization of choices in a number of various lexicogrammatical systems; and these intonational systems interact with other systems in the grammar (realised by wording), primarily in the interpersonal region but also in the logical region.

The analysis of the phonological system into seven tones is the first step; these are the 'primary' tones. These may be more delicately distinguished into various 'secondary tones', such as high fall / mid fall / low fall, which will be introduced in Part II. Meanwhile we turn to the other intonation systems TONICITY and TONALITY.

3.4.2 TONICITY and information focus

We saw above (3.3) that every tone unit contains a Tonic element, which occurs either alone or preceded by a Pretonic. The Tonic element carries the defining pitch contour of the tone unit; and this may be either 'simple' (one contour) or 'compound' (two contours, of which the second always selects tone 3). We referred to the simple Tonic as having 'single focus', the compound Tonic as having 'dual (major plus minor) focus.' This now needs to be explained.

Let us first look at it from the phonetic end. Given any tone unit, where does the Tonic segment begin? Phonetically, the onset of the Tonic is marked by a kind of prominence; this is often heard as loudness (and in phonemic theory was called 'primary stress'), but it is actually more complex than that. Tonic prominence is mainly a matter of pitch movement: it is the place where the greatest amount of pitch movement occurs, relative to the range of pitch change that is available as the potential range decreases from wide potential at the beginning of the tone unit to much narrower potential at the end. Tonic prominence will be established not by the greatest fall or rise, but by the greatest relative fall or rise, according to the tone selected.[2]

It may also be characterised by a movement of greater duration. But duration of what? Pitch movement over what segment of speech?

The most obvious candidate here is the syllable. Typically, in fact, the Tonic prominence is clearly allocated to one particular *salient* syllable, which stands out because of its combination of amplitude, duration (timing), and change of pitch along one or other of the (tone) contours. We can refer to this as the 'tonic syllable'. The tonic syllable marks the beginning of the Tonic element of the tone unit.

The limiting case of a tone unit is one that consists of only one syllable, like // 1 stop // or // 1 why // or // 2 cream // ('Do you want cream with your coffee?'). Here, there is no choice as to where the tonic element begins — no choice in *tonicity*, as we call it. As soon as there is more than one syllable in the tone unit, as in the great majority of instances, there is a choice in tonicity. Tonicity means the location of the Tonic element; this is initiated by the tonic syllable, which is realised phonetically as that syllable carrying prominence of the kind described.

3.4.2.1   A note on SALIENCE

The syllable that carries the tonic prominence will always be a *salient* syllable: one that already carries a prominence of its own because of its position in the wording.

Let us mark out the salient syllables in that previous paragraph, as they will appear if it is read aloud. The salient syllables are all those immediately following the slash.

the / syllable that / carries the / tonic / prominence will / always be a
/ salient / syllable: / one that al/ready / carries a / prominence of its
/ own be/cause of its po/sition in the / wording.

Phonetically this salience appears as greater amplitude and duration. Salient syllables are generally heard as both louder and longer than the non-salient, or **weak**, syllables surrounding them.

How do we know which syllables will be salient? English words of two or more syllables have one syllable (more than one in very long words) which is *accented*; this is often the first syllable, but not always. In the example above, the words *syllable, carries, tonic, prominence, always, salient* and *wording* are accented on the first syllable, the words *already, because* and *position* on the second. Such accented syllables will normally carry salience in connected speech, simply by virtue of their prominence within the word. In addition, some monosyllabic words will typically be salient: namely, those which operate lexically, as 'content' words (in open sets). We could change the end of the above example to

...be/cause of its / place in the / text

where both *place* and *text* would be salient. Monosyllabic words which operate grammatically, as 'function' words (in closed systems), like *that a the of,* are normally not salient. Many words lie on the borderline: common adverbs like *just* and *soon* and *out*, numbers, 'person' words like *myself* and *own,* modal auxiliaries; and these regularly occur either salient or non-salient.

When you listen carefully to continuously flowing English speech, you find there is a tendency for salient syllables to occur at fairly regular intervals, and this affects the syllables in between: the more of them there, the more they will be squashed together to maintain the tempo. Thus the syllables in /*prominence of its* will be shorter than those in /*tonic* or /*own be-*. This means that there is a level of organization of the speech sound in between the tone unit and the syllable, a unit that contains one salient syllable plus any following weak (non-salient) syllables before the next salient one. This is rather like a bar, in music, which always begins with the beat; both arise from the same bodily urge for a regular pulse or *rhythm*. It is also what lies behind the metric foot in verse; so the name *foot* has been taken over from metrics to refer to it.

Our phonological rank scale is thus made up of tone unit, foot, syllable, and phoneme: a tone unit consists of one or more feet, a foot of one or more syllables, and a syllable of one or more phonemes. This means that we can talk about the first foot in the tonic segment of the tone unit as the ***tonic foot***; the ***tonic syllable*** is then the salient syllable that begins the tonic foot. The notion of tonic foot is valuable because the critical movement in the tone unit, while mostly concentrated on the tonic syllable, is typically distributed over the tonic foot as a whole.

3.4.2.2 Information focus

We could set up tonicity as a system at the phonological stratum, as we did with tone (tone 1, tone 2......). If we did this, the primary contrast would be between marked and unmarked tonicity, the unmarked being defined as 'Tonic element beginning on the final salient syllable in the tone unit'.

However, whereas with tone the generalization that can be made at the phonological stratum is extremely powerful, with tonicity there is little point in trying to systematize purely in phonological terms; the generalizations would be both more complicated and less powerful. Instead, we need to look into it straight away from the standpoint of the lexicogrammar — and this is where the concept of 'focus' comes in.

At the lexicogrammatical level, as we saw in 3.4.1 above, the ***tone unit*** corresponds to (i.e. realizes) a unit of information. This ***information unit*** is not identical with any of the units in the grammatical rank scale, but in the unmarked case it is coextensive with a (ranking) clause (see 3.4.3 below). Within the information unit, one element is singled out as the focus of information; and it is this that is realized by tonicity — the Tonic syllable signals the element that is under focus. For example, *the salt* in

// please pass me the **salt** //.

More specifically, the Tonic syllable is the last salient syllable in the focal element. So, for example, in

// I've just been having a conversation with one of the best-informed newspaper correspondents you could ever expect to **meet** //

the item under focus is the whole of the phrase *with one of the best informed newspaper correspondents you could ever expect to meet.*

The system of INFORMATION FOCUS makes a clear distinction between an unmarked and a marked option:

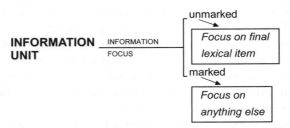

Figure 3.4.2a

for example, if the information unit contains the wording *too many cooks spoil the broth*, there is one unmarked focus, realized phonologically as follows:

// too many cooks spoil the **broth** //

Locating the focus anywhere else than the last lexicalized item constitutes marked focus, as in phonological realizations such as

// too many cooks **spoil** the broth //

or

// too many **cooks** spoil the broth //.

Putting these last two points together, we can now see why we were able to define the unmarked option in tonicity as 'Tonic element beginning on the final salient syllable in the tone unit'. This is where the tonic syllable will occur when the information focus is in its unmarked location.

We will not pursue the analysis much farther at this point; but we do need to take one further step in the analysis of the information unit. The general formula for the structure of an information unit is '(Given +) New'. Note that this lacks the ordering symbol ^ that we find in the (Pretonic ^) Tonic formula for a tone unit. In other words, '(Given +) New' specifies that an information unit must have the functional element

New in its structure, and may have an optional element Given; but it does not specify the order in which these occur.

How do these relate to the focus of information? There are three basic principles at work.

(1) The focal element itself is New. In

// 1 ∧ I /bought a / new com*/**pu**ter //
PLAY ◀ Sound 3.4.2b

the Tonic syllable is */**pu**. This comes in the nominal group *a new computer,* and makes *a new computer* focal. *A new computer* is New.

(2) In an information unit with marked information focus, all elements following the focal element are Given. In

// 1 ∧ I /bought a /new com*/**pu**ter for the /office //

the phrase *for the office* comes after the focal element, and so is Given.

(3) Elements preceding the focal element (whether the information unit is marked or unmarked) may be either Given or New — with the proviso that here the Given, if present, must come first. Put another way, the focal element is either the entire New or the culmination of the New. The phonological system does not determine this. Other information from the lexicogrammar (such as deixis, pronoun reference, lexical prediction and so forth) will help determine the matter. So by itself

// 1 ∧ I /bought a / new com*/**pu**ter //

could realize an information unit with the structure

Lexico-grammar	Given	New	
	I	bought a new computer	
Phonology		Pretonic	Tonic
		// 1 ∧ I /bought a /new com	*/**pu**ter //

This structure might occur in the little dialogue:

A: What did you do today?
B: I bought a new computer.

Here in B's answer, everything apart from *I* is New.

Alternatively, the same tone unit could realize a different Given New structure:

Lexico-grammar	Given	New	
	I bought	a new computer	
Phonology	Pretonic		Tonic
	// 1 ^ I /bought a /new com		*/**put**er //

PLAY 🔊 Sound 3.4.2b

This structure might occur in the little dialogue:

A: What did you purchase?
B: I bought a new computer.

Here the *bought* in B's answer follows the *purchase* in A's question and figures as part of the Given in the information unit. In a real life situation the two would be likely to differ, since in the first case the speaker would probably jump up in pitch on the word *bought*; this would reflect the shift from Given to New taking place at that point. This difference could be brought out with a more delicate phonological analysis.

For the interpretation of Given and New, and for more detailed treatment of the information unit, see Chapter 5 below.

3.4.3 TONALITY and information distribution

TONALITY is concerned with setting the boundaries of the tone unit. As with TONICITY, we can look at it from the phonetic point of vantage: there are moments where one pitch contour is overtaken by another. Note that there are typically no pauses between tone units; the melodic contour of spoken discourse is continuous, and a pause is much more likely to occur in the middle of a tone unit — for example before a rare or unexpected word — than at the point where a tone unit ends.

In fact there are no clear boundaries between tone units in connected speech; but we can take a theoretical decision by saying that a tone unit continues up to the point where a new tone choice is embarked upon. This may be either one of the five tones described above, or a 'secondary tone' functioning as Pretonic to one of the five tones. Phonetically this 'embarking on a new tone choice' takes the form of a marked change of direction, or upjump (and occasionally a downjump) occurring on a salient syllable.

However, as with the location of the Tonic, so also with the boundary of the tone unit the significant issue is the relationship of the tone unit to units set up in the grammar. We have noted already that the tone unit in phonology realizes the information unit in the grammar; but how does the information unit, in turn, relate to the clause, or the group or the word?

Here again we can make a clear distinction between a marked and an unmarked option. As pointed out in the last section, in the unmarked case the IU is coextensive with (i.e. is mapped on to) one clause; we specified this further as a 'ranking' clause, which means a clause that is functioning clausally — that is not rankshifted (downgraded, embedded) to function as, or as part of, a nominal element. Thus, other things being equal, a stretch of language that we recognize on phonetic / phonological grounds as a tone unit will be (the realization of) an information unit in the grammar; and this, in turn, will have the same extent as a grammatical clause. Here is an example:

		John and I	are staying	on the **farm**	all week
PHONOLOGY	TONE UNIT	// Pretonic		/ Tonic	//
GRAMMAR	INFO UNIT	((⟵————————————— New —— (focus)| Given))			
GRAMMAR	CLAUSE	nominal group	verb group	prep. phrase	adv. group
	(MOOD)	Subject	Finite/Pred'r	Adjunct	Adjunct
	(TRANSITVITY)	Actor	Process	Loc./Spatial	Ext./Temp.

Figure 3.4.3a

Any other mapping between the information unit and the structural units of the grammar (those on the grammatical 'rank scale') is considered marked, and hence needing to be explained in terms of its discursive environment. .

The system of INFORMATION DISTRIBUTION can be shown as follows:

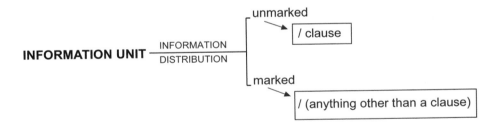

NOTE: in realization statements the slash (/) = 'conflates with (is mapped onto)'

Figure 3.4.3b

In

// 1 ʌ we can */**do** that . . . *// 3 **on** // 1 the . . . /week */**end** / maybe //
PLAY ◄ Sound 3.4.3

there is only one clause, but there are three information units: These are clearly (and unusually) separated by long periods of silence.

The first information unit consists of most of the clause: *we can do that*. The next consists of the word: *on* by itself. The final tone unit consists of the three words *the, weekend* and *maybe*.

This unusual set of choices within the INFORMATION DISTRIBUTION system is the result of a discursive environment which is unique indeed. A researcher is discoursing with a bonobo (the species of ape which is closest to humans), and is 'shadowing' part of her talk by pointing to the symbol for *on* on a lexigram board (which the bonobo shares and uses to communicate with the researcher). The first part of the conversation directed to the bonobo is quite normal in terms of its spontaneity and pace, and the information distribution is almost unmarked: the Subject, Finite, Predicator and Complement of the clause, *we can do that* are conflated with the initial tone unit. All that remains are the phrase *on the weekend* and a concluding modal adverb *maybe*. But these two units are not conflated, together or separately, with an information unit. Instead, the single word *on* is conflated with an information unit, and then the final information unit contains the group *the weekend* together with the concluding expression of uncertainty *maybe*.

In this way the system of TONALITY opens up a vast range of possibilities in the way the constituents of clause structure may be distributed into quanta of information — all of which make a significant difference to the overall meaning of the message.

Notes

1   Note the terminological distinction between 'intonation systems' (i.e. systems of intonation, in the phonology) and 'intonational systems' (i.e. systems which are realised by intonation but are themselves located in the lexicogrammar).

2   This may be a glide, or, especially where there are voiceless consonants involved, may take the form of a downward jump or upward jump.

4 The linguistic environment of intonation

4.1 Systems and system networks

In the previous sections we have examined the phonological resources of intonation in English, and shown in outline what contribution these resources make to the construction of meaning. In this section we shift our angle of vision so as to foreground the meanings rather than the sounds. We shall still be concerned mainly with those meanings that are, at least in part, realized by choices in intonation. But first we shall try to show how the meanings themselves are organized as systems of choice, and how meanings that are realized prosodically fit in to the general picture of the semantics and grammar of English.

The set of possible options at any stratum is represented in the form of a system network. We have already introduced system networks as the way of representing the phonological systems of intonation; the network shows the total potential of the system, up to whatever degree of delicacy is required (or can be attained). Grammatical and semantic networks have the same properties and the same notational conventions. They represent the potential at the levels of wording and of meaning.

It is an essential feature of systemic theory that its most abstract representations are paradigmatic. A language is construed not as an inventory of structures but as a semiotic system: that is, as a potential for creating meaning. Structure has to be accounted for, of course; but it comes in as part of the process whereby the meaning is made manifest through functional configurations of various kinds (like the elements of a tone unit, of a foot or of a syllable). This has one important consequence: it means that we do not first describe something and then ask how it can be related to everything else. In a system network, describing something actually consists in relating it to all other possibilities. Each feature in the network is defined by reference to what it might have been; the network thus makes explicit the notion that meaning is discrimination as well as substance. Meaning arises at the 'fault line' between competing alternatives.

4.2 Strata

We have referred to the four strata of language as the semantic, the (lexico)grammatical, the phonological and the phonetic. The stratum of phonology is the sound system of a language: its articulatory and prosodic resources. The prosodic systems of English are those of intonation and rhythm. We shall raise elsewhere the concept of 'prosodic' as a way of theorizing about phonological systems of any kind; here we want to concentrate on the categories of intonation and rhythm in order to locate them within the overall stratal framework.

In terms of the opposition between 'content' and 'expression', phonological systems are obviously systems of expression, more specifically systems of expression in sound. If we talk of the 'plane of expression', we mean the phonological system of a language together with its realization in phonetics.

The 'plane of content' includes the lexicogrammatical and semantic systems. In the simplest terms, we can think of content and expression as a sign: the content is the dark side, the expression is the light side. Using this very simple model, we could set up a system showing a choice in expression, between 'falling tone' and 'rising tone', realizing a choice in content, between 'certainty' and 'uncertainty':

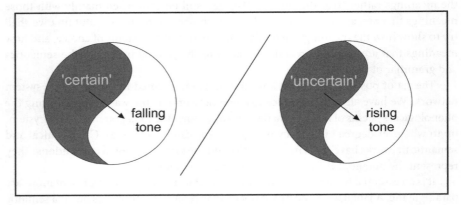

Figure 4.2a

In this picture, the content plane is collapsed into a single stratum, without any distinction being drawn between semantics and lexicogrammar. This model in fact works reasonably well for a human infant's protolanguage, because the protolanguage is made up of systems of simple signs; it will also work for the 'language' of other, non-human species.[1]

For a language in the usual sense, however (post-infancy human language), this model will not work. Language as we know it has evolved further, through the content plane expanding to the point where it has split into two: a level of meaning (semantics) and a level of wording (lexicogrammar). What has happened is that the content plane has replicated within itself the same semiotic relationship as that which obtains between it and the expression plane — except for one critical feature, which we shall pick up below. So while content is realized in expression, within the content meaning is realized in wording; and this gives us two strata of content instead of just one. Our model now looks more like Figure 4.2b

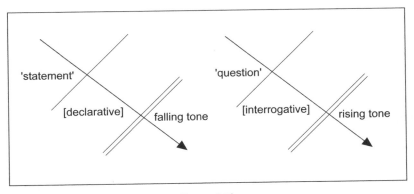

Figure 4.2b

This says that the falling tone realizes a lexicogrammatical category declarative which in turn realizes a semantic category of 'statement', while the rising tone realizes a lexicogrammatical category of interrogative which in turn realizes a semantic category of 'question'. (We shall modify this way of looking at it later on, to something more like that shown in the yin/yang format recast as in Figure 4.2c.)

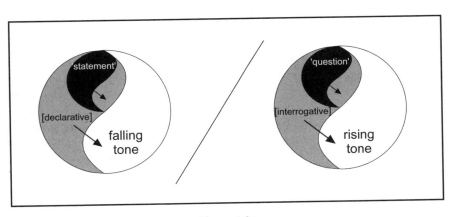

Figure 4.2c

Here the simple content system of 'certainty / uncertainty' has been replaced by a two-stage model in which a meaning system 'statement / question' is realized as a wording system 'declarative / interrogative'. (Note that this is not the way this particular corner of English will be analysed when we come to present the systems of English in detail; it is used here to provide a simple illustration of the model.) It is clear that, taken by itself, this second version has become more complex: we have stated 'content' twice over, once semantically and once grammatically. In the 'local' context of any small illustration, that is how the difference will appear. Globally, however, the effect is greatly to simplify, because the stratified version enables us to bring out, and to explain, all the intricate interconnections that arise between meaning and wording; and it is the flexibility of these interconnections that enables the meaning potential of a language to be openended. As long as there are only the two planes of content and expression, as in the protolanguage of infancy, the system remains closed; the only way it can be extended (and this is how the infant does expand his/her powers of meaning) is by adding to the inventory of signs. Such a system has no semogenic (meaning-creating) power. Once there is further stratification within the content plane, the system can expand indefinitely, through constant coupling, decoupling and recoupling of the bonds between the meaning and the wording. From then on, the only limit to the size of a language is the capacity of the human brain; and that, while it is certainly not infinite, is such as to appear virtually inexhaustible.

Such an enormous potential could, however, get out of hand and run amok, eventually lapsing into total semiotic disorder. So why does this not happen? The reason is to be found in the caveat referred to above, which is that the relationship within the content plane (between meaning and wording) does not exactly replicate that between the one plane and the other. The proportion

meaning : wording :: content : expression

does not strictly hold. The difference lies in the feature of arbitrariness. (Note that this term carries no negative connotations! It was originally introduced in translation from the French *arbitraire*, which is not negatively loaded. A better term in English is 'conventionality'.) The relation between the two parts of the original sign, the content and the expression, is prototypically conventional: this is obvious because the same content has quite different expressions from one language to another — given a content 'H$_2$O', it may be realized as *water* or *aqua* or *air* or *pani* or *shui* or *mizu* or ...: the only constraints are those imposed by the articulatory systems of the language concerned. There are, of course, some features of the content-expression relationship which are not purely conventional (in which intonation holds a key position, as we shall see later); but these stand out clearly as being marked features. Within the content plane, however, the pattern is reversed: the realization of meaning in wording is prototypically natural, or iconic, not conventional. It is not the case that any semantic patterning may be realized by any kind of lexicogrammatical patterning. So (to return to our simplified example), rather than saying that 'the falling tone realizes a lexicogrammatical category of declarative which in turn realizes a semantic category of 'statement' ' we would say something like 'the falling tone realizes a complex feature consisting of declarative realizing 'statement' ' (cf. the revised yin/yang diagram above).

So in our treatment of intonation in this book we shall use this two-level schema, interpreting intonation systems both at the grammatical and at the semantic strata. This will increase the local complexity of particular parts of the description; but it will reduce the complexity overall, since we will be able to refer at various points to the same set of grammatical systems, whose terms recur frequently in different combinations in the realization of different semantic options. A term such as interrogative, which is defined in the MOOD system in the grammar, embodies a powerful generalization about systemic options in wording; at the same time, this particular grammatical feature has a multiplicity of functions in construing systemic options in meaning, and this is typical of the relationship that obtains between the semantics and the grammar.

Meanwhile there is one further aspect of the organization of language that we need to take into account: the fact that a language 'means' in more than one way. This will be the topic of the next sub-section.

4.3 Metafunctions (1): experiential, interpersonal

We have referred to the strata of semantics and lexicogrammar as together constituting the 'content plane' ('le plan du contenu', in Hjelmslev's terminological framework), where 'content' is being used in opposition to 'expression'. But the term 'content' has certain associations which are unfortunate when one is dealing with language. It suggests that language is some kind of a container, in which some separate and distinct substance called 'meaning' is cut into pieces and packaged, presumably so that it can be transported from speaker to listener. This is a very persuasive, semi-learned view of language; it is also a very pernicious one, because it leads in to a number of quite untenable conclusions.

Language does not 'contain' meaning. Language *consists of* meaning; there is no meaning until it is brought into being in the form of language. Meaning does not exist, in the air, so to speak — or in the mind, waiting to be 'expressed' or 'encoded' or packaged into a container. Meaning is created in language; and what we call the content plane is the meaning-creating, or semogenic, facet of the linguistic system. And the meaning that is created by language is of more than one different kind.

In the first place, meaning consists in interpreting human experience, in terms of categories and relations between categories. This is the kind of meaning that it is perhaps natural to think of first, because it relates to our perceptions of the real world: what is going on 'out there', and also what is going on 'in here', within the realm of our own consciousness. (And it is this kind of meaning to which the term 'content' is usually applied.) So we have names for classes of things and events and qualities, ways of expanding these, ways of configuring them into schemas, and ways of expanding the schemas into complex patterns and sequences. Grammatically, we have verbs, nouns, verbal and nominal groups, adverbs and adverbial groups, prepositional phrases, clauses, clause complexes and so on; and these impose order on the flux of our collective experience. The categories that are embodied in the grammars of human languages are not 'given' to us in the real world; they are construed, or rather we construe them, and language evolved as the resource with which we do so. This kind of meaning is that whereby language becomes the resource for construing experience; we call it *experiential* meaning.

In the second place, alongside this experiential mode, language has another, more active mode of meaning: we use language to enact our social relationships. Most obviously, perhaps, this takes the form of engaging in dialogue: we set up particular dialogic relations one with another, giving or demanding either information or goods-&-services

of some kind, and exchanging attitudes and judgments within the immediate context of the situation. Grammatically, we exploit a variety of moods, modalities and the like: declaratives, interrogatives, imperatives, exclamatives; judgments of likelihood and of obligation and so on. But above and beyond the immediate context, we are all the time constructing the social order, and our own identities as defined and maintained within it — all this, again, in the form of language; and we are enacting the ongoing relationships in which we find ourselves, in family, neighbourhood, workplace and other institutional contexts. This is the *interpersonal* mode of meaning; here language can be thought of as the resource for enacting social processes.

These kinds of meaning, the experiential and the interpersonal, are the functional contexts in which human language evolved. They are not different 'uses' of language; they are the underlying functions that have shaped the form that every language takes — hence they are unavoidably implicated in everything we say or write. We refer to them technically as *metafunctions*. Here is an analysis of one example showing the mapping of experiential and interpersonal components in the grammar of the English clause (Figure 4.3a).

	can	you	get	that little tag		off	the bread	
[experiential]		Actor		Goal		Location		
	Process					Process	Range	
[interpersonal]	Finite	Subject	Predicator	Complement		Adjunct		
						Predicator	Complement	
	Mood			Residue				

Figure 4.3a

Figure 4.3b shows the systemic features, experiential and interpersonal, that are realized in this example.

[experiential] material process : (effective : active / dispositive) / locative: motion from
[interpersonal] indicative : (interrogative : polar) / modulated : readiness / positive

Figure 4.3b

What happens here is this. The meaning potential of each metafunction can be represented in the form of a grammatical network, showing the options that are available at each rank. At the rank of the clause, the experiential system is that of TRANSITIVITY; the interpersonal system is that of MOOD, including MODALITY. Figure 4.3c(1) shows the most general (least delicate) portions of the network for these two systems in English.

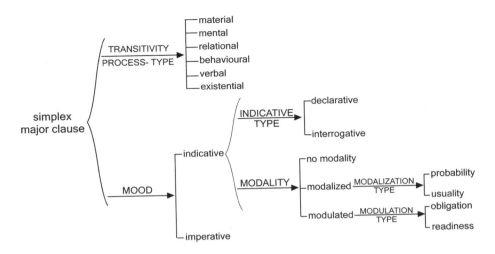

Figure 4.3c

Selections of features within each of these networks are realized as different functional configurations, like Finite followed by Subject realizing interrogative; these configurations are mapped one on to the other and realized, in turn, as a unified syntagm — that is, as a sequence of groups and phrases. The example above consists of verbal group *can get* + nominal group (1) *you* + nominal group (2) *that little tag* + prepositional phrase *off the bread*, the last of these in turn consisting of preposition *off* + nominal group *the bread*. Every "major clause" in English selects in this way both for transitivity and for mood.

That is to say: the clause 'means' simultaneously in two distinct and complementary ways. Experientially, it construes an experiential figure: (process) 'remove', (participant, affected) 'little tag', (participant, agentive) 'individual human', (circumstance: spatial location of origin) 'bread'. Interpersonally, it enacts an interpersonal dialogic relationship: (persons) 'you & me', (give goods-&-services) 'I want you to ...', (modulation) 'if you are willing/able'. The experiential and interpersonal meanings are bound together in the system of language; they cannot be realized independently, but only together in a single semiotic act.

4.4 Metafunctions (2): textual, logical

We shall see in a moment where intonation fits in to the total picture so far: its special contribution to the interpersonal aspect of meaning. Meanwhile however there are two further metafunctional components to be taken into account; and intonation has some part to play in these as well.

One of these is the ***textual*** metafunction. The textual is that aspect of the meaning of language that is concerned with the creation of text, the ongoing flow of discourse that is systematically related to the context of the situation. The system of INFORMATION FOCUS, whereby the information unit is structured in terms of Given and New (see Chapter 3, Section 3.4.2 above), is a system of the textual metafunction. The 'information unit', as we saw, is a grammatical unit that is specific to this particular kind of meaning. It is not another kind of clause, or part of a clause; it is a structure in its own right which associates freely with the experiential/interpersonal units. In the typical case, it gets mapped on to the clause; but it creates its own flow of information without being constrained by the boundaries set up in these other metafunctional structures.

There is in addition a textual system that is located at the clause: the system of THEME. This system enables the speaker to structure the clause as a message, a two-part arrangement consisting of a Theme and its development, or Theme + Rheme in grammatical terms. The Theme is the speaker's point of departure; it is realized in English by initial position in the clause (the exact delimitation is rather complex; see Halliday ed. Matthiessen, *Introduction to Functional Grammar*, Chapter. 3). The remainder of the clause then constitutes the Rheme. Figure 4.4a shows the same example analysed as a thematic structure, together with the textual features involved.

can you	get that little tag off the bread
Theme	Rheme

[textual] unmarked theme : polar ('yes or no?', i.e. 'can or can't?') / + Subject ('you')

Figure 4.4a

We can now see how these two textual systems, that of INFORMATION FOCUS and that of THEME, interact with one another in the construction of text. In the typical case, one information unit is mapped on to one clause, which then becomes the locus of the intersection between Theme + Rheme and Given + New. When this happens, the information focus, since it is typically located at the end of the information unit, will be mapped on to (part of) the Rheme; and the Theme, in turn, will be constituted of some element that is non-focal, Given rather than New. In the example above, the actual focus was on *tag*, the clause was on a rising tone (tone 2), and this was the peak of prominence — the locus of the steepest rise. In this way *off the bread* was shown to be Given; while the New element began with the pretonic prominence on *get*. Combining Theme + Rheme with Given + New, we can represent the textual structures as in Figure 4.4b.

		can you	get	that little **tag**	off the bread
	THEME:	Theme	Rheme		
[textual]					
	INFO. FOCUS:	(Given)	New ————→ Focus		Given

Figure 4.4b

The textual metafunction includes (just as the other metafunctions already referred to do) many aspects other than those that are sketched in here. Taken as a whole, we can interpret it as the resource for engendering text — managing the speaker's or writer's flow of discourse. The continuous flow of melody and rhythm, as the speaker ongoingly activates the resources of the phonological system, serves both as means and as metaphor: it is the means whereby the speaker keeps the discourse flowing, and also the metaphor for the seamless flux of experience and of personal interaction.

The fourth, and last, of the metafunctions of language is the **logical**. This has links with all the other metafunctions, particularly in some regards with the experiential; but it is also distinct from all of them by virtue of the ways logical meanings are realized in grammatical structure.

It is perhaps a good idea to gloss the term logical as 'logical-semantic', to make it clear that the name refers to the logic of natural language (which we could think of as 'grammatical logic') and not to formal and symbolic logic — forms of logic that were in the first instance derived from natural language but then tidied up, and subsequently (rather perversely?) turned round and used as sticks with which to beat their progenitor (natural language being dismissed as 'wholly illogical'). The logic of grammar is just as coherent as the logic of mathematics; but it is different. For one thing it is fuzzy, although not in the specific sense of 'fuzzy logic' (which is fuzzified mathematical logic); and for another thing it is dynamic — the premises change at every movement of the discourse. But it contains the raw material out of which formal logics have been constructed.

Logical meanings are those which construe relationships, either between elements (of the same kind), or between successive configurations of elements (successive figures). In principle, any group or phrase, or any clause, can be combined with another one of the same functional potential to form a logical nexus. (See Chapter 5, section 5.3 below.)

It will be noted that there is variation in the degree of dependency between the pairs forming a logical-semantic nexus. The nexus is either paratactic, having two members of equal status, neither of which is dependent on the other, or hypotactic, one member being dependent on the other. The difference is important, because it affects the kind of primacy that is established between one clause and the other.

Within a paratactic nexus, the primacy is determined solely by the sequence: the primary clause is the one that comes first. Hence if the sequence of two figures is reversed, the primacy is also reversed:

hear all,	but say nothing		say nothing,	but hear all
1	2		1	2

Figure 4.4c

In a hypotactic nexus, on the other hand, the primacy has nothing to do with the sequence; the dependent member remains dependent whether it occurs following the dominant member or preceding it:

you'll hear all	if you say nothing	if you say nothing	you'll hear all
α	β	β	α

Figure 4.4d

For analyzing and interpreting intonation, it is the clause nexus that will be significant; other logical aspects of intonation can be derived from those associated with the logical relations between clauses. This is in effect the same principle that applies throughout the system: since there is a typical, unmarked association between the clause and the information unit, wherever the domain of an intonational choice is something other than a clause its meaning can be explained by reference to that which it would have in a clausal environment. This does not mean that the meaning will always be the same; but since the prototypical mapping between the flow of discourse and the flow of experiential/interpersonal meanings is that of one information unit (realized phonologically as one tone unit) with one clause, this has shaped the semantic value of the overall intonation system. (Note that this is not to assert that in every discourse this pattern of association will be the most frequent, and in some registers (e.g. news reading on radio or television) it clearly is not. Rather, it is asserting that this is the way the system first evolved — and this can be verified at least circumstantially from the way children first construct the grammar of English as a mother tongue.)

In the next section (4.5) we examine the different types of structure that are typically associated with the various metafunctions. This will help us to understand the meanings of intonational choices in their different metafunctional environments.

4.5   Types of structure associated with the four metafunctions

We have discussed the notion of metafunctions, the different kinds of meaning that are incorporated in every language. They are present in every instance of language use — they are a feature of language as a system, an inherent aspect of the organization of human language as such. They are called 'metafunctions' because they are functional at a very abstract level: they represent the functional contexts within which language was enabled to evolve. Every linguistic act on the one hand makes reference to the categories and relations of human experience (like the 'tag' and the 'bread', the process of 'detaching' one from the other, the notion of 'ability' and so on), and on the other hand sets going, or keeps going, some kind of interactive process (like 'I want you to do something for me', 'tell me if you are able and willing', 'you and I are intimates' and the like); and gains its effect by fusing these into a single expression which has a place in the overall flow of the discourse, with 'you (the child)' and 'your ability' as the point of departure, the 'tag' as main focus and 'off the bread' as a secondary moment of prominence. The metafunctions are thus part of a general theory of language; they are an aspect of the explanatory model we use to understand the workings of language and its relation to its social and material environment.

In presenting them in this way, we are looking at the metafunctions as it were 'from above' — from the standpoint of their role in the semantics of language, in its powers of meaning. Let us now alter our perspective, and look at the metafunctions 'from below' — from the standpoint of language's powers of expression. Do we still see them as distinct, from this end? In other words: are there also different kinds of expression in language? and if so, do these correspond in some way to the different kinds of meaning we have been able to establish?

In order to try to answer this question, we need to ask where the idea of metafunctions comes from in the first place. This takes us back to the concept of the system network. We have said that each stratum in a language — the semantic stratum, the lexicogrammatical stratum, the phonological stratum — may be represented as a network of individual systems (sets of options); such a network states the total resources, the potential that is available at that stratum. Each individual system has a way in (an *entry condition*), and this enables us to show how all the resources are interconnected: which choices are independent of each other, and which are associated; and where two or more choices are associated, what kind of association there is between them.

When grammars are written structurally, as most of them still are, while local associations may be brought in to the picture no general principle of organization will emerge. When grammars are written systemically, based on paradigmatic relations, the general pattern stands out rather clearly. If we represent the systems graphically with lines and arrows, as we have been doing here, the system network for the clause blocks out into three clearly defined topological regions, such that within each region there is very dense 'wiring' (showing a high degree of association among the systems making up the region), whereas between one region and another the wiring is relatively sparse — there is still some association between the blocks, but significantly less than within each. It is these regions that constitute the metafunctions as seen from within the grammar.

Here the perspective is no longer from above — we are not defining them as different ways of meaning; but it is not yet from below either. We are looking at the metafunctions from inside the grammar, where they are construed. The system network for the English clause shows up the three clearly-defined regions of mood-&-modality, transitivity, and theme; and it is these (together with related regions of the networks at other ranks) that we are able to interpret in semantic terms as interpersonal (enacting social relationships), experiential (construing experience) and textual (engendering discourse). The different modes of meaning explain why the grammar evolved in the way it did.

But does this pattern of organization also show up 'from below'? Are there systematic differences in the forms of expression that are associated with the different metafunctions? We remarked earlier that, whereas the relationship between the lexicogrammar and the semantics is typically non-arbitrary (so that we expect this kind of resonance between them), the relationship between the lexicogrammar and the phonology is typically arbitrary, or conventional; there is no a priori reason why the metafunctional components of the grammar should be expressed in different ways. But we also emphasized that these tendencies are not absolute — they are tendencies. So while, by and large, individual lexical items (words and morphemes) do not bear any natural relationship to their meanings, these very fundamental and all-pervasive distinctions within the grammar do resonate somewhat in the forms of expression; and they do so in ways which are critical to the role of intonation in language.

We want to be cautious at this point. We shall state the differences in expression that are associated with the different metafunctions as we find them embodied in English, treating them as descriptive features, not as part of a general theoretical model. They may be properties of every language, and similar patterns can certainly be found in very many languages — but it is not yet clear how to theorize them in suitably abstract terms. So what we are offering here is an account of the situation in English. We will refer to each of the metafunctions in turn.

(1) Experiential metafunction. Here the principal system of the clause is TRANSITIVITY: types of process, with associated participant functions, and circumstantial elements. These are typically realized in the form of **constituency**, or constituent structure: configurations of fairly clearly delineated segments each of which plays a part in the organic construction of the whole. This has always been taken as the norm for linguistic structure; partly because constituency is the simplest form that structure can take (clearly defined and differentiated parts making up a clearly defined whole), but partly also because experiential meaning has always been taken as the norm for meaning in general — meaning as reference, prototypically reference to clearly defined perceptual phenomena.

(2) Interpersonal metafunction. In the interpersonal metafunction, the principal system of the clause is MOOD, together with the closely associated systems of POLARITY and MODALITY: the dialogic relations between speaker and listener ('speech functions'), speaker's judgment of probabilities and obligations, and the like. These are typically realized in the form of some kind of **prosody**, a colouring of some particular stretch of the discourse: the 'spin' given to the clause by final particles, the build-up of motifs within the wording, and melodic or other sound patterns that stretch across the passage as a whole.

(3) Textual metafunction. Here there are two related systems with distinct though overlapping domains, one a system of the clause, the other a system of the information unit. The former is THEME, the organizing of the message around the speaker's point of departure; the latter is INFORMATION, putting in focus what is offered as newsworthy to the listener. These are typically realized in a culminative pattern, peaks of prominence at beginnings and endings; and this sets up a **periodicity** as one movement succeeds another in a continuous discursive flow.

We may liken these three modes of expression to the notions of particle, field and wave. Experiential meanings tend to be construed in a particulate form, made up of segments which (although, of course, they run into each other uninterruptedly at the phonetic level) are identifiable as discrete entities. Interpersonal meanings tend to be construed as field-like: they spread across regions of text, without clear boundaries. Textual meanings tend to be construed in an oscillating pattern, an ebb and flow analogous to the ebb and flow of air pressure that constitutes the sound wave. And it is the fact that these different kinds of meaning are realized in different ways that makes it possible to combine them with each other freely and with minimal constraint.

4.6   The place of intonation in the metafunctional scheme

We can now ask how the resources of intonation relate to this general pattern. Intonation is a continuous melodic movement punctuated by moments of relative prominence. The melodic movement, or 'pitch contour', is prosodic in nature: it stretches over extended portions of speech. The prominence is culminative: it provides focus and so defines rather regularly occurring boundaries, or periods. Phonologically, we refer to the melodic movement as 'tone'; and to the prominence as 'tonic prominence' — thus the system which locates tonic prominence is called 'tonicity'.

As an initial generalization, we can postulate the principle set out in figure 4.6.

tonicity	realizes meanings of the texual metafunction
tone	realizes meanings of the interpersonal metafunction

Figure 4.6

In other words, intonation functions in the grammar in a way that is consistent with the other realizational resources. In its prosodic aspect, as pitch contour, intonation relates to the prosodic features of the syntagm, those run as motifs through the clause: mood (e.g. *you're . . . aren't you, eh?*), modality (e.g. *I think . . . perhaps . . . might*), and expressions of attitude such as appraisals, intimacies and oaths. In its culminative aspect, as tonic prominence, intonation relates to the culminative features of the syntagm, those which assign prominence and so give periodicity to the discourse flow: e.g. theme, and systems of predication and identification (what structural grammars call 'cleft and pseudo-cleft constructions').

As far as the logical metafunction is concerned, it seems natural to expect that intonation would play no part: logic would lie at the opposite end of the semantic spectrum from something like mood. But this is not in fact the case. In the construction of mood falling pitch is associated with making a statement and rising pitch with asking a question. Underlying this, however, is a more fundamental distinction, that between complete and incomplete: a question is an incomplete act of meaning, because it seeks an answer. In the logical metafunction, this motif of complete / incomplete turns up in another guise: rising pitch is associated with a dependent clause, or with a non-final clause in a co-ordinate sequence. Thus tone has a systematic part to play in constructing logical meanings.

The one part of the lexicogrammar to which intonation makes no contribution is the experiential. At first sight this might seem to be the difference between English and a tone language such as Chinese or Vietnamese: in these latter, one of the features discriminating among lexical morphemes is tone (pitch movement), and lexicalized distinctions are, as in every language, typically experiential. But this is misleading; there is no systematic lexical meaning that is construed by this or that tonal opposition. The tone simply functions as a part of the set of phonological resources that are available on the expression plane (and historically it alternates with articulatory features — in Chinese, for example, falling tone evolved as the reflex of lost final voiced obstruence in the syllable). In some West African languages, such as Akan, there is a tonal unit within the clause, extending over more than one syllable; but it is defined by mood, not by transitivity. We do not know of any language in which intonation functions systematically in the realization of experiential meaning (as it could do if, for example, a rising tone always meant something small).

This is a further reason why we prefer not to reduce tone (pitch contour) to a schema of pitch levels, or pitch heights. We agree with 't Hart et al. on their reasons for rejecting this analysis when reasoning 'from below' — that is, when considering the phonological options and their resolution in phonetic shape. But we would add a further consideration when reasoning 'from above', from the semantic point of view. Treating tone as a sequence of pitch heights makes it analogous to the constituent-like structure that is typical of experiential meanings; and, as we have seen, this is the one kind of meaning in which intonation plays no part at all. Of course, it is always possible to reduce other structural modalities (other modes of expression) to the model of constituency; we do this with prosodical and culminative structures in the grammar anyway, so (it might be argued) why not do it with intonation? We do it with the resources of wording because it is easier to represent lexicogrammatical structures in constituency terms (and it always has been done that way!). But we recognize that this is a form of reductionism, since it distorts the nature of prosodic and culminative structures, imposing discreteness on both axes where there should be continuity and 'fuzz'. With intonation, however, reducing pitch contour to pitch heights seems simply perverse. It is not, in fact, easier to represent intonation patterns as discrete segments; it is virtually impossible to derive either the paradigmatic or the syntagmatic continuities from sequences of pitch levels. What we should be attempting, rather, is the reverse: we should try to use intonation as the general model from which to derive representations of interpersonal and textual meanings. In this way mood and modality would appear as a melodic movement in the wording of the clause, (we might note in this connection the high, median and low degrees of probability and obligation; cf. Halliday ed. Matthiessen 2004, Chapter 10); and theme would be shown as a periodic diminuendo from a peak of speaker-oriented prominence.

In other words, we do not think it helpful to treat intonation, or other prosodic features of a language, as a kind of secondary resource, something that is added on at the perimeter of a language to contribute a few extra refinements to its meaning potential. We would argue that the prosodic resources of the phonological system, its intonation and rhythm, are every whit as central to the workings of a language as are the resources of articulation, the repertory of vowels and consonants. We should not be misled by the fact that, in writing systems that are phonologically organized, like that of English, the prosodic aspects of the system are not represented. In fact, it is not entirely true that they are not represented; the punctuation system is a device for bringing in to the picture some of the essential contrasts that are construed by intonation and rhythm, although it is not usually taught as such in school. In any case our aim throughout this book will be to show how intonation and rhythm are integrated into the total semogenic potential of the English language; and how they can be studied in a way which is at once both highly theoretical and grounded in close and accurate observations of the sounds of everyday speech.

4.7   Intonation in infants' language development

It may be pertinent to include here a short note on the place of intonation in the development of language in infancy. Some time between the ages of six and eighteen months, before they embark on learning their mother tongue, children typically develop a protolanguage: a systematic resource for meaning that they construct for themselves in interaction with those who are closest to them.

The meanings they express cannot be exactly translated into adult language; but they are understood, by those within the infant's meaning group, in terms that we could gloss as 'that's interesting! —what is it?', 'hullo: nice to see you', 'do that again!', 'I want that', 'that tastes good' and so on. Likewise, the sounds that infants use cannot be adequately represented as adult speech sounds; they are not articulated as contrasting and bounded segments. Rather, they are constructed posturally, as patterns of movement between the three basic postures of the human articulatory organs, y, w and a:

y: lips spread, front of tongue raised forwards (as in ye)
w: lips rounded, back of tongue raised backwards (as in woo)
a: lips open, tongue lowered (as in ah)

By moving among these postures infants produce sounds such as wa, ayi, wiyuwiyu; they then learn to combine these with consonantal postures, producing protosyllables such as na, da, bu, gui; and to explore intermediate and recombinant vocalic configurations such as [e] and [o] — by which time they are able to model the adult forms.

Along with the three basic postures of y, w and a, the other phonic resource that infants control early is tone: they very soon master the contrast between falling and rising pitch. When they come to construct their protolanguage, they first tend to combine tone and posture into fixed packages, like *da* on falling tone, *a* on rise fall and so on; but they soon discover that the two can be varied separately — the same syllable can be spoken on different tones. For some children this is the first step into grammar, a move which they make along with the move from 'proper' to 'common' terms (from names of individuals to names of classes). Whether or not they adopt this particular strategy, combining intonation with articulation is a condition of entry to the phonological system of every adult language.

We can notice how, in the very first phase of life, both intonation and (proto) articulation are prosodic: that is to say, the configurative patterns and movements that we have called postural are more like continuous contours than like sequences of distinct segments. Of course, adult articulation does not consist in enunciating strings of consonants and vowels one after another. Nevertheless there is a clear constituent-like organization in adult speech: in English we pronounce (and hear) a distinction between, say, bad and bud as one of /æ/ contrasting with /ʌ/ while /b/ and /d/ remain constant; and we are aware of /b/, /æ/ and /d/ occurring in sequence. Not all languages have the phoneme as a prominent feature of their phonological organization: in Chinese, for example, the syllable carries most of the functional load; but there is always some system of phonological constituency. This is why most languages have come to be written phonologically, as strings of syllables or phonemes or something in between the two. Such a representation is not at all suitable for early protolanguage, for which we would need a notation more analogous to pitch accents, as in Figure 4.5a

Figure 4.5a

This would mean something like Figure 4.5b, using the standard vowel triangle.

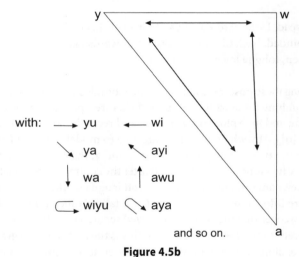

Figure 4.5b

We are not introducing any such notation here. But for understanding the way that intonation works in adult speech it is relevant to point out that intonation itself, and vocal postures having the same prosodic quality, are developmentally prior to segmental articulation — and were probably prior to it also when language first evolved.

4.8 Systemic phonology

We have been assuming that language is organized, and therefore is to be analysed, in terms of strata, phonology being one such stratum; and we shall continue to use this well-established metaphor. But when we are considering the place of phonology within a systemic-functional framework, it is perhaps helpful to be reminded that it is a metaphor, and that stratification is not the only way of thinking about how language works. Firth (1935, 'The technique of semantics') used the metaphor of a spectrum: the linguist's task was to split up meaning in the way that light can be split up into a spectrum. The analyst is able to split up light in this way because of the physical nature of the light rays; but there are also conditions, like a rainbow or a thin film of oil, under which the spectral pattern will appear of its own accord. And we can think of analogous conditions in language, where the usually hidden organization is revealed — for example in forms of verbal art, and in various language games. The bands of colour within the spectrum are not clearly bounded, and this indeterminacy is part of the force of the metaphor: phonology can be thought of as one band, but it is not located within clearly defined limits.

In European linguistics, phonology had first evolved as a historical concept: the language family could be established by tracing speech sounds backwards through time. Saussure formulated a synchronic linguistics in which the speech sounds of a language were represented as a phonological system. Among Saussure's successors, Trubetzkoy developed an abstract model in terms of phonemes and archiphonemes: the system was maintained in equilibrium with sets of contrasting features sharing out the total functional load. Hjelmslev stressed the parallelism between the expression plane and the content plane, and defined the system in terms of paradigmatic and syntagmatic relations; Martinet interpreted the stratal organization as a 'double articulation' with phonology as 'functional phonetics'. Firth added theoretical depth to the paradigmatic and syntagmatic axes with his concepts of system and structure, and in working out these concepts in phonology he developed his distinctive model of 'prosodic' phonology (1948, 'Sounds and prosodies'). This was in sharp contrast to the American structuralist view of phonology, which was grounded in the concept of the phoneme — and usually called, simply, 'phonemics'. For Firth, phonological features were abstract systemic constructs associated with stretches of speech that could be of any extent; furthermore these might be identified not only within the phonological level (such as a syllable) but also at the level of grammar and lexis (e.g. a word).

Systemic functional phonology is based closely on Firth's prosodic theory; but it has had a significant input also from other sources. Before studying with Firth, Halliday had been trained in traditional Chinese phonological theory, under two leading Chinese scholars Luo Changpei and Wang Li. Chinese phonology was based on the analysis of the Chinese syllable into two aspects, an onset and a rhyme; it was an entirely abstract theory, with no labelled categories and no phonetic representations (Halliday 1981, 'The origin and early development of Chinese phonological theory'). Chinese scholars had also set up a prosodic system of four syllabic tones: level, rising, falling and stopped. There were no phoneme-like segments of any kind. After some centuries of indigenous evolution, Chinese phonology came to be influenced by linguistic scholarship from India. Indian phonology was strikingly different, being based on very accurate phonetic observation and explicit descriptions. These of course were derived from Sanskrit, and so did not fit the phonological system of Chinese; but the Chinese scholars adapted the phonetic categories, and used some of them to classify the syllables prosodically, with every syllable assigned to one of four 'grades' on the basis of the prosodic colouring of the setting.

Firth's prosodic phonology was entirely compatible with the Chinese theories, as he found out when working on dialects of modern Chinese. But Firth's own special field of research was in Indian languages (he had taught at a university in India before joining Daniel Jones' department at University College London); and, at a time when very few western linguists were aware of the scholarly traditions of other cultures, he gained a considerable knowledge of Indian theories of language [cf. Brough 1953, 'Some Indian theories of meaning', *Transactions of the Philological Society* 161–176.; Allen 1953, *Phonetics in Ancient India*]. Firth recognized the strength of the Indian tradition in phonetics and in semantics, and this resonated with the distinctive slant taken by his own theory. Unlike the phonemicists, whose categories were largely distributional (on the principles of avoiding the 'mixing of levels'), Firth saw no virtue in trying to insulate one level of analysis from another; his prosodic phonology faced 'outwards' from the sound system itself — and it faced in both directions, both towards meaning and towards sound. In other words, Firth's concept of 'theory' in phonology meant explaining not only phonological patterns (eg. systematic vs. random gaps) but also patterns at higher levels — and also phonetic realizations: descriptions framed in prosodic terms could predict the phonetic exponents considerably more accurately than descriptions based on phonemes and their allophones.

As already remarked, the conception of phonology in systemic functional theory is essentially prosodic, in Firth's sense; but with the phonological features, both prosodic and articulatory, represented in system networks in a way that is analogous to the grammar (and other strata). Each network displays the potential open to a particular phonological unit: thus there are networks for tone unit, foot and syllable in English; and, where applicable, for the phonological features of a particular grammatical unit (e.g. the word in vowel harmony languages). Such units in phonology are often not clearly delimited — in any given language there may be some that are more and some that are less determinate;[2] and while this is true also of the grammar, the principles behind this variation are different at the two strata. In grammar, the driving force comes 'from above', from the way meaning is organized on metafunctional lines: ideational elements tend to be clearly segmental, interpersonal ones much more fluid.

In phonology, on the other hand, the driving force comes 'from below'. Some features, such as pitch movement, are inherently prosodic; others, such as consonantal plosion and closure, are segmental; while features like nasal / oral resonance, front / back vocalization, may be segmentally organized in one language (or one part of a language) and prosodically organized in another. Thus while phonological features, like features at other strata, can always be shown to be systemic, with a definite point of origin for each network, their phonetic reach can be very varied; a syllable prosody, for example, may be realized at syllable initial or syllable final only, or even somewhere outside the syllable altogether.

Relative to the now fairly extensive systemic publications concerned with grammar, semantics and discourse (and with context and genre, and with other modalities than language), there has been rather little systemic functional work in phonology; see Tench, ed; 1992 for a representative selection of papers. On the other hand, within phonology, intonation has been fairly strongly represented. Far from being seen as fringe areas, as in phonemics and many other approaches, in systemic phonology intonation and rhythm are regarded as central. There are a number of reasons for this view. (1) As pointed out already, intonation plays a primary role in early language development; in the protolanguage, articulation begins as a special kind of prosody, rather than the other way round. (2) A language is a meaning-making system, and phonology is an essential component in the making of meaning; systemic phonology foregrounds this aspect, in which intonation is implicated in the most direct manner. (3) Intonation is the most clearly iconic of all phonological features, and hence enables us to modify the view that phonology is totally arbitrary. (4) Intonation tends to realize meanings of the interpersonal kind, and systemic grammarians (uniquely among their kind!) have always given interpersonal meanings equal weight with those of other metafunctions. (5) Intonational systems display proportionalities very clearly, and so serve as a model for the systemic nature of sound systems in general (we have already said that we reject the claim that analysis in terms of pitch levels is more abstract, or more theoretically powerful, than analysis in terms of pitch contours). (6) Intonation features are more stable in time and place (diachronically and dialectally) than features confined to small articulatory segments. (7) Intonation displays general systemic properties, paradigmatic and syntagmatic, which allow powerful generalizations (from all three perspectives: from above, from round about, from below) and hence carry important implications for language typology, and for clinical linguistics, for language teaching, for text-to-speech (and speech-to-text) programs, and perhaps other applications as well. There is a sense in which intonation (or, as we would see it, the complex phenomenon formed by intonation and rhythm) stands out, within phonology as a whole, as being at one and the same time means, model and metaphor for language itself.

Notes

1 Recent research on bonobo apes has shown that not only are they able to manipulate symbols but also they can also combine symbols into structural configurations of their own com-position. It would be wrong to try to identify these abilities with any particular stage in the development of the human child; the bonobo are a distinct species with their own evolutionary path. The observed behaviour is not part of the bonobos' normal individual development; it is a product of their involvement in human social processes. But it seems clear that their semiotic potential is well above that of what is characterized as 'primary consciousness'

2 For example, in Chinese the syllable is a clearly defined unit; but within the syllable the constituent structure is rather hazy: in Mandarin the entire system is framed as a move from an initial to a terminal posture, and there are no phonematic units at all. In English, on the other hand, the syllable is rather fuzzy (are words like *button, tower, police* one syllable or two?), but the phoneme-like segments are relatively clear — though not perhaps as clear as in Italian or Czech.

Appendix to Part I

A.I.1 How sound makes meaning in a short text

We can illustrate many of the points discussed in Part I using two small segments from a doctor-patient interview in Anne Thwaite's *Language in Contexts*. (Thwaite has generously allowed us to include a number of her videos in the CD which accompanies this book.)

Video A.I

In both segments the field of discourse is non-technical general medicine: use of medication and drugs; the tenor relationship is a relaxed but typical professional / client orientation; and the fully engaged spontaneous interactive mode shows language taking a central place during this particular phase of diagnosis and treatment (in contrast, for example, with X-ray analysis where language is ancillary to the main tasks of placing joints in the right place, pushing buttons and processing results). The video clip through which it is presented gives us direct access to the physical setting in the doctor's office; to the 'body language' of the interacting participants (particularly their gaze and facial expressions), and to the process of language creation in real time as interpersonal and experiential threads weave a texture of new meanings around gradually shifting points in the field and tenor of the unfolding discourse.

A.I.1 The first segment deals with previous reactions to drugs:

Doctor:	// 2 ∧ what / happens when you / take peni*/**cill**in //
Patient:	// 4 well it's / so long a */**go** //
Patient:	// 4 but um / when I was a */ **child** I //
Patient:	// 1 broke out in . . . / red */ **rash** //
Doctor:	*// 1 **ah** // 13 **fair** e*/**nough** *// 1 **yeah** //

80

The doctor begins with an information question. Figure A.I.1a shows how meaning is being shaped through choices in the MOOD system, with the final choice realized through intonation.

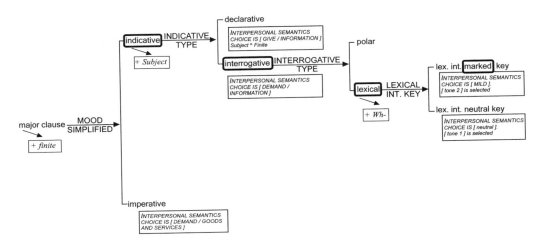

Figure A.I.1a

The simplified system shows the MOOD choices made by the Doctor. Since this is the information gathering phase of the diagnosis procedure, the doctor is not demanding goods and services, and the clause is indicative rather than imperative. And since she is at this point demanding rather than giving information, she selects interrogative mood rather than declarative. The patient has already established that she has a reaction to penicillin, so the polar choice yes versus no is not at issue. But the kind of reaction to penicillin has not yet been determined, and the doctor's clause continues the 'other things being equal' pattern and selects lexical interrogative. In the LEXICAL KEY system, however, there *is* reason for a marked choice. The doctor's professional manner is relaxed — she is drawing out the patient. Had she spoken with a falling tone 1, which is the unmarked choice for a lexical question, her gentleness would not have been established. Instead she selects a mild interpersonal meaning. The rise of tone 2 neutralizes the polar certainty inherent in the lexical form of interrogative. The doctor is, of course, quite certain of polarity — but her intonation masks this certainty, making the question more open and inviting. The intonation through which this choice is realised is shown in Figure and sound A.I.1b. There is movement in the Pretonic, but the Tonic syllable is clear in the jump up to the 'cill' in penicillin.

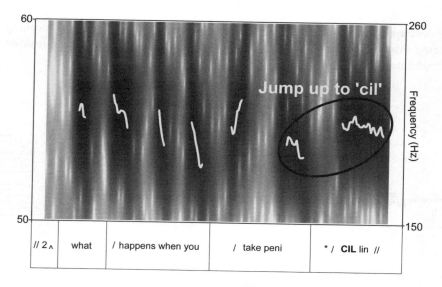

Figure A.I.1b PLAY

The patient's reply,

// 4 well it's / so long a */**go** //

PLAY Sound A.I.1b1

is a declarative clause (she is giving information), but she must make a further choice in the DECLARATIVE KEY system, which can be followed in Figure A.I.1c.

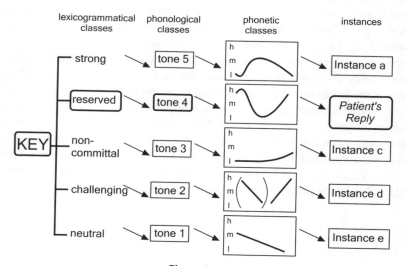

Figure A.I.1c

This is a typical tone 4, with the two Pretonic feet following a fall rise contour which anticipates the final fall rise on the final tonic foot */**go**. As you listen to the sound you will hear the reservation she is expressing through this choice of key. The tone 4 expresses the initial lack of certainty she feels in answering the doctor's question.

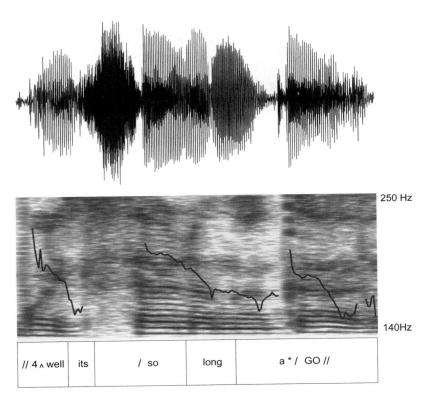

Figure A.I.1d PLAY ◀

Her next clause,

// 4 but um / when I was a */ **child** I //

PLAY ◀ Sound A.I.1e

is also tone 4, but for a different reason. Here the tone 4 is expressing a logical meaning. This clause, expressing a temporal qualification, is in an unequal status relationship with the clause which follows. (See Chapter 5 section 2.3.1 below.) Figure A.I.1e again shows the two pretonic feet following a falling rising pattern foreshadowing the intonation of the tonic foot */ **child** I. And note how it is the slightly higher position of the final syllable I which rounds the intonation upwards, in contrast with what would happen in a tone 1, where I would have continued the fall to the bottom of the speaker's range.

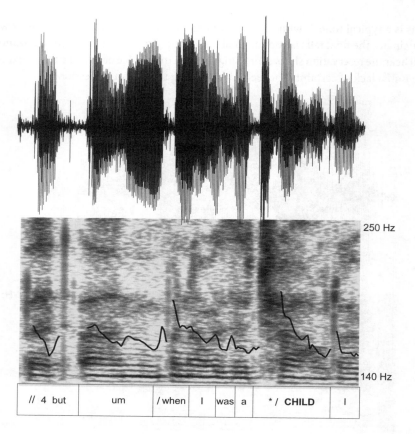

Figure A.I.1e PLAY 🔊

By the time she reaches her next clause, the patient is no longer hesitant. So there is a double effect of her choice of tone 1: it shows that it has the higher status relationship with the previous clause, and it also shows an uncomplicated polar certainty in her declarative statement. This, in fact, is further emphasized by very clearly articulated *red* modifying *rash*.

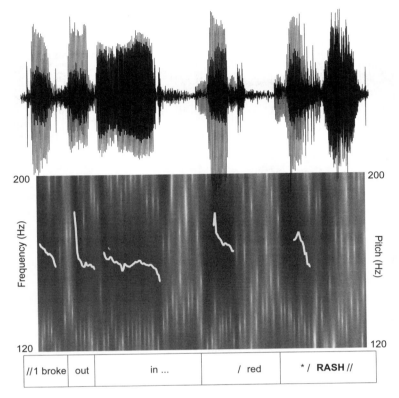

| //1 broke | out | in ... | / red | * / **RASH** // |

Figure A.I.1f PLAY 🔊

The final line in our little dialogue,

*// 1 **ah** *// 13 **fair** e*/**nough** *// 1 **yeah**

PLAY 🔊 Sound A.I.1g

is a study in polar certainty. The fall in the tone 1 of the initial *ah* shows certainty. This is repeated in the next foot */ **fair** e/. This is, however, forced to share its role as New information with the next foot, */**nough**, because the word *enough* is not being treated as Given. It, too, is New, having been 'raised' through its presentation as the second information point in the compound choice of tone 1–3. (Note that this is the tone typically used with this particular expression.) A final tone 1 on *yeah* nails down the doctor's certainty.

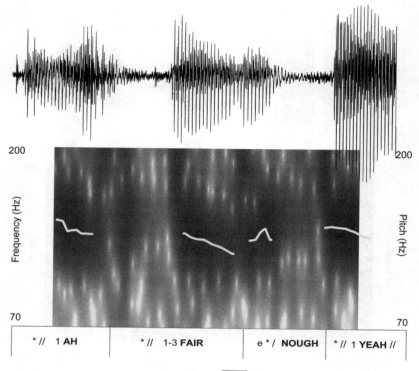

| * // 1 AH | * // 1-3 FAIR | e * / NOUGH | * // 1 YEAH // |

Figure A.I.1g PLAY 🔊

A.I.2 Smoking

In the next, somewhat more challenging, section the doctor moves from the effects of penicillin to the subject of nicotine which she deals with in two sets of questions. These, although different in length, are similar in structure, for medical examinations are a very stable ritual in the culture, in which the doctor opens a topic, probes, and concludes with evaluation or prescription. The smoking passage runs through two cycles, dealing with present and past time:

Doctor: // 1 um / ∧ / what about */ **smok**ing //
Patient: *// 1 **no** //
Doctor: // 3 nope */ **good** //
Doctor: *// 2 **ever** / smoked //
Patient: *// 1 **nev**er //
Doctor: // 3 nope */ **great** //

PLAY 🔊 Sound A.I.2

There are seven tone units in the text. The first, *um*, is not language, and is minimally functional in the discourse; the second, *what about smoking* is language and is completely functional in the discourse, even though not having the formal properties traditionally associated with an independent clause. This and the remaining five fall within the scope of the system as discussed in the present chapter.

// 1 um / ∧ / what about */ **smok**ing //

PLAY ◀ Sound A.I.2a

The 'um' is fully describable in phonetic terms as human vocal sound. It has amplitude, frequency and vowel and consonant quality:

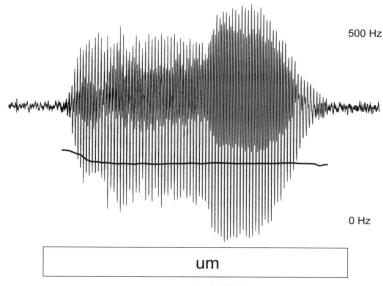

500 Hz

0 Hz

um

Figure A.I.2b PLAY ◀

[ʌm] is, therefore, a member of a recognizable class of sounds. It is iconic to the ear in the way a cross is to the eye, or a particular perfume is to the nose, or the taste of salt to the tongue. Given one instance of any of these, we lump it together with other instances.

When an icon is recognized, it can be understood in two ways. If we link it directly to context, with no intermediary systems of coding and recoding, the meaning is indexical. A particular perfume is an index when we link it to the wearer.

[ʌm] lets us recognize *um* in this way. We recognize the sound qualities as coming from the doctor and not the patient, and we recognize the vowel consonant profile [ʌm] as typical of a particular phase in discourse — when one speaker is in the middle of a turn, is collecting thoughts, and wants to retain the role of speaker. So the *um* is understood perfectly well, and does its job: the patient does not interrupt the doctor's flow of talk.

But the understanding has not been dependent on any decoding of content. There have been no intervening strata between the sound and its context.

There is no phonemic contrast between /m/ and /n/ involved. *Um* means *um*. Full stop. It does not mean *not un*. Nor does it mean *not am*. It resembles an utterance in protolanguage in being posturally rather than phonemically defined. It has been uttered as a sound in its own right — a sound of English, but not functioning as a realizational component in the phonological system.

This means that it can not construe lexicogrammatical meaning. When we have phonetic [ʌm] but no phonological contrast involving /ʌ/ or /m/,. there can be no lexical or grammatical word "um".

The non-symbolic nature of *um* can be seen even more clearly when we consider *er* and *ah,* two of the other sounds used to mark time in a discourse. *Er, um* and *ah* are different sounds, but they do not have grammatical class. They are not nouns, adjectives or verbs. Nor do they have grammatical function. They do not enter into meaningful structural configuration patterns with elements such as Subject Predicator Complement or Adjunct.

And with neither phonological nor grammatical pattern to work with, nothing has been done with them at the semantic stratum. *Er, um* and *ah* have not built up a meaning nexus in which 'um' contrasts with 'er' — although this could be done and would be understood instantly:

'I'll have proper speaking Sir. Um me no ums, and er me no ers'

Here we have phonemes, nouns and verbs, Predicators and Complements, and semantic components of Process and Participant with ideational meaning in the field of non technical good manners in speaking. These *ums* and *ers* have entered the language. The doctor's *um* has not.

This is true for the intonation of the doctor's *um* too. It has very describable pitch. It is quite musical — almost sung. It is not, however, a tone in the English system. It is not a tone 1, 2, 3, 4 or 5. The reason is not that it doesn't have the phonetic shape of one of these five tones. It could be argued that its contour is in some respects 3-like. But even if it does fall into a broad tone three phonetic classification, it does not enter into meaningful contrast with the other four tones.

The lexically empty *um* could, however, select for phonological tone. And if it did so it would have become, partly, language. It would contrast, and carry a meaning which would be understood.

Suppose that someone said to me *Proper speech never includes hesitations.* If I responded by making the sound // 4 um //, my // 4 um // would mean that I had a clear reservation about the proposition. A more linguistically conservative colleague might well utter // 1 um // or perhaps // 5 um // showing strong agreement. And if I had been in a more challenging mood I might have uttered // 2 um //. The doctor, however, was making none of these choices.

Contrast her *um* with the next part of her utterance: *what about smoking?* Every vowel and consonant in *what about smoking* is phonologically systemic: /wɔt/ contrasts with /wɒz/ and so forth. And these sequences of phonemes are realizing three words of the classes pronoun *what*, preposition *about* and non-finite verb *smoking*. The words so construed are operating in recognizable functional structures like the prepositional phrase *about smoking* or the intonational pattern Pretonic ^ Tonic. While *what about smoking* is not a fully explicit interrogative clause, the wh- word lets us know that its meaning is a question. But the patient's response *no* suggests that in the context it was interpreted as the kind of question more typically worded as a polar interrogative *do you smoke?*

In its *do you smoke?* form a polar question asked in this context would involve the speaker in the system of INTERROGATIVE COMMITMENT. The doctor would have three choices. A level rising // 3 do you */ **smoke** // would show a distinct lack of commitment. She would be building an interpersonal relationship in which the patient was 'just another number'. A rise falling // 5 do you */ **smoke** //, on the other hand, would show considerable involvement. The remaining option, the rise // 2 do you */ **smoke** // would show neither commitment nor disinterest.

The doctor, in fact, avoids the pointed focus of a direct polar question. Her

// 1 what about */ **smok**ing //

clearly signals 'information required', but through the choice of the wh- item *what*. This leads into a different set of intonational choices, within which falling tone is the neutral pattern. This is what the doctor selects here.

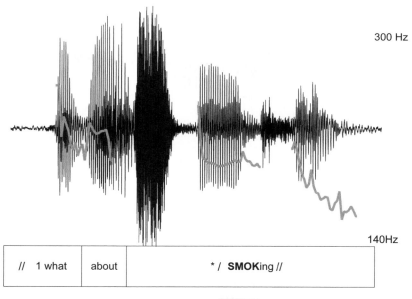

300 Hz

140Hz

// 1 what	about	*/ SMOKing //

Figure A.I.2c PLAY ◀

*// 1 **no** //

PLAY ◀ Sound A.I.2.d

The patient's reply *no* is fully engaged in the choices available at all strata.

She is playing her expected discourse role by providing a response as the context demands. The interpersonal meaning is statement, not question, command or offer; the experiential meaning is negation of the material Process 'smoke'.

Lexicogrammatically we have extreme ellipsis: the negative polarity of the Mood element *I do not*. And this interpretation is supported by its possibilities of intonation.

Intonationally *No* could be uttered with the full range of tone choices available for a declarative clause statement:

> // 5 no // (I really mean it. I am fully committed.)
> // 4 no // (I don't smoke often, but in fact I do light up in some social settings.)
> // 3 no // (to be followed with *and I don't drink, either.*)
> // 2 no // (how dare you suggest that!)
> // 1 no //

The patient's choice is simply the neutral

> // 1 no //.

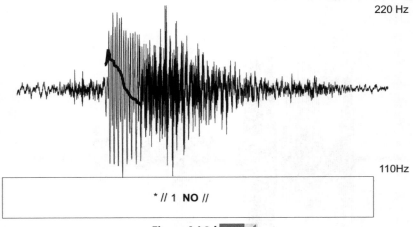

220 Hz

110Hz

* // 1 **NO** //

Figure A.I.2d PLAY 🔊

// 3 nope */ **good** //

PLAY 🔊 Sound A.I.2e

Interpersonally, this is precisely what the doctor should do in the context, because that is the semantic patterning that makes up this kind of text. The doctor's question required the patient's answer. And the answer in turn requires acknowledgement and evaluation. *What about smoking?* got *no* which in turn got *nope — good*. The patient's giving of information as answer has been responded to by the doctor's giving of information in the form of acknowledgement and evaluation.

But if 'statement' is clearly the interpersonal meaning involved, what about the stratum below? Is the MOOD system at work in this one word utterance? We would argue that it is, through ellipsis. But the argument must be carefully made. Saying that a structure relies on something that has been omitted is a tempting way to escape problems.

We would argue that *good* is an Attribute, and that the implied full structure is *nope — [that's] good.*

Textually this makes sense: *[that]* would pick up the previous New *no* and bring it in as point of ideational Theme which is now conflated with Given..

[That], the patient's non smoking, has, in addition to the functional roles Theme and Given, also the role of Carrier.

The Theme also includes the non-ellipted interpersonal component, *nope,* thematising the doctor's act of acknowledgement (through repeating the patient's negative polarity) of the patient's statement. In this structure the Rheme *'s good* makes perfect sense, with the Predicator *s* linking the Carrier *[that]* to the Attribute *good.*

The structure *[that's]* makes sense in terms of MOOD, too. Declarative is the unmarked choice for the semantic option which textualized the patient's move in the discourse.

This may all be very plausible, but without an existing clause to depend on, what can we produce as evidence for our interpretation in terms of an ellipted structure?.

The answer is to be found in the phonological system. The range of intonational choices for *good* is the same as that for the unellipted *that's good.*

Committed:	*// 5 **good** //	// 5 that's */**good** //
Reserved:	*// 4 **good** //	// 4 that's */**good** //
Approving:	*// 3 **good** //	// 3 that's */**good** //
Challenging:	// 2 not */**good** //	// 2 that's not*/**good** //
Neutral:	*// 1 **good** //	// 1 that's */**good** //

Here is the doctor's tone of approval — tone 3. (Note that this is a rare instance of tone 3 being level phonetically as well as phonologically.)

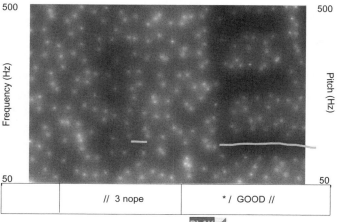

Figure A.I.2e

*// 2 **ev**er / smoked //

PLAY ◀ Sound A.I.2f

Having dealt with the present, the doctor turns to the past. The two cycles are parallel: question — answer — evaluation; question — answer — evaluation.

A question (with falling intonation for the wh- type and rising intonation for the polar type) is followed by a one word answer on tone 1. This is followed by the doctor's evaluation presented as Attribute in an ellipted Carrier ∧ Process ∧ Attribute structure.

The elliptical analysis of *ever smoked* as *[have you] ever smoked* is dealt with in Halliday ed. Matthiessen 2004, Chapter 4: a subjectless clause on tone 2 will be interpreted as having 'you' as subject. Here it is clearly supported by the context and by the intonation options available to it.

A demand for information is appropriate at this point in the discourse. Semantically, this means a question, for which the unmarked mood choice is interrogative. The clause is modalized by *ever*, the indefinite form of the temporal adverb. The previous information was that she does not smoke, with negative polarity combined with present tense. *Ever* raises the question of polarity again with reference to the past. The anticipated answers are *no* or *never*, which would be offered comfortably as single words in an elliptical structure: *Have you ever smoked? Never / no.* If the expected answer was not the one forthcoming, the interpersonal pressure would make a non-elliptical clause the more probable, with, perhaps, an accompanying hedge: *Well, I used to smoke frequently.* The sequence *Did you ever smoke? Frequently.* is far less likely. *[Have you] ever smoked* fits the context and the semantic environment, and on its own stratum it gets support by eliciting the appropriate response *never*.

We may also consider the options open to such a clause.

// 2 [have you] */ **ev**er /smoked //

is the unmarked intonation for an interrogative polar question. It sounds very comfortable and natural — as does the actual

*// 2 **ev**er /smoked //.

On the other hand,

// 1 [have you] */ **ev**er /smoked //

is marked as strong — more of an interrogation than a relaxed question. Here the doctor's choice of *// 2 **ev**er /smoked // is in accord with the relaxed nature of the interview evident in the speakers' voice qualities and in their gesture on the video.

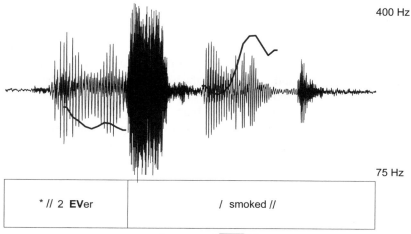

400 Hz

75 Hz

* // 2 **EV**er	/ smoked //

Figure A.I.2f PLAY

*// 1 **nev**er //

PLAY Sound A.I.2g

The patient's reply *never* follows the pattern established above. It is contextually appropriate, semantically unmarked, and in a declarative elliptical relationship with 'have you ever smoked?'. Intonationally it selects the unmarked tone 1. (The fall is very breathy and does not show up in the Praat pitch line, but it is very evident in the sound when you listen to it, and is clearly shown by the first harmonic.)

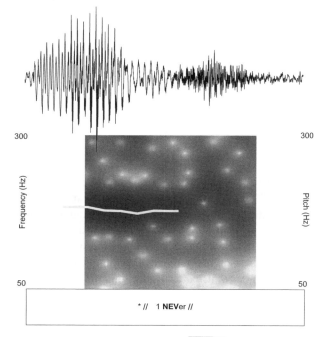

300   300

Frequency (Hz)   Pitch (Hz)

50   50

* //   1 **NEV**er //

Figure A.I.2g PLAY

// 3 nope */ **great** //

PLAY 🔊 Sound A.I.2h

Again the doctor signals her approval with an evaluative attribute; this is again a tone 3, which is less definitive and judgemental than a tone 1 would have been, and less patronizing than a tone 5 (which would carry a prosody of 'oh, haven't you done well! — I'm really pleased', as often used when talking to a child). Like in the earlier example, the *nope* comes as Pretonic, in the way such acknowledging 'yes's' and 'no's' usually do (whereas if they are responding to a question they carry the tonic).

The difference between the two is not so much that between *good* and *great*, which are pretty well synonymous in this context, but that between the low Pretonic and the mid. The low, which the doctor uses on the first occasion, is so to speak markedly casual: 'that's what I would have imagined, so not an issue'; whereas the mid Pretonic, which she uses this second time, gives her observation more substance. It is still a lightweight tone 3, as opposed to tone 1, but it makes clear to the patient that she has heard and is approving.

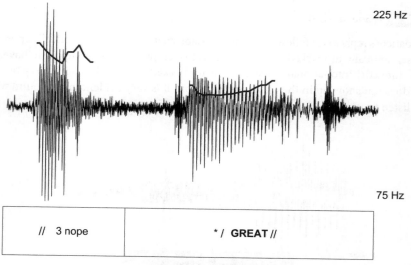

225 Hz

75 Hz

// 3 nope	* / **GREAT** //

Figure A.I.2h PLAY 🔊

These little fragments illustrate how much meaning is embodied in the prosodic patterns of ordinary speech. Such prosodic features are not random and they are not paralinguistic; they are instantiations of the system of the language, and they get their meaning, as always, by the selection of 'this, rather than that or the other' — what is meant, against the background of what might have been meant but was not. In Part II we shall try to give some indication of the range of meanings that the English language construes through the resources of its patterns of intonation.

Part II

Intonation and meaning

5   Intonation in meaning

It is obvious that intonation contributes fundamentally to the flow of discourse; this is a feature of every spoken language. On the other hand, the exact contribution it makes will differ from one language to another: in the last resort, in this as in other respects, every language is unique.

As we saw in the last chapter, one useful guide to the part played by intonation is provided by the metafunctional analysis: we can ask how intonation contributes to making meaning in textual, interpersonal, experiential and logical terms. And here we can make one broad generalization, one that is valid for English and can serve as a starting hypothesis when investigating intonation in other languages. (See for example Verdugo 2002.) Broadly speaking, systems of TONE (falling, rising &c.) construe interpersonal meanings, while systems of TONALITY (division into tone units) and TONICITY (location of prominence within the tone unit) construe textual meanings. *Tone sequences* (the sequential choices of tone in successive tone units) play some part in construing logical meanings. The one metafunction to which intonation makes no contribution is the experiential.

This enables us to distinguish between intonation and what is usually just called 'tone', as in a 'tone language'. A tone language is one in which contrasts of pitch (pitch movement and pitch level) figure alongside those of articulation (vowels and consonants) in the realization of morphemes, or other lexicogrammatical units. Here, as pointed out in Chapter 4, the actual distribution of the tones is arbitrary, just like that of consonants and vowels; whereas the distribution of pitch contours (intonation) is in the last resort iconic. Most, perhaps all, tone languages also make some use of intonation (though not the other way around), so the distinction between these as language types is in any case fuzzy. But it is useful to separate intonation from 'tone' in this specific sense, and here we can invoke the metafunctional criterion, that intonation does not construe meanings of the experiential type.

In the next few sections we will consider the role of intonation in English in relation to the textual, interpersonal and logical metafunctions in turn.

5.1   Intonation in the textual metafunction

Let us come back to the notion of the 'flow of discourse'. We use this term in preference to 'flow of information', since that term privileges the experiential, with 'information' being usually understood in the sense of content — that is, experiential meaning.

The flow of discourse in English is organized primarily by the systems of TONAL-ITY and TONICITY. We shall see later (§2.3 below) that the system of TONE also enters the picture, in the form of sequences of tone choices, which combine the textual and interpersonal into a system of logical relationships. The basic taxonomy of intonation systems in English is thus as in Figure 5.1.

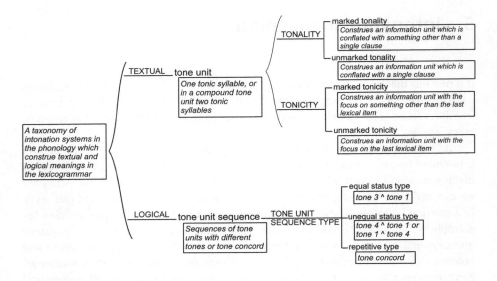

Figure 5.1

5.1.1 Tonality

Tonality systems are the choices concerned with how the discourse unfolds as a succession of units of information. A 'unit of information' is a quantum of discourse that is organized into some configuration of 'given' and 'new' material.

The simplest way of introducing this is with a nursery rhyme:

// Little Miss Muffet //

// Sat on a tuffet   //

// Eating her curds and whey //

// Along came a spider   //

// Which sat down beside her   //

// And frightened Miss Muffet away //

PLAY Sound 5.1.1a

Here (in this reading) each line of the verse is one tone unit; the double slash // marks the boundary between one tone unit and another. (We shall normally enter it only once.) Note that there is no pause at this point. A pause is not impossible, of course; but it is not necessary, and it plays no part in the identification of the tone unit.

What then does define the tone unit? The tone unit is a unit of English phonology, and it can be defined as one melodic contour — one line of spoken melody. It is no accident that one line of melody corresponded in our nursery rhyme to one line of the verse, because that is how the 'line' in verse form originated: it evolved as the poetic reflex of one tone unit. It is not difficult to find poems that read quite naturally in this way, like the following from Blake's Songs of Innocence:

// When the voices of children are heard on the green,

// And laughing is heard on the hill,

// My heart is at rest within my breast,

// And everything else is still. //

PLAY ◀ Sound 5.1.1b

— although the third line may read better as two tone units:

// My heart is at rest // within my breast //

PLAY ◀ Sound 5.1.1c

More often, however, when we speak poetry aloud we find ourselves cutting across the metric line, sometimes combining two lines into one tone unit, or two tone units into one line, or overriding the verse lines altogether, as in this poem also from Blake:

// O rose // thou art sick

// The invisible worm

   That flies in the night

// In the howling storm

// Has found out thy bed

   of crimson joy

// And his dark secret love

// Does thy life // destroy //

PLAY ◀ Sound 5.1.1d

What then is the relationship between the tone unit and the *information unit*? As we have made clear, the tone unit is a unit of the phonology; it is the highest unit in the hierarchy: tone unit ('line') — rhythm unit ('foot') — syllable — phoneme. The information unit, on the other hand, is a unit of the lexicogrammar; it is defined (from below) as that grammatical unit that is realized by one tone unit.

Thus the two units, the phonological 'tone unit' and the grammatical 'information unit', correspond one to one; but since they are located on different strata, their boundaries do not correspond exactly. In fact, both are fuzzy: the boundaries are not clearly defined in either case. But to show their semogenic power we need to model them in terms of the different strata, defining the tone unit boundary phonologically and the boundary of the information unit grammatically. The tone unit, then, is made up of (a whole number of) rhythm units, or 'feet'. Here is a passage of conversation, marked up to show the tone units:

// You were telling me that you were in the army   //

— // Yes //

— // And, er — could you tell me a little bit about it? //

— // Yes … I // joined … I was // in what they called the local territorials …
like a ci//vilian army be//fore the war … I was ap//prenticed engineer at a
// big truck and bus factory … called // Leyland Motors //

It will be easier to follow this if we mark it up for feet (rhythm units):

// ∧ you were / telling me that / you were in the / army //

— // yes //

— // ∧ and er ∧ / could you / tell me a / little bit a/bout it //

— // yes ∧ I // joined /∧ /∧ I was // in what they / called the / local terri/torials ∧
like a ci//vilian / army be// fore the / war ∧ I was ap//prenticed engin/eer at a
// big truck and / bus factory ∧ called   // Leyland / Motors //

PLAY 🔊 Sound 5.1.1e

The foot boundary is marked by a single slash / . Note that the tone unit boundary // is
also a foot boundary. The symbol ∧ marks a silent beat.

Let us now interpret this in terms of information units, and match these up with the
familiar grammatical units of clause, phrase and group. Here each line in the transcription is one information unit:

A.	‖‖ You were telling me ‖ that you were in the army ‖‖‖	clause nexus
B.	‖‖ Yes ‖‖‖	[clausette]
A.	‖‖ And, er … could you tell me a little bit about it? ‖‖‖	clause
B.	‖‖ Yes ‖‖‖	[clausette]
	‖‖ I joined … I was in what they called the local territorials	clause …
	‖ like a civilian army	phrase …
	[before the war]	phrase
	‖‖ I was apprenticed engineer	clause …
	‖ at a big truck and bus factory	phrase …
	[[called Leyland Motors]] ‖‖‖	embedded clause

Boundary markers:
‖‖   clause complex (one or more clause nexuses)
‖   clause
‖   phrase or group
[[ ]] embedded clause
[ ]   embedded phrase or group

Speaker B has been asked to give information, about his past; it is all news to speaker A, so he 'chunks it up' — organizes it into units of information many of which are less than a whole clause. And that in itself gives us a clue: it suggests that the typical quantum of information is one (ranking) clause. That in fact turns out to be the case: in continuous dialogue, typically around 60% of the information units are mapped into one complete clause. Here is what the above passage would sound like if this 'unmarked tonality' (one information unit = one ranking clause) was maintained throughout:

> // Yes … I // joined … I was // in what they called the local territorials …
> like a civilian army before the war … I was ap//prenticed engineer at a big
> truck and bus company called Leyland Motors //

PLAY◀ Sound 5.1.1f

We can see from this that the information unit is a grammatical unit that runs in parallel with the units of the grammatical rank scale but is not identical to any of them. One could talk of it as a unit of 'informational grammar' as opposed to 'clause grammar'. It is of course specific to the spoken language, being realized by intonation and rhythm — although the punctuation system of written English, if used sensitively and with understanding, can go a long way towards giving a written text what Firth used to call the 'implication of utterance'.

We can also see why the boundaries of the information unit and the tone unit do not exactly correspond: the former maps into units of the (clause) grammar, while the latter is a unit of the phonology. The reason for analysing in this way is that it allows us to explain the internal workings of each system. The information unit is organized in configurations of Given and New. The tone unit is organized as a structure of (optional) Pretonic plus (obligatory) Tonic, each with its own systems of tone choices; but such choices only become available where there is a new rhythm group, or foot: hence every tone unit must begin at a foot boundary, i.e. with a salient syllable. (For the structure of the foot, including silent feet and silent beats, see Section 2.4 below.) The tone unit will thus always consist of a whole number of feet.

5.1.2 Tonicity

Whereas tonality concerns the organization of discourse into quanta of information, *tonicity* refers to the internal organization of each one of these information quanta. This is called 'tonicity' because it revolves around the location of the *tonic*, the prominent portion of the tone unit.

The information unit embodies the principle that discourse proceeds as a kind of alternating current, an oscillation between the two poles of familiarity, the known and the unknown. Familiarity is of course a cline: something can be more or less familiar to the listener, and in any case it is the speaker who is organizing the discourse at any given moment, even if the total enterprise is dialogic and collaborative. The information unit is the speaker's resource for *managing* the cline of familiarity, as a balanced alternation between what is familiar and what is news — that is, between what that speaker chooses to present as being one thing or the other.

This cannot take the form of a clearcut organization into two constituent-like elements, because the distinction into a known part and an unknown part is not, as a rule,
clearcut. At the same time, there can be elements within the utterance that fall clearly
into one category or the other: if speaker A says 'What would you like?' and speaker
B replies 'I'd like some coffee', it is very clear that in B's response 'I'd like' is already
given whereas 'some coffee' is essentially new (we will stipulate that there has not been
any prior discussion of their desires). So the information unit compromises between
determinacy and indeterminacy: it allows for a gradual move between the given and
the new, but also for 'moments' of real discontinuity: and it has a clearly defined climax
which focuses the new information.

We shall continue to use use these three terms, 'given', 'new' and 'focus'; so we should
comment briefly on their use as technical terms.[1] There has been extensive discussion
of the concepts of 'given' and 'new' since the work of linguists of the Prague school
in the 1930s and 1940s; much of it fruitful, but some of it empty because based on a
misapprehension of the nature of such category labels. In labelling grammatical and
semantic categories, using a language (e.g. English) as its own metalanguage, we try to
choose words which give an indication of the core meaning or function of the category.
But all such categories are in fact strictly ineffable: they mean themselves, and no simple
label or even lengthy gloss can provide a definition against which to match individual
instances. When we discuss tense, for example, we do not argue about the label 'present'
or insist that some particular instance cannot be present tense because doesn't fit the
label we have chosen to assign to it — it refers to some time in the past, perhaps, or in
the future. Likewise 'given' and 'new' were adopted to suggest the core meanings of these
categories; we can offer helpful glosses, such as saying that 'given' means that which is
known or at least recoverable to the listener; but these are not definitions, and (while
we may certainly bear them in mind when engaged in discourse analysis) they cannot
be conscripted to decide whether some particular instance is or is not a 'given' element
in the information unit.

A typical information unit is English discourse is organized something like this:

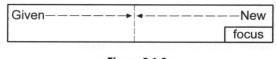

Figure 5.1.2a

For example:

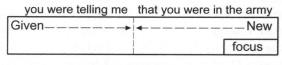

Figure 5.1.2b

Let us start at the end, with the 'focus'. If we wanted to gloss the meaning of the information focus, we might say that it is the portion that the speaker is drawing particular
attention to. It typically comes, as it does here, at the end of the information unit;
whether this is so or not, it always marks the culmination of the New, so that anything
that comes after it, but is still in the same information unit, is explicitly marked as being
Given. Here is an example:

// ∧ so in/stead of / getting / ∧ /seven / shillings a */ **week** |

// got about / fif*/**teen** / shillings a / week //

PLAY ◀ Sound 5.1.2a

Expressing this grammatically we get:

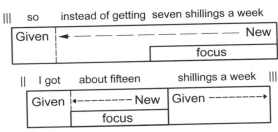

Figure 5.1.2c

Here *shillings a week* had appeared in the first clause, so it was not surprising to find it
marked as Given when it appeared again in the second one.

    Other than such final Given segments, however, the dynamic of the information
unit is a crescendo movement from the familiar to the newsworthy; with one element
(typically a group or a phrase, i.e. an element in the grammatical structure of the clause)
shown culminatively as the main news — that is, we can tell exactly when it ends. We
cannot tell quite so clearly when it begins, although there are some ancillary signals
which play a part (see Section 2.5 below). The critical feature phonologically is that of
tonic prominence: one foot, the *tonic foot*, and within that foot the initial syllable, the
tonic syllable, is auditorily and acoustically more prominent than the remainder of the
tone unit. Acoustically this prominence is complex, but it is typically made up of

(1) either steeper pitch movement (on a straight tone, i.e. falling or rising) or change
     of direction (on a curved tone, i.e. fall-rise or rise-fall);

(2) extended duration, and

(3) slightly greater intensity.

Each information unit, then, will contain some matter that is New; this is criterial — no
quantum of information lacks a focus. Phonologically, this means that every tone unit has
a tonic segment, or 'tonic nucleus' as it has sometimes been called. The Given element,

however, is optional: it is possible (and not uncommon) to have an information unit that consists solely of New material. Speaker B's narrative includes some examples.

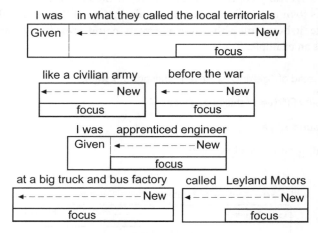

Figure 5.1.2d

Speaker B is pursuing his narrative, adding further information point by point; the two clauses are constructed each as three information units, and the only Given material is the *I was* at the beginning of each clause.

Where does the tonic prominence actually fall? We have said 'at the end of the New', which usually means on the final lexical item in the tone unit. This needs to be further clarified. The lexicogrammar of a language is, as we have said, a single stratum, in which the word classes lie along a continuum: the most open classes, verbs, nouns and adjectives, lie at one end, and the most closed, operators (verbal auxiliaries), determiners and pronouns, at the other; adverbs have various subclasses which lie at different places along the line, and prepositions and conjunctions come somewhere toward the middle. Two comments may be made regarding tonic prominence.

(1) Operators and determiners seldom occur finally, because they come at the beginning of the group (operator at the beginning of the verbal group, e.g. *wasn't, may have* in *wasn't going, may have gone*; determiner, e.g. *the, any*, at the beginning of the nominal group); pronouns often occur finally, but they are inherently 'given', like the *it* in this example:

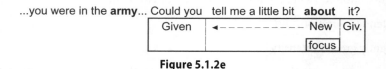

Figure 5.1.2e

(2) Compound words have their accent on the first lexical element, e.g. *bus* **factory** not *bus* **factory**; this does not make the second element Given — it merely shows

that such compounds behave phonologically like single words. (But a coordinate sequence '*a* and *b*' has the accent on the '*b*'; hence the expected pattern here is *truck and **bus** factory*.

5.1.3 Information unit and clause

To provide a rounded picture of the way intonation and rhythm contribute to the texture of discourse we need to combine these two perspectives, that of the clause and that of the information unit.

The tone unit, as we have seen, constructs a quantum of information by intersecting two forms of order: linear sequence in time, and acoustic / auditory prominence. These are used to make textual meaning in ways that we can recognize as iconic: lineally, the movement goes from what is familiar to what is new; and the moment of greatest prominence marks the climax of the new matter. The combined effect is that the information unit builds up a crescendo of information — but on a microtextual scale.

The clause, while it is the principal organizing unit of grammatical structure, where experiential, interpersonal and textual meanings are all construed together, is from the textual point of view similarly a micro unit. But while the information unit typically moves towards a peak of prominence at the end, in the clause the textual prominence comes at the beginning — though it is prominence of a significantly different kind.

Consider this from the speaker's point of view. The speaker begins the clause by enunciating a particular point of departure, which serves as grounding for the message; we refer to this as the Theme. The remainder of the clause, following the Theme, is called the Rheme. Since the clause is more clearly configured as a constituent structure than the information unit (because of its role in the other metafunctions), it is not difficult to depict Theme + Rheme also as a constituent structure; and if we examine the way this clausal feature is used to construct discourse, building up the succession of microtexts into larger text units, we find that the thematic 'grounding' takes in just one topical element — that is, just one element that has a function in the experiential structure (as Actor, circumstance of Place or Time, and so on). Whatever comes *before* this first topical element also functions thematically; whatever comes *after* it is part of the remainder, the Rheme.

Much of the time, in informal dialogue, the topical Theme is simply *I* or *you*:

			you	were telling me
that			you	were in the army
		could	you	tell me a little bit about it
			I	was in what they called the local territorials
			I	was appointed engineer at... Leyland Motors
textual	inter-personal		topical	
Theme				Rheme

Figure 5.1.3a

Here there are just two pretopical items: *that*, marking the structural status of the clause as a projection, and *could*, showing (by its position) the mood of the clause as interrogative — one aspect of the thematic grounding of the clause being to signal if its function is something other than a simple independent declarative (which is what the other four clauses all are). The topical Theme in each case is *you / I*, both referring here to speaker B, whose past experience is the topic under discussion. Later in the same dialogue we have:

	one day	my commanding officer said to me
Look Alan|he		I said
inter-personal	topical	
Theme		Rheme

Figure 5.1.3b

— where a new stage in the narrative is initiated by a time expression *one day*, and then the projection (this time paratactic, i.e. as 'direct speech') is marked by the interpersonal *look* (addressing) plus *Alan* (vocative).

There is a certain amount of arbitrariness in treating Theme + Rheme as a constituent structure with the boundary at this point — though not much, for three reasons: (1) the clause, unlike the information unit, has a constituent-type structure (both experientially and interpersonally); (2) when a clause is mapped into two information units, in a clear majority of cases the boundary coincides with that between Theme and Rheme as here defined; (3) the evidence from discourse, where the thematic progression is highly functional [cf. Matthiessen, 1992 and 1995], also supports this analysis. But if we think of it in the other way, as a gradual progression from a thematic to a rhematic pole, we can see Theme + Rheme as a diminuendo complementing the crescendo of the information unit's typical progression from Given to New, as in Figure 5.1.3c below:

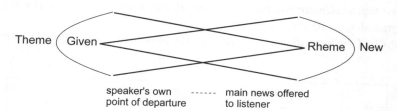

Figure 5.1.3c : Clause as wave flowing from speaker to listener

This is, of course, a theoretical model; but it is one to which any given instance may be related, and it suggests the kind of dynamic that makes up one unit in the micro-cycle of the discourse. This textual unit is a little wave, a ripple, travelling from speaker to listener: from 'where I'm starting from' to 'where you are to pay attention'. Or we could vary the metaphor and think of it as a form of gift: discourse is a giving by the speaker to the listener, in small repetitive allocations, with the roles of giver and receiver changing from time to time. The listener may not always want the gift that is being offered — but that is true of material as well as semiotic gifts! and the listener can refuse, by no longer listening. The gift analogy brings out the interpersonal aspect; the wave analogy foregrounds the dynamic continuity. Like all analogies from the material world, they should not be carried over unthinkingly into the world of meaning.

We have stressed that the mapping of information unit on to clause is merely the default condition: other things being equal, the two will correspond. We can apply the 'good reason' principle: where they do not match, we can find a reason for it (as in the examples above; whereas when they do match, there is nothing further to be explained). There will be other examples throughout the following sections. Meanwhile we return briefly to the point made at the beginning of the present section, where we showed the relationship of rhythm group to foot and of tone unit to line. If we consider this now along a dimension of time (which can be either evolutionary time or developmental time — the history of the language or the learning of the language by a child), we can postulate an earlier moment when there is a single undifferentiated unit at each of these two ranks: an element, at the lower rank, and a configuration of elements at the higher. Each of these then evolves, or develops, into three distinct units: those of (1) lexicogrammar [metafunctional], (2) phonology and (3) verbal art. See Figure 5.1.3d.

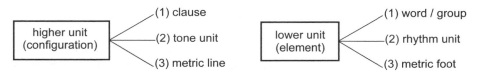

Figure 5.1.3d

As language evolves, each of these units takes on a life of its own. At the higher rank, the tone unit comes to function as a quantum of information (textual meaning), while the *clause* becomes a quantum of experience (a happening) and of interaction (a speech event), the mapping of ideational and interpersonal meaning; tone unit and clause can now vary independently, but with one-to-one mapping remaining as the default condition. Similarly with the poetic *line*: this is now, as it were, a quantum of verbal art, and can be varied independently of the other two. And the same thing happens at the lower rank, though here there are other complications: the *word* expands into a (word) *group*, and words themselves come in various shapes and sizes — but they maintain their contact with the *rhythm unit* in the form of *accent*. The rhythm unit, in turn, gives birth to a smaller quantum of verbal art, the metric *foot*. Thus, as with the higher rank, at the lower rank also we now have three independently varying units, [lexicogrammatical] word / group, [phonological] rhythm unit and [metric] foot. As always, new meaning is created by the dissociation of associated variables, where (as in Figure 5.1.3e)

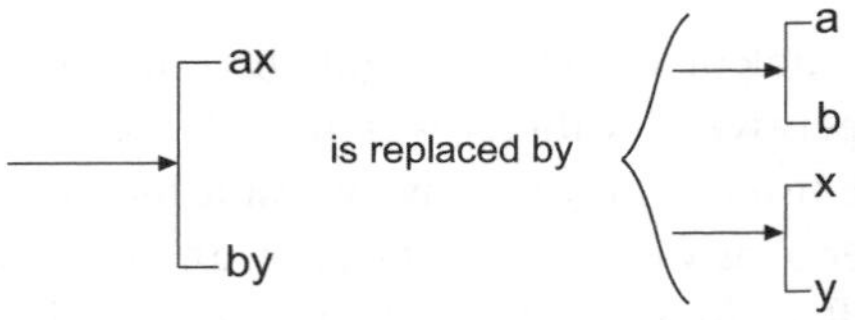

Figure 5.1.3e

— which is why the evolution of independent poetic forms (like the iambic pentameter line) increases the total meaning potential of the system. When these, in turn, come to be felt as straitjackets (i.e. when the constraining force of the structure comes to exceed the enabling force), this is not because the meaning potential has shrunk but because the demand for meaning potential always goes on increasing.

5.1.4 Combining tonality and tonicity

Thus the combination of tonality (the organization of discourse as a successivity of tone units) and tonicity (the organization of each tone unit around a particular point of prominence) is an immensely powerful resource for creating what we call 'textual meaning': a flow of discourse at the micro level that (i) engenders information (in the grammatical sense, as a balanced oscillation between the given and the new), and (ii) enables this to be mapped freely into the clause-based structures of experiential and interpersonal meaning. The tone unit construes a quantum of information in this grammatical sense: this is what is meant by saying that one tone unit realizes one information unit.

The prototypical mapping, as we have seen, is defined by relating the information unit grammar to the clause grammar. This occurs where one information unit is mapped on to one clause ('unmarked tonality'), and within this unit the focus falls on the final lexical item ('unmarked tonicity'). This unmarked, or default, condition is not defined by frequency, although it does tend to be the most frequent choice in most varieties of text. Rather it is defined as that choice that is made in the absence of good reason for choosing anything else. Any 'marked' option, such as the (also frequent) splitting of the clause into two information units, one for Theme and one for Rheme, plays a meaningful part in the overall unfolding of the text.

It may be that, in some very general sense, in the co-evolution of human language and the human brain, a metafunctional principle has evolved whereby quanta from each metafunction are mapped into one another: as the base line, one quantum of experience (clause as transitivity) equals one quantum of personal exchange (clause as mood), which in turn is 'packaged', or construed, as one quantum of discourse. If so, what we are examining is the particular form in which this principle is embodied in English. Every language will do it in its own way. It may be that intonation always plays some part; again, what we are looking at is the part played by intonation in the overall construction of meaning in English. In the next section we shall look into the role of intonation in the interpersonal metafunction, as an essential part of the semogenic resources within the general system of MOOD.

5.2   Intonation in the interpersonal metafunction

In Section 5.1 we discussed intonation in its 'textual' function, showing how the regularities of the tone contour, and the feature of tonic prominence, give order to the flow of discourse. We modelled this by setting up the information unit as a constituent in the grammar that is realized by the phonological resources of the intonation system, in particular the complex syndrome of features of pitch, loudness and length serving collectively to give prominence to certain moments within the stream of speech. We shall return later, in Section 5.3, to a consideration of the information unit in its function of creating complex logical sequences. But that requires a prior treatment of the system of TONE; so first we turn to the discussion of intonation in its 'interpersonal' function; specifically, of tone in its relation to the clausal systems of mood and modality. Here we will be focussing on choices that are available to each individual information unit.

5.2.1   MOOD

As we noted in Chapter 1, the principal interpersonal system in the clause is that of MOOD. This is the choice between imperative and indicative; within indicative, between declarative and interrogative; within interrogative, between polar ('yes/no') and non-polar (lexical, 'WH-'), and so on.

The MOOD system is systemically related to the system of TONE in phonology. This relationship is highly productive, in the semogenic sense: it is the source of a large network of meaning potential. Hence it is somewhat complex; in order to deal with it we will first move 'up' to the semantic stratum, looking at the semantic system of SPEECH FUNCTION. This will then enable us to explore the interplay between the two sets of categories, those of mood and those realized by tone.

The basis of the SPEECH FUNCTION system is extremely simple. Consider an initiating act of meaning in a dialogic exchange. The speaker has certain options; and these options are of two kinds. (1) He may give, or he may demand; that is, he may take on one of two roles in the exchange, and in doing so assign to the listener the complementary role in responding: either (a) 'I give: you accept', or (b) 'I demand: you give'. (2) He may exchange goods-&-services, or he may exchange information; that is, he may exchange one or other of two commodities, which we could characterize as either (a) non-verbal, 'give ... to', 'do ... for', or (b) verbal, 'say ... to', 'ask ... for'. These two variables define a matrix of primary speech functions, as in Figure 5.2.1a.

COMMODITY EXCHANGED / ROLE IN EXCHANGE	goods and services	information
give	offer	statement
demand	command	question

Figure 5.2.1a

The notion of giving and demanding, as roles set up by the speaker in initiating the exchange, is clear enough: we are considering for the moment only the initiating speech functions, although the pattern of responses can be specified in similar terms: either 'accept / acknowledge what is being given', or 'give what is being demanded'. (These are of course only the most generalized speech functions; we shall extend them further in a moment.) The notion of 'commodity exchanged' is more complex. What this refers to is the substantive nature of the exchange: whether it is material ('goods-&-services') or semiotic ('information'). Exchanging goods-&-services means using language as a means to a (typically non-linguistic) end; e.g. (offer) *Shall I see you home?*, (command) *Don't come back!*. (It includes those cases where a semiotic process is turned into a 'material' commodity, as in *I'll tell you* a *secret*.) Exchanging information means using language as an end in itself — a much more complex notion, since 'what is being exchanged' is just language; there is no other process that is being furthered by the speech event. In making a statement, or asking a question, the entire event takes place on the semiotic plane. (This is why it takes young children significantly longer to master the principle of exchanging information.)

The critical feature of the system of SPEECH FUNCTION is this: that the major options within it are realized by combinations of MOOD and TONE.

Let us first set out the typical realizations of these general categories (Figure 5.2.1b).

SPEECH FUNCTION	realization in MOOD	realization in TONE
statement	declarative	falling (tone 1)
question: polar	interrogative: yes / no	rising (tone 2)
question: non-polar	interrogative: wh-	falling (tone 1)
command	imperative	falling (tone 1) or level-rising (tone 3)
offer	(various)	(various)

Figure 5.2.1b

It will be clear right at the beginning that this system has considerable potential for semogenic extension, on the principle of the dissociation of associated variables already alluded to. In principle, any mood could combine with any tone. (In addition, of course, both mood and tone embody many more delicate options; these we shall return to later.) Here is a short passage of conversation between a mother and her $3^1/_2$-year-old daughter which we can use to illustrate some of the categories listed so far: first in orthography, then in prosodic transcription.

M: Sit up and finish your lunch! [child obeys] Do they sit — they make you sit up straight like that at kinder, do they?

C: No.

M: I remember sitting up like that when I was at school. The teacher'd say 'Sit up straight!', and everyone sat up looking like that. [stiffening her body]

C: Why did they?

M: I don't know; 'cause they thought it made them look straighter, I suppose.

C: Why did the teacher at your school say 'Sit up straight!'?

M: // 1- sit up and / finish your */ **lunch** //

     // do they / sit — // 1 they / make you / sit up / straight like / that at */ **kind**er

     *// 2 **do** they //

C: *// 1 **no** //

M: // 1 I remember / sitting up like / that when / I was at */ **school** the

     // 1 teacher'd say / sit up */ **straight** and // 2 everyone / sat up / looking like */ **that** //

C: // 5 why */ **did** they //

M: *// 2̲ I don't */ **know** 'cause they // 13 thought it / made them look / */**straight**er I sup*/**pose** //

C: // 5 why did the / teacher at / your school say / sit up */ **straight** //

Here some of the tones match the selection of mood according to the default pattern set out in the table; others do not. Of those that do not, the mother's *everyone sat up looking like **that*** has the high rising tone accompanying the posture of the body; the child's two tone 5s have the added exclamatory prosody common in young children's speech; the mother's ***I don't know*** has the final rise characteristic of declaratives of protestation, and her low rise on *I suppose* is typical of a modality added on as afterthought. All these are systemic choices in the broadly defined semantic domain of speech function.

5.2.2 Intonation and mood

We now consider each of the four primary speech functions in turn, noting the typical, or 'unmarked', tone associated with each, and the meanings that are produced by systematic variation from the typical (the 'marked' alternatives). Only the primary tones will be elaborated in this section.

5.2.2.1   Statements

(a) Clearly the unmarked realization of a statement is a declarative clause comprising one tone unit spoken on a falling tone (tone 1).

> // 1 ∧ it's / very ef*/**fic**ient //
> `PLAY` 🔊 Sound 5.2.2.1a1

> // 1∧so /Lombok's em em /flora and /fauna is /very like Aus*/**tral**ia's //
> `PLAY` 🔊 Sound 5.2.2.1b

This does not embody any other features or imply any particular discursive or situational conditions. The declarative mood realizes 'give + information'; the falling tone realizes '[polarity] known, move independent'. The mapping on to one tone unit has already been discussed; it realizes the feature 'one information unit'.

Keeping the tonality (clause / information unit mapping) constant, let us vary the other features one at a time: first the tone, and then the mood.

(b) Declarative clause, falling-rising (tone 4). The dynamic of fall followed by rise means 'seems, or seemed, certain, but isn't'. This tone adds a feature of reservation, 'this statement has a 'but' about it somewhere'. It is easily the most frequent tone for declaratives after tone 1; the discursive contexts for it are numerous and varied, ranging from mildly provisional to strongly contrastive. Note that we are concerned here with tone 4 on independent clauses; its association with dependent clauses and marked Themes will be taken up in Section 3.

> // 4 ∧ it's a / bit of a */ **risk** //
> `PLAY` 🔊 Sound 5.2.2.1b1

> // 4 and /∧ he dis*/**cov**ered //
> `PLAY` 🔊 Sound 5.2.2.1d

> // 4∧ he / did re*/**search** //
> `PLAY` 🔊 Sound 5.2.2.1b3

> // 4∧ he's in/credibly */ **nice** about it //
> `PLAY` 🔊 Sound 5.2.2.1b4

(c) Declarative clause, rising-falling (tone 5). The dynamic of rise followed by fall means 'seems, or seemed, uncertain, but isn't'; including, as a special case of that, 'surprising, but is so'. In other words, the 'certainty' of the fall cancels out the 'uncertainty' of the rise, just as in tone 4 the 'uncertainty' of the rise cancels out the 'certainty' of the fall. This tone is commonly used by children — and also by adults in talking to children, each reinforcing the predilection for it of the other. It is characteristic of expressions such as *Wow! Far from it! No way!*

// 5 ∧ he wasn't / telling the */ **truth** //
PLAY◀ Sound 5.2.2.1c1

// 5 but it was */**fab**ulous //
PLAY◀ Sound 5.2.2.1c2

(d) Declarative clause, high rising tone (tone 2). The rising tone is in direct opposition to the fall, and may realize any one of three rather different features.

(i) The clause functions as a query, querying a statement that has been made or implied. See 2.2.2.2(g) below.

// 2 Peter isn't */ **here** yet //
PLAY◀ Sound 5.2.2.1d-i1

// 2∧ just 'cause you / do / get up */ **ear**ly //
PLAY◀ Sound 5.2.2.1d-i2

(ii) The clause functions as a challenge, protesting or contradicting a statement that has been made or implied.

// 2 ∧ no I */ **have**n't / got the / tickets //
PLAY◀ Sound 5.2.2.1d-ii

(iii) The clause functions as a response, satisfying a question that has been asked or implied.

// 2 um / probably a/bout ah / ∧ / ∧ / three */ **bot**tles //
PLAY◀ Sound 5.2.2.1

(In answer to 'How much alcohol do you drink on average in a week?'). It is arguable whether these are all identical in sound. Those of type (ii), for example, may carry a more assertive prosody, being louder and/or longer, or covering a greater pitch range, than the others; those of type (iii) sometimes seem to reach a higher terminal pitch. But it is not clear how consistent these variations are. There also seem to be dialectal preferences, type (i) being more frequent with North American speakers, type (ii) with British and type (iii) with Australians and New Zealanders. Type (iii) in particular is recognized in Australia as a regular, if relatively recent, phenomenon — so regular that with some speakers it appears to be the unmarked version of a statement. But all types are found at least to some extent in all these dialect regions.

(e) Declarative clause, level-rising tone (tone 3). The level-rising tone is the neutral one, that as it were opts out of the choice between falling and rising. (For a discussion of level rising tone, see Yves Talla Sando Ouafeu 2006). For this reason it is often referred to as 'level'; this is appropriate phonologically, but in practice it is hard to find one that is actually level in pitch: there is almost always a final rise, ranging from one that is barely perceptible until stretched, to one that overlaps with the high rise of a tone 2. The basic meaning of declining to choose between rise and fall is some kind of a lack of commitment; but there are various ways of being uncommitted, which we can most helpfully group into three types:

(i) The statement is uncommitted in the sense that the speaker is tentative, suggesting rather than asserting; or else unconcerned, disclaiming any interest in the question at issue. In this sense it contrasts with the highly committed tone 5.

> //-3 ∧ I / don't sup/pose it / really */ **mat**ters //
> PLAY 🔊 Sound 5.2.2.1e-i

(ii) The statement is uncommitted in the sense that it signals agreement with something said or implied before. In this sense it contrasts with the contradictory tone 2, as in type (d.ii) above.

> // 3 ∧ I'll / see what / I can */ **do** //
> PLAY 🔊 Sound 5.2.2.1e-ii

(iii) The statement is uncommitted because it is incomplete: it is not, in fact, assigned to any speech function, being conjoined to a following clause. As with the analogous function of tone 4, this type will be taken up under the 'logical' metafunction in Section 3.

> // 3 ∧ al/though he was */ **tired** he // 1 couldn't */ **sleep** //
> PLAY 🔊 Sound 5.2.2.1e-iii1

This tone (tone 3) is often used by a speaker wishing to hold the floor; and by a reader reading aloud from a written text (e.g. a radio newscast) to break up passages which are inappropriately dense for the spoken channel. It is also the characteristic tone used in enumerating lists, in this way merging with the 'listing' pretonic of tone 1 (see Chapter 7 section 7.4 below).

> // ...1 one / two / three */ **four** //
> PLAY 🔊 Sound 5.2.2.1e-iii2

(f) Declarative clause, falling plus level-rising (tone 13, to be read 'one three', not 'thirteen'). This is an unmarked statement of type (a), to which is appended a secondary focus; typically either (i) a circumstantial element of Place, Time &c., or (ii) an element that is already given (and could have been structurally Given, realized post-tonically) but to which the speaker assigns a status of secondary prominence.

// 13 ∧ there are */ **deer** in those */ **woods** //
PLAY 🔊 Sound 5.2.2.1f1

// 13 ∧ it's a / real */ **nuis**ance / that */ **dog** //
PLAY 🔊 Sound 5.2.2.1f2

(g) Declarative clause, rising-falling plus level-rising (tone 53, 'five three'). This bears the same relation to a tone 5, type (c), as a tone 13 declarative does to one of tone 1.

// 53 ∧ he / didn't come */ **home** last */ **night** //
PLAY 🔊 Sound 5.2.2.1g

(h) Statements realized by other than declarative clauses. These are of two types, one pseudo and one real. The pseudo type is an elliptical declarative clause, in which some element or elements must be presumed from the (verbal or situational) context. These are in fact declarative clauses, and types (a) to (g) above all apply.

The real types are those which are interrogative or imperative in mood. These are rare. Most of those usually cited fall into what we consider the distinct category of exclamations; see Section 5.2.2.5 below. Others are dependent clauses, having no speech function of their own, such as the first (imperative) clause in *do that once more and I'll never speak to you again*; for these see Section 5.3. Those that occur are usually fixed expressions having their own characteristic tone, like the *far from it* cited in (c) above. Here are a few examples.

// 1 good */ **mor**ning //
PLAY 🔊 Sound 5.2.2.1h1

// 1 how do you */ **do** //
PLAY 🔊 Sound 5.2.2.1h2

// 1 how */ **are** you //
PLAY 🔊 Sound 5.2.2.1h3

// .3 good */ **bye** //
PLAY 🔊 Sound 5.2.2.1h4

// .3 good */ **eve**ning //
PLAY 🔊 Sound 5.2.2.1h5

*// 1+ **glad**ly //
PLAY 🔊 Sound 5.2.2.1h6

*// 5 **cert**ainly //
PLAY 🔊 Sound 5.2.2.1h7

For declarative clauses functioning as questions, commands or offers, or in minor speech functions, see under the relevant sections below (5.2.2.2 to 5.2.2.7).

5.2.2.2 Questions

(a) The unmarked realization of a question is an interrogative clause, comprising one tone unit, spoken either on a rising tone (tone 2) or on a falling tone (tone 1) depending on which type of interrogative it is.

   If it is a 'yes/no' question, the unmarked realization is a polar interrogative clause spoken on tone 2:

   // 2 does the / Wallace Line go / round the whole */ **globe** //
   PLAY ◀ Sound 5.2.2.2a1

   // 2 ∧ are we /back to trans*/**crib**ing now //
   PLAY ◀ Sound 5.2.2.2a2

   If it is a 'WH-' question, the unmarked realization is a non-polar interrogative (lexical interrogative) spoken on tone 1:

   // 1 how's */ **Fran**cis //
   PLAY ◀ Sound 5.2.2.2a3

   // 1∧ what / time do /you get */**up** //
   PLAY ◀ Sound 5.2.2.2a4

The rising tone signals uncertainty; and particularly, uncertainty as to the polarity: 'is it yes or no?'. So this tone is naturally associated with the polar type of interrogative, where it is precisely the polarity that is at issue. For the same reason, the non-polar, lexical type of interrogative does not demand a rising tone; there is no uncertainty about the polarity — the clause is simply a declarative with a missing piece, which the respondent is called upon to supply. So while the unmarked tone of the polar interrogative is the rising tone, tone 2,the unmarked tone of the lexical interrogative is the same as that of the declarative, namely tone 1. Each type of interrogative then displays a paradigm of marked alternatives, in the same way as the declarative does, but differing in their systemic alignments and in their significance in the discourse. We will consider the marked alternatives for each type of interrogative in turn.

(b) Polar interrogative clause, falling tone (tone 1). The falling tone has the effect of enforcing attention to the question; it embodies a demand for an answer, often calling for reassurance or explanation. An explanation is more likely to be forthcoming in answer to a yes/no question spoken on this tone than to one spoken on tone 2.

   // 1 are you */ **sat**isfied //
   PLAY ◀ Sound 5.2.2.2b

(c) Polar interrogative clause, rising-falling tone (tone 5). Here the effect of the rising-falling sequence is to turn a question of type (a) into one of type (b). A typical instance of this type is one introduced by *yes but* … at the beginning of the clause; the meaning is 'no it's not just a simple question; it's something I need to have explained or to be reassured about'.

> // 5 why */ **did** they //

(d) Non-polar interrogative clause, rising tone (tone 2), neutral tonicity. The rising tone with a WH- type question has the effect of making it milder; it is a question that is modulated by a request for permission to ask (and the speaker may add *may I ask?* at the end). Often there is also a prosody of puzzlement in the questioner's approach.

> // 2 what's the */ **time** //
> PLAY 🔊 Sound 5.2.2.2d

(e) Non-polar interrogative clause, rising tone (tone 2), marked tonicity. This is a special type of rising tone non-polar interrogative, in which the information focus is on the WH- item itself. These are what are known as 'echo questions', where the questioner is repeating or alluding to a previous utterance some element of which he didn't hear, or has forgotten, or can't bring himself to believe.

> */ / 2 **who** is that / man over / there //
> PLAY 🔊 Sound 5.2.2.2e

(f) Non-polar interrogative, rising-falling tone (tone 5). As with the declarative, there is a movement here from uncertainty to certainty; at the same time, as with the non-polar interrogative on tone 2, type (d) above, the initial rise gives a prosody of puzzlement or surprise — which is then, however, overtaken by the expected movement of the fall, showing that there is, in fact, a framework within which some information is to be supplied.

> */ / 5 **why** do you / do that //
> PLAY 🔊 Sound 5.2.2.2f

(g) Questions realized by other than interrogative clauses. We have already referred to one of these, in 5.2.2.1 type (d.i): one of the functions of a declarative clause on tone 2 is not so much a statement as a type of question. This is in fact the most usual instance of a non-interrogative question; its meaning is that of 'statement held up for query', seeking confirmation or denial. In many cases it represents a speaker's inference (which may be signalled by a final *then*) which the speaker regards as needing to be checked.

> // 2ʌ just 'cause you / do / get up */ **ear**ly //
> PLAY 🔊 Sound 5.2.2.2g

Other examples were given in 5.2.2.1d above.

Other than this type, we are not certain whether instances of declaratives functioning as questions should be regarded as systemic. We are probably all familiar with individuals who ask questions using a declarative clause on tone 1 or tone 5; but it is noteworthy that such utterances are often misinterpreted as statements, which suggests that they are not part of a systematic grammar of question types. Here is an example constructed to illustrate this type.

> // 1 ∧ they / haven't */**sent** it //
> ('Am I right in thinking that they haven't sent it, then?')
>
> PLAY ◀ Sound 5.2.2.2h

5.2.3 Offers

Offers are interesting in that they have no special category of mood associated with them. All the primary mood types may realize an offer: declarative, as in *I'll help you*; polar interrogative, as in *Shall I help you?*; lexical (non-polar) interrogative, as in *How can I help you?*; imperative, as in *Let me help you!*.

The tone is usually that which is the unmarked choice for the mood concerned: tone 1 on imperative and non-polar interrogative, tone 2 on polar interrogative. The declarative type is the exception; it tends to be combined with tone 3, in the tentative sense that we saw in 5.2.2.1 (e.i) above. This may be a tone 3 tone unit, as in

> // 3 I'll */ **help** you //
> PLAY ◀ Sound 5.2.2.3a

or a tone 13 tone unit, with the major tonic on the Subject (the person offering — especially if the speaker is someone else making the offer on that person's behalf!):

> *// 13 **Mary'll** */ **help** you //
> PLAY ◀ Sound 5.2.2.3b

With offers realized by the imperative, tone 3 is also frequent, probably in about the same proportion as it is with imperative commands. For these, and also suggestions (which are a combination of an offer and a command), see the following section.

5.2.4 Commands

(a) The unmarked realization of a command is an imperative clause. This is not to say that the imperative is always the form most frequently taken by a command; that will depend on the register of the discourse. (We should perhaps add a reminder here, not to be trapped by the commonsense meaning of the technical terms. A 'command' includes everything from a polite request to a forthright military order.)

In contexts where the tenor relations are notably skew, with an unequal distribution of power as in parents to children or participants at different levels in some institutional hierarchy, the imperative will tend to predominate. The more even the tenor, on the other hand, the more likely it becomes that other moods will supplant it: especially modulated declaratives and interrogatives (see (c) and (d) below).

What is the unmarked tone for an imperative clause? The most likely candidate is tone 1, which is clearly typical of a positive command of the more peremptory kind. But in many contexts the level-rising tone, tone 3, appears equally 'unmarked'; so we will treat them together. The contrast between them is similar to that in declarative statements: tone 3 gives a prosody of lower commitment, greater tentativeness — hence, with a command, it is more 'polite'. It is clearly typical of expressions such as *Take your time!*, as well as formulaic commands like *Have a nice day!*. But with positive commands as a whole, tone 3 still appears as a marked variant; we code it as 'mild command'.

// 1 tell me / all a*/**bout** it //
PLAY Sound 5.2.2.4a1

// 3 tell me all a*/**bout** it //
PLAY Sound 5.2.2.4a2

With negative commands, on the other hand, the tone 3 form seems to be the unmarked one; a negative command (or 'prohibition') on tone 1 seems marked as carrying an additional degree of peremptoriness. We code it as 'strong' command.

// 3 don't stay / out too */ **long** //
PLAY Sound 5.2.2.4a3

// 1 don't stay / out too */ **long** //
PLAY Sound 5.2.2.4a4

(b) Imperative clause, falling plus level-rising (tone 13). With a negative imperative, e.g. *Don't do that!*, and also with a 'marked positive', e.g. **Do** *hurry up!*, the option arises of using a compound tone unit with the tone 1 tonic falling on the imperative verbal operator *don't / do*. What this does is to treat the mood marker itself as the major focus of information, foregrounding the sense of 'I'm telling you (not) to do something!'.

*// 13 **do** tell me / all a*/**bout** it //
PLAY Sound 5.2.2.4b

(c) Imperative clause, falling-rising (tone 4). This is a compromising command, with a prosody of 'well at least ...'. This is clearly related to the sense of 'with reservation' that tone 4 has with a declarative clause; but the context of a command gives it a somewhat different significance. Note its use in more or less ritual expressions such as *Be reasonable!*, *Have a heart!*.

// 4 give him a */ **chance** //
PLAY Sound 5.2.2.4c

(d) Imperative clause, rising-falling (tone 5). Here again the meaning is related to that of the same tone with a declarative clause; but again the imperative context makes the meaning somewhat different. A tone 5 imperative has an insistent flavour, often with an added sense of 'do it yourself — don't expect me to do it for you'.

> // 5 ∧ you */ hand it / **over** / to me //
> PLAY ◄ Sound 5.2.2.4d

(e) Imperative clause, high rising (tone 2). This is actually a query (cf. 5.2.2.2 (g) above); it is analogous to the tone 2 declarative, querying a statement, but with an imperative what is being queried is the command — the sense is 'is that what you want me to do?' Such a query may be a challenge, or it may be something closely akin to an offer (see Section 5.2.2.7 below, on responses).

> // 2 make the */**cof**fee // ('shall I?)
> PLAY ◄ Sound 5.2.2.4e

(f) Suggestions. A suggestion is a combination of offer and command, typically realized in English by an imperative clause with *let's*. Tonally, these follow the pattern of imperative commands: if positive, tone 1 is neutral, tone 3 is 'mild'; if negative, tone 3 is neutral, tone 1 is 'strong'. The negative form has either *don't let's* or *let's not*. Again as with commands, there is a marked alternative of tone 13 both with negative (focus on *don't*, or on either *let's* or *not*) and with marked positive **do** *let's* (focus on *do*); with a suggestion this tone often has the force of a plea.

> // 1 let's go and / see if we can / get a / copy of the re*/**port** //
> PLAY ◄ Sound 5.2.2.4f

> // 3 let's go and / see if we can / get a / copy of the re*/**port** //
> PLAY ◄ Sound 5.2.2.4g

> *// 13 **let's** go and / see if we can / get a / copy of the re*/**port** //
> PLAY ◄ Sound 5.2.2.4h

(g) Commands realized by other than imperative clauses. In many contexts, the typical form of a command is not an imperative but a modulated declarative, such as *You must help me₂*, or a modulated interrogative, e.g. *Will you help me?*. The tonal options are those of declarative and polar interrogative clauses, respectively. It is the grammar that specifies the combinations of tone with mood (this being one important reason for treating intonational systems as grammatical). The interpretation in any given instance will of course depend on the semantic environment.

Modulation is one type of modality, and modality is dealt with in a separate section below (Section 5.2.4) — with particular reference to one tonal contrast that is foregrounded in modalized declarative clauses. This becomes clearest when the modality itself is under focus, which is often a feature of modulated declaratives functioning as commands, e.g.

// 13 ∧ you */ **must** / try to be more */ **care**ful //
PLAY ◀ Sound 5.2.2.4i

These in turn relate closely to the imperative clauses of type 5.2.2.4 (b) above, where the mood marker carries the major information focus, the substance of the command being given secondary status.

In general, the more highly elaborated the form of a command, the less it will sound like a command in terms of its intonation (and of its voice quality). Elaborate circumlocutions such as *You might want to help me with this.* are virtually indistinguishable from ordinary statement-type declarative clauses.

5.2.2.5 Exclamations

The characteristic tone of an exclamation is the rising-falling tone 5. This often maps on to a clause structure that is a hybrid of declarative and lexical (non-polar) interrogative, as in *What a fuss you're making!*, *How the world has changed!*. A text example:

// **5** what a / gorgeous */ **col**our that / is you're / wearing //
PLAY ◀ Sound 5.2.2.5

Many straightforward declaratives with this tone may also function effectively as exclamations; there is obviously no clear line between an exclamation and a statement, and lots of instances could be interpreted as either. If someone says *he's a menace* and the response is *Is he?*, it is being interpreted as a statement, whereas if the response is *Yes, isn't he* (on tone 1), then it is being interpreted more as an exclamation.

Polar interrogatives, typically in the negative, often function as exclamations; here the distinction between an exclamation and the unmarked function as a question is usually rather clear — if someone says *Wasn't that amazing!* (likewise on tone 5), it is unlikely to be responded to as a question. The other common form of exclamation is a minor clause, again typically on tone 5: *What a mess!* (and cf. 5.2.2.1 (c) above).

For the continuum linking tone 5 to the high falling (wide) variety of tone 1, see Chapter 7, on secondary tone, below.

5.2.2.6 Calls, greetings (including valedictions) and alarms

These are often known as 'minor speech functions' (sometimes exclamations are also included in this category); they are typically realized as minor clauses ('clausettes') — that is, clauses that do not select in the systems of transitivity and mood.

The consequence of this is that such expressions tend to display the meanings of the different tones in a rather unmixed form. This happens in one of two ways.

On the one hand, many of these are 'set phrases': fixed or formulaic expressions each of which has its own characteristic tone, with perhaps some very minor variation:

Speaker A: // 3 good */ **morn**ing //
PLAY ◀ Sound 5.2.2.6

Speaker B: // 1 good */ **morn**ing //
PLAY ◀ Sound 5.2.2.6a

On the other hand, a vocative can occur on all possible tones, and the distinctive meaning of the tone comes through clearly in every case:

*// 1 **Ei**leen // ('come here!', 'stop that')
PLAY ◀ Sound 5.2.2.6 1

*// 2 **Ei**leen // ('is that you?', 'where are you?')
PLAY ◀ Sound 5.2.2.6 2

// 3 Ei*/**leen** // ('listen!', 'I've got something to say to you')
PLAY ◀ Sound 5.2.2.6 3

*// -3 **Ei**leen // ('I'm warning you!')
PLAY ◀ Sound 5.2.2.6 4

*// 4 **Ei**leen // ('listen carefully!', 'don't tell anyone', 'be honest')
PLAY ◀ Sound 5.2.2.6 5

*// 5 **Ei**leen // ('now I've told you before!', 'take a look at that!')
PLAY ◀ Sound 5.2.2.6 6

*// 5̲ **Ei**leen // ('you shouldn't have done that')
PLAY ◀ Sound 5.2.2.6 7

Minor speech functions thus have a useful role in helping people to become aware of the tonal system operating in the language.

5.2.2.7 Responses

A response is not a separate speech function. Initiating and responding are separate moves in dialogue; the prototypical form of a response is a switch to the complementary role in the EXCHANGE system:

statement → question	It's raining. → Is it?
question → statement	Is it raining? → Yes, it is. No, it isn't.
offer → command	Shall I ask them? → Yes, do! No, don't!
command → offer	Ask them! → Shall I?

The response takes on the range of tonal variants associated with the mood selected: polar interrogative, declarative, or imperative.

Responses are often elliptical, like those above. This of course affects the tonicity, since it limits the possible location of the tonic prominence; one of the meanings of choosing an elliptical clause is precisely that it redefines the 'unmarked focus'. But the choice of tone — and the meaning of that choice — is the same in elliptical as in 'full' (non-elliptical) clauses.

5.2.3 Speech function, mood, and tone

As we have seen, there is a pattern of typical, or 'unmarked', relationships between the semantic categories of (major) speech function and the grammatical categories of mood: statements realized by declarative clauses, questions by interrogative and commands by imperative — only offers have no special mood associated with them. We also find 'marked' alternatives, the most important of which have been discussed and illustrated: questions realized by declarative, commands by interrogative and so on. These get their distinctive meanings precisely by departing from the unmarked pattern.

As long as the realizations are unmarked, it does not matter whether we refer the tonal variation to the semantic category (e.g. 'kinds of statement') or to the grammatical one (e.g. 'kinds of declarative clause'); it comes to the same thing. But when there is a departure from the unmarked pattern of realizations, the question arises: do we explain the tonal variants in terms of the semantic categories, or in terms of the grammatical ones? Intuitively, since the choice of tone is clearly meaningful in a systematic way, we might expect it to be the semantic category that determines the specific meaning of a particular choice of tone. In fact, however, it is the grammatical category that turns out to be the more significant. In other words, if we want to specify what the contrast between (say) tone 1 and tone 3 means in a particular instance, we need to know, not whether the clause in question is functioning as statement or as offer, but whether the clause in question is declarative or imperative in mood. This, as we pointed out, is one major reason for locating the tonal systems themselves within the grammar: it is the grammatical environment which determines their systemic value and their meaning. What we attempt to bring out are the different sets of tonal oppositions that are associated with the different moods, and what each term in each set of oppositions means. Thus the combination of a tone 5 with an imperative clause means something like 'have you thought of doing that?' or 'don't expect me to do it for you'; whereas the combination of tone 5 with a declarative clause has the sense of 'this is indeed so, surprising as it may seem'. But this variation in meaning is obviously not arbitrary or random. Essentially, there is a constant meaning associated with each of the different tones, deriving (as we said at the beginning) from the basic prosodic opposition between rising and falling. But these constant meanings are highly general, so general that even if we could gloss them adequately (and that is impossible, because they are not susceptible of definition) it would not help us much in explaining particular instances. To get closer to the instance we try to find a more specific meaning, by relating the tonal category to its grammatical environment.

This is where we find that the relevant category in the clause grammar for determining the meaning of the tones is the interpersonal system of mood; and this shows that the systems realized by tone are interpersonal systems. We find that there are unmarked associations between tone and mood: typically, each mood has its characteristic tonal mapping. But these are not obligatory; there are also alternative 'marked' mappings — and here we see the same fundamental semogenic process taking place as we saw with tonality. We can postulate (and this is backed up by observations about how children learn their first language) an earlier state in which there is an absolute tie-up between, say, polar interrogative mood and high rising tone: all yes/no questions are realized by the combination of the two. This embodies a redundancy; at the next stage, this redundancy is deconstrued, so we get a polar interrogative mapped on to a falling tone, and a rising tone mapped on to a declarative — this has doubled the number of possible options. The original association remains as the unmarked choice, the default option in the system. Such a state of affairs often persists — it is perfectly stable; but it may evolve further, to a state in which there is no one unmarked mapping and hence all combinations are equally (un)marked.

We have suggested in the coding framework how these tonal categories may be represented systemically, as sets of features that can be shown to contrast semantically in the same environment; and we have labelled them according to the dimension of contrast, with terms which we hope will be seen to be relevant to some instances — though certainly not to all (but, as we have pointed out, this is true of all names of grammatical categories). The point to be stressed is that these tonal systems are themselves also systems in the grammar. Their point of origin is the information unit, not the clause; but it is the information unit as a bearer of speech function, either a proposition (statement or question) or a proposal (command or offer) — that is, the information unit when it is mapped on to a clause: specifically, on to an independent major clause, or at least that part of it which selects for mood. Put more simply (though slightly less accurately), we could say that these are systems of the information unit with tonality unmarked.

It is perhaps helpful to have a single term with which to refer to this entire complex of tonal systems; for this we have suggested the term *key*. A number of the individual systems are in fact coded as one or another specific kind of key, so it is not inappropriate to use this as a generic label for all. Despite the variation in their meaning in association with different moods (which made it impossible to set them up as a separate category independent of mood), there is a unity about them, a sense that they make as a whole a distinctive contribution to the creation of meaning in the spoken language.

What about these same tones in contexts of marked tonality, or where even if the information unit is mapped on to a clause the clause is not selecting independently for speech function? Consider an extract such as the following:

// 4 and / you know the / major */ **foods** in those / south pacific / islands are
// 3 things like _ em */ **bread**fruit *// 3 **ta**ro _ em and // 4 those kinds
of in/credibly */ **bor**ing // 1 horrible */ **things** //

PLAY ◀ Sound 5.2.3

The tones are exactly those that we have been discussing. Moreover, each instance exemplifies a feature that is systematically related to the features in the various systems of KEY: the tone 4 on the initial Theme, the tone 3 on the items in the list, are not only phonologically identical to the tone 4, and tone 3, that we saw functioning with declarative and imperative clauses — at a deep level they are also related semantically. But the grammatical environment is different: here they are not selecting for speech function. We will come back to these at a later section in this chapter (5.3). Meanwhile we take up the final aspect of the association of tone with mood: its relationship to the various systems of MODALITY.

5.2.4 Intonation and modality

Closely aligned with mood in the grammar of English is the system known as 'modality'. This is actually a rather complex set of sub-systems having to do with the speaker's attitude to the statement, question, offer or command that he or she is construing. Modality is realized in many ways, one of which is by the verbal operators *can could may might (shall) should will would must ought to* and sometimes also *be to, have to, need* and (now much less commonly) *dare* — the so-called 'modal verbs' or 'modal auxiliaries'. Another form of realization is through 'modal adverbs' such as *perhaps, probably, usually*, and adjectives such as *able to, supposed to, willing to*.

What the MODALITY systems do is to open up the semantic space between 'yes' and 'no'. To see how this happens, let us establish terms for the two columns of 'commodity exchanged' in Figure 5.2.1a above. We will refer to the speech functions in the 'goods-&-services' column, namely offers and commands, as **proposals**; and to those in the 'information' column, namely statements and questions, as **propositions**. Now, consider the system of POLARITY associated with each. With a proposition, the positive / negative poles mean 'it is so / it isn't so'. With a proposal, on the other hand, the positive / negative poles mean 'do so / don't do so'. But instead of construing this as a simple switch between two states, as the polarity systems do, the systems of modality reveal it to be a continuum. They construct meanings such as 'maybe so, maybe not', 'should do, but needn't' and so on.

Let us first set out a paradigm of modal expressions, beginning by giving them all a positive value:

('high' value)	Certainly.	Always.	It must be.
('median' value)	Probably.	Usually.	It will be.
('low' value)	Possibly.	Sometimes.	It may be.

If we now take these as complete utterances, so that the modal expression is carrying the tonic, we find that they are typically associated with two particular tones, as follows:

// 1 certainly // PLAY		// 1 it must be // PLAY	
// 1 probably // PLAY	// 4 probably // PLAY	// 1 it will be // PLAY	/ 4 it will be // PLAY
	// 4 possibly // PLAY		// 4 it may be // PLAY

Figure 5.2.4 Intonation and modality

As we should predict, the 'high value' modals commonly combine with a declarative-type tone 1, the tone of assertion; whereas the 'low value' modals favour tone 4, the tone of reservation ('there's a 'but' about it'). The 'median value' modals take either tone 1 or tone 4, both equally unmarked, but with one or other being more likely according to the context: tone 4 suggests a move down from the position of 'certain', e.g.

> [They're bound to notice. —]   // 4 ∧ they */ **prob**ably / will, but ... //
> PLAY ◀ Sound 5.2.4b1

whereas tone 1 suggests a move up from 'just possible', e.g.

> [It sometimes works. —]   // 1 ∧ it */ **us**ually / works //
> PLAY ◀ Sound 5.2.4b2

What we have illustrated here is the type of modality that accompanies propositions. In a proposition (statement or question), the positive and negative poles are 'it is so' and 'it isn't so'; the system of modality fills out the space between these two poles, along one of two trajectories: (1) '*either* yes *or* no', i.e. degrees of probability; (2) '*both* yes *and* no', i.e. degrees of usuality. The first is the dimension of 'certain – probable – possible'; the second is the dimension of 'always – usually – sometimes'.

There is a second type of modality, that which accompanies proposals (commands and offers). Here the positive and negative poles are 'do it!' and 'don't do it!'; again the modality fills out the space in between, and again there are two possible trajectories, although the relation between the two is rather different. One of the trajectories is related to commands, and construes degrees of obligation:

('high' value)	You must do it.	You're obliged to.
('median' value)	You should do it.	You're supposed to.
('low' value)	You may /can do it.	You're allowed to.

These are, of course, declarative clauses, and they are not restricted to having 'you' as Subject; any entity (though it is usually one that is considered to be endowed with consciousness!) can function in this slot, e.g. *let Fred do it, Fred's supposed to do it, they've got to stop shouting, no-one's allowed to leave*, &c. &c. There is a similar association of the different degrees of obligation with the two tones, tone 1 and tone 4, if the modal expression is carrying the tonic:

> // 1 you */ **must** do it //   PLAY ◀
>
> // 1 you */ **should** do it //   PLAY ◀
>
> // 4 you */ **should** do it //   PLAY ◀
>
> // 4 you */ **can** do it //   PLAY ◀

with the tone of the median value again reflecting the direction of approach:

> [Do we have to pay? —]   // 4 ∧ you're sup*/**posed** to, but ... //
> PLAY ◀ Sound 5.2.4d1
>
> [You can if you like. —]   // 1 ∧ in / fact I / think you */ **should** //
> PLAY ◀ Sound 5.2.4d2

The other trajectory is that of 'readiness'; this is related to offers, and comprises two aspects of readiness, (1) inclination, and (2) ability. Like offers themselves, the degrees of readiness are less clearly defined in the grammar; but we can illustrate them with examples as follows:

(inclin.: 'high' value)	He must / is determined to have his own way.
(inclin.: 'median' value)	We would rather / are anxious to know.
(inclin.: 'low' value)	Frank will / is willing to do the job.
(ability: 'low' value)	Jill can / is able to understand Italian.

Likewise the tonal associations are less clearcut. There are one or two characteristic patterns where the modal is under focus, e.g.

// 4 ∧ if you */ **must** / know ... //
PLAY ◀ Sound 5.2.4e1

// 5 you */ **would** / spoil it * // 1 **would**n't you //
PLAY ◀ Sound 5.2.4e2

These are both examples of inclination, high and median value respectively; and the tonic on the modal adds a sense of 'perversely': 'if you insist on knowing', 'you chose to spoil it (as I would expect of you)'. (In both cases the tone would typically be the low variant; see Chapter 7 section 7.7 below.) In general, however, the modal in this type of proposal does not carry the tonic, and the pattern is just that which is typical of declarative clauses; with the low values it is perhaps more than usually common to have (marked) tonic prominence on the Subject, in which case the tone is often a compound 13 (or 53):

*// 13 **Roger**'ll / take you */ **home** //   ('so don't worry')
PLAY ◀ Sound 5.2.4f1

*// 53 **Jill** can / understand I*/**tal**ian //   ('you thought noone could')
PLAY ◀ Sound 5.2.4f2

We have illustrated the association between intonation and modality using simple constructed clauses, mainly with the modal expression carrying the tonic prominence, and with the polarity positive throughout. With negative polarity the pattern is not essentially different; but it is more complex because there are two types of negative polarity: those where the negative is on the proposition (PROP-N; sometimes called 'straight negative'), e.g.

It may not be so. Possibly it isn't so. Possibly it may not be so.

and those where the negative is on the modality (MOD-N; 'transferred negative'):

It can't be so. It isn't possibly so. It can't possibly be so.

If the negative is transferred from the proposition to the modality, there is a switch between the high and low values; note that the tone continues to match the value, whichever way it is expressed:

(MOD-N, 'high' value)   // 1 ∧ it / can't */ **pos**sibly be / so //
PLAY ◄ Sound 5.2.4g1

(MOD-N, 'low' value)   // 4 ∧ it / needn't neces*/**sar**ily be / so //
PLAY ◄ Sound 5.2.4g2

The median value involves no switch, of course, and the tone may be tone 1 or tone 4 exactly as would be expected in the positive:

(PROP-N, 'median' value)   Probably it won't be so. (tone 1 or tone 4)

(MOD-N, 'median' value)   It isn't likely to be so. (tone 1 or tone 4)

What should be stressed, however, is that the association of a particular tone with a particular type of modality, as we have illustrated it here, follows naturally from the systemic association of tone with mood; it is not based on any different principles. In fact we could say that modality presents the fundamental contrast between tone 1 and tone 4 (which are the two most frequent tones in connected discourse) in its prototypical guise, as the distinction between unconditional assertion (tone 1) and conditional assertion — assertion modulated by reservation (tone 4). In most instances of modality, the focus is not on the modal expression itself — it is at its unmarked location in the information unit; and the general principles outlined in Sections 5.2.2.1 – 5.2.2.4 hold good. Even when the focus is on the modal, the whole range of tone choices is still available; but because the meaning of modality is being foregrounded, the marked tonal variants are rather less likely. So, for example, while an instance such as

// 4 ∧ you / certainly / won't get a*/**way** with it //
PLAY ◄ Sound 5.2.4h1

is entirely unremarkable, with the tone 4 attaching the feature of reservation to the proposition *not get away with it* ('even if you think you can', &c.), utterances such as

*// 4 **cert**ainly //
PLAY ◄

or

*// 4 **cert**ainly / not //
PLAY ◄

are somewhat unlikely, because here the high value probability (i.e. certainty) actually constitutes the focal point of the information, and this does clash with the note of reservation conveyed by the tone 4.

5.3   Intonation in the ideational metafunction

The ideational metafunction is the grammar in the role of construing the world we inhabit, as already noted (Chapter 4 section 4.3). The term 'construing' is carefully chosen; what it signifies is that the grammar transforms human experience into meaning — semioticizes it if you like. It thus contrasts both with the interpersonal metafunction, where the grammar is enacting — enacting human relationships, in the innumerable micro-encounters of daily life; and with the textual metafunction, where (as we saw) the grammar is engendering the flow of discourse that makes possible, and integrates, the other two.

We distinguish two components of the ideational metafunction: the experiential, and the logical. In a sense both are concerned with the construal of human experience; but they are concerned with different aspects of it, and these call up different resources within the grammar.

On the one hand, the grammar construes *happenings:* the happenings that go on around us, and also within ourselves. These it typically construes as a configuration consisting of a process together with its participating entities and circumstantial factors — that is, as a clause, with its functional roles of Process, Actor, Location and the like. This is what we refer to as the ***experiential*** component.

On the other hand, the grammar construes *the relations between happenings:* sequences of happenings linked by time or cause or other potentially iterative relationships. These it construes as tactic complexes, such as the 'compound and complex sentences' of our traditional grammar books. This is what we refer to as the ***logical*** component.

In many languages, intonation plays an important part in the experiential component, either as an inherent property of a word or morpheme or as a marker of the grammatical relationship between words or morphemes (or both). Such languages have usually been labelled distinctively as 'tone languages'. English, obviously, is not a tone language in this sense. Intonation plays no part in the realization of experiential meanings in English.

With logical meaning, the situation is a little different. One reason for distinguishing the logical from the experiential, in fact, is that logical meanings, while ideational in origin (that is, evolving as the construal of relationships between happenings), extend very naturally into the interpersonal and textual realms. And intonation does play a part in construing logical meanings in English.

It is beyond our scope here to explore the full potential of intonation for the construction of English discourse. For this see especially the work of Paul Tench (1990). But we will take the first steps, showing how intonation contributes towards the construction of patterns at a higher rank. This is achieved by starting from the role that intonation has in defining and giving meaning to the information unit (as described in Sections 1 and 2 of this chapter) and extending the same principles to establish a semantic relationship between one such unit and another — again with the same kind of interaction with the clause-based systems of the grammar. In this case, however, the interaction is not with the individual clause but with the clause complex; more specifically, with the kinds of clause nexus (systemic pairing of two clauses) out of which the clause complex is built. We will find that there is an information unit nexus which is independent of the clause nexus but is related to it by the same default principle as we found with the systems of tonality and tone.

Two intonational patterns are involved. One is tactic sequences; the other is tone concord. The two in fact overlap, since tone concord construes one particular kind of tactic sequence; but it is clearer to describe them as separate systems. These will be the topic of the next two subsections.

5.3.1 Intonation in tactic sequences

We saw in Section 2.2 above how tone 1 is typically associated with a declarative clause functioning as an assertive statement. It is something complete and final in itself — there the matter ends. On the other hand, tone 3 is the tone of opting out; this means that it suspends any decision about speech function. In that regard, tone 3 is incomplete. Tone 4 may well be a completed statement; but it carries a strong reservation — more could be said, which might modify the whole picture.

Now consider a sequence of two clauses, each one congruently construing a single happening. How might the two happenings be related to one another? We will construct a simple paradigm.

(a) It's stopped raining. I'm going out.

(b) It's still raining, and I'm not going out.

(c) Unless it stops raining I'm not going out.

Grammatically, (a) is two unrelated clauses; (b) is a paratactic clause nexus, while (c) is a hypotactic clause nexus. What this says is that, in (a), the two happenings are not connected; in (b) and (c), on the other hand, they are connected, but there is a difference in their relative status. In (b) they have equal status; in (c) the status is unequal, the first one having no speech function of its own and dependent on the second for acquiring one.

Assuming unmarked tonality (each clause one information unit), the typical tone pattern would be as follows:

// 1 ∧ it's / stopped */ **rain**ing // 1 ∧ I'm / going */ **out** //
PLAY ◀ Sound 5.3.1a1

// 3 ∧ it's / still */ **rain**ing and I'm // 1 not going */ **out** //
PLAY ◀ Sound 5.3.1a2

// 4 ∧ un/less it / stops */ **rain**ing I'm // 1 not going */ **out** //
PLAY ◀ Sound 5.3.1a3

Here the clause grammar and the information unit grammar are in cahoots, each reinforcing the picture construed by the other.

But, as always, the two can vary independently; we might have

// 1 ∧ un/less it / stops */ **rain**ing I'm // 1 not going */ **out** //
PLAY ◀ Sound 5.3.1a4

where the hypotactic concessive clause is combined with the definiteness derived from the meaning of tone 1 as an assertive statement ('strong force' in our coding). Or we might have:

// 3 ∧ it's / stopped */ **rain**ing // 1 ∧ I'm / going */ **out** //
`PLAY` ◀ Sound 5.3.1a5

where the first clause, while having no structural (clause grammar) linkage with the second, is presented as informationally non-final: as anticipating that there is something more to follow. Or, again,

// 4 ∧ it's / still */ **rain**ing and I'm // 1 not going */ **out** //
`PLAY` ◀ Sound 5.3.1a6

where the clause grammar (paratactic clause nexus) is in tension with a sense that here is a conditioning factor, conveyed by the tone 4. All combinations of tone with tactic structure are possible; and all the marked variants have a different meaning deriving from the tension between the features selected in the two domains of the grammar (clause grammar and information unit grammar).

What is happening here is simply an extension of the principle noted in Section 2.1 of this chapter, whereby the information unit grammar and the clause grammar become dissociated; new meanings are created through the recombination of what have become independent features — once decoupled, they can be cross-coupled in all possible ways. Here the process is taking place at a higher rank, that of the clause complex / information unit complex; but the principle is the same. Alongside the clause nexus, with its system of TAXIS (paratactic / hypotactic), we can recognize an 'information unit nexus' which has a system that is analogous but not identical in meaning (since the two can vary independently), where the tonal options are 1+1, 3+1, 4+1. The question then arises: how is this system to be coded? what does the choice of tone sequence actually mean?

Three points need to be noted:

(1) We have illustrated this system with the information units mapped on to clauses (unmarked tonality). But what we are considering is an information unit nexus, which is independent of the clause; it is in fact frequently mapped on to a single clause, with one information unit as Theme and one as Rheme. The frequency of this mapping gives a good insight into the significance of the Theme + Rheme structure.

(2) Secondly, just as the clause complex is not limited to a single clause nexus, likewise the information unit complex can be extended to longer sequences, 4+4+..., 3+4+ ... &c. The terminal information unit usually has tone 1, less frequently tone 5 — a tone ending with a fall, signing off so to speak.

(3) To get a richer sense of the logical meaning of these tone sequences, we should consider both the meaning of the various tones in isolation (i.e. as terms in the KEY systems associated with mood; cf. Section 2.2 above) and their association (by

default) with terms in the logical systems of the clause. To do this would take us more deeply into the grammar than can be attempted here. We will just illustrate with another constructed example, this time of a single clause with a tone unit boundary corresponding to Theme and Rheme.

// 3 no-one */ **else** would have // 1 known what to */ **do** //
`PLAY` 🔊 Sound 5.3.1b1

// 4 no-one */ **else** would have // 1 known what to */ **do** //
`PLAY` 🔊 Sound 5.3.1b2

// 1 no-one */ **else** would have // 1 known what to */ **do** //
`PLAY` 🔊 Sound 5.3.1b3

Note the difference in meaning among the three forms: 3+1, 4+1, 1+1.

5.3.2 The meaning of tone concord

As we have seen, any nexus of two clauses may be either paratactic (equal status) or hypotactic (unequal status: one dependent on the other). We refer to this as the system of *interdependency*, or *taxis*.

Combining with this is another system, that of the *logical-semantic relation* linking the two clauses. The primary network for these systems is as in Figure 5.3.2.

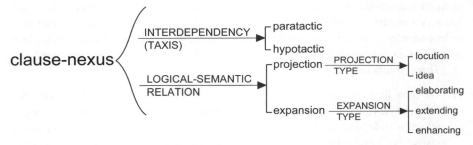

Figure 5.3.2

We need to explain briefly the logical semantic relations which can obtain between a pair of clauses forming a nexus.

The relations of *projection* are those where one clause 'projects' another either as speech (*locution*) or as thought (*idea*). These combine with parataxis, as 'direct' speech and thought, or with hypotaxis, as 'indirect', or 'reported' speech and thought.

The relations of *expansion* are those where one clause 'expands' another by (i) repeating, paraphrasing, exemplifying, etc. (*elaborating*); (ii) adding to it, either simply or as alternative or adversative: 'and', 'or', 'but' (*extending*), or (iii) qualifying it, by time, cause, condition, concession etc: 'when', 'because', 'if', 'although' (*enhancing*). Again, these combine with both parataxis and hypotaxis.

Table 5.3.2

	parataxis	hypotaxis
locution	Mary said ' we're leaving this evening'	Mary said they were leaving that evening
idea	Peter thought 'I can stay here until tomorrow'	Peter thought he could stay there till the next day.
elaborating	we're leaving now, we're just setting out	we're leaving now, which will just be in time
extending	we've locked up, and we've also closed the shutters	as well as locking up, we've closed the shutters
enhancing	we've locked up, so we can leave at any time	since we've locked up, we can leave at any time

We saw in the last section that intonation construes these tactic relations, either (by default) in harmony with the clause grammar or (markedly) in tension with it. We introduced this system in the context of a nexus of the expansion type, which is where it applies; but, while this is valid for extending and enhancing relations, those of the elaborating kind have a distinct intonation pattern of their own.

Unlike the extending and enhancing types, which are marked in the grammar by conjunctions (paratactic *and or but so then yet* etc, hypotactic *besides instead when because if although* etc), elaborating nexuses generally have no such markers in speech. They are often indicated in writing by symbols like *i.e. viz. e.g.* — because writing does not show intonation; but in speech they are clearly signaled by **tone concord**. What this means is that the two parts have the same tone pattern, which in the typical case is repeated very exactly.

Elaborating favours parataxis, so these are often paratactic nexuses, and may contain more than two clauses. But there is a hypotactic analogue, which is what is often called a 'descriptive, or non-defining, relative clause'; this usually displays tone concord with the segment containing its antecedent:

// 4 ∧ whereas */ **Ba**li which is / four — // 4 four hours a/way on a */ **boat** // 1 ^ is that / lush */ **trop**ical / ^ kind of / stuff //

PLAY ◀ Sound 5.3.2a

This is analogous to the pattern that is found with clause sequences which construe some kind of a list:

// -3 ∧ you've got to know / where your */**pass**ports /are // -3 ∧ you've got to know / where your */**tick**ets / are // -3 where your */**board**ing cards / are //

PLAY ◀ Sound 5.3.2c

The 'listing' Pretonic to tone 1 is another manifestation of the same principle: see Chapter 7 section 7.4. In these cases the relation between the parts is of the extending kind, but each one of them stands in the same relation with respect to some larger unit (in this example all are manifestations of 'having a system': see *Analysis*: texts with detailed commentary in Appendix to Part II).

By the same token, the resource of tone concord is also exploited when the speaker breaks up what would otherwise be an inordinately long tone unit. This can happen with any tone; for example in asking a question, if the tone selected is tone 2, each tone unit before the last anticipates the tonic movement at the end. Similarly, where the tone is fall-rising (tone 4), each segment repeats the same fall-rising pattern; and this same pattern is found in one of the Pretonics to tone 4, where the fall-rising movement is a feature of each Pretonic foot.

What is common to all these occurrences of tone concord is that the two or more stretches that share the same pitch movement have the same function in some wider context. The use of tone concord in an elaborating clause nexus is one application of this very general principle.

Finally, in a clause nexus of projection, whether hypotactic or paratactic, the pro-jecting clause typically does not form a separate information unit, unless it contains a lot of additional matter, or the sayer/thinker is being contrasted with a previous one. In connected spoken discourse the projecting clause normally comes first; in written narrative, with 'direct speech', it may come in the middle or at the end, in the latter case often being quite long — but even then, if it is read aloud it becomes post-tonic, a 'tail' added to what has gone before:

[paratactic locution]
   // 5 why did the / teacher at / your school say / sit up */ **straight** //

[hypotactic idea]
   // 1–3 ∧ they / thought it / made them look */**straight**er I sup*/**pose** //

5.3.3 Summary of intonation in the logical metafunction

So there are three basic principles involved where intonation realizes meanings in the logical metafunction.

(1) Where the logical-semantic relation in the nexus is one of expansion, between elements that differ in kind and in discourse function, '*a* and *x*', '*b* if *y*' etc, the intonation matches the relative status of the two. The contrasting possibilities are:

   no tactic relation   // 1 // 1 //

   paratactic relation   // 3 // 1 //

   hypotactic relation   // 4 // 1 //, // 1 // 4 //

This is the default pattern, in the sense that these are the tone sequences that match the relationships construed in the clause nexus. It then serves as the base line from which the system takes off on its own, and becomes a resource for creating new meanings in tension with those construed by the clause grammar.

(2) Where the logical semantic relation in the nexus is one of expansion, but between elements that are identical in kind and in discourse function '$c = z$', the intonation construes this as a repetition of the same pattern, matching not only in tone selection but in the entire tone contour. Again, this then becomes a strategy for creating a relationship of this kind; the tone concord is telling the listener that in the flow of the discourse these two chunks are carrying the same message. Note that such repetition, far from being unnecessary or 'redundant', contributes to the meaning of the discourse no less than the other forms of expansion. One familiar example of this is the word *too* which typically forms an information unit on its own, in tone concord with whatever has preceded. PLAY Sound 5.3.4

(3) Where the logical semantic relation is one of projection, between elements one of which is providing the grounding for the other, 'm says/thinks n', the intonation typically construes the 'm' element, the sayer or thinker, simply as an appendage to the 'n' element, that which is said or thought. The effect is, here again, to set up a tension with the clause grammar: the clause complex construes projection as a relationship between two processes, while the information grammar construes it as a single unit with the projecting element as a subsidiary part PLAY Sound 5.3.4a, rather as if 'Mary said' was to be worded as *according to Mary*. PLAY Sound 5.3.4b

In this chapter we have attempted to summarize the ways in which intonation interacts with the systems of clause grammar in the making of meaning in English. The next chapter presents a detailed analysis of a short passage of discourse, with exposition of the effect of the choices in intonation that are made at each move. In the final chapter we look more closely into the TONE system and discuss the finer distinctions of meaning that are construed by the secondary tones.

Note

1 We might have used the terms 'information' and 'redundancy', or 'informative' and 'redundant', taken from information theory. But we avoid using these particular terms for two reasons. First, these concepts as defined in information theory are valuable in linguistics just in their technical sense, where they enable us to quantify the information contained in a grammatical system (Halliday & James 1993). But information in the sense in which we are using it here is quite different: it is a property of the stream of speech, not of the system that lies behind it (i.e. it is syntagmatic and instantial, not paradigmatic and systemic); and (therefore) it is definitely not quantifiable. Secondly, 'informative' and 'redundant' are used in commonsense discourse with an affective loading: information is positive and good, redundancy is negative and bad. Here again the sense is quite different from our 'new' and 'given': information as a discursive concept has to be the product of the alternation between the two.

6 A detailed demonstration: how sound makes meaning in the microtext 'Prince Lazarus'

6.1 Text and representation

6.1.1 The microtext
`PLAY` ◄ Sound 6.1.1

'Prince Lazarus' is a 'microtext', that is, a short stretch of language having a recognizable beginning, development and ending. A microtext will have a semantic unity, but is not defined as a formal unit; it is a stretch of text chosen to be studied in respect of some features of its language. Here our interest centers on the intonation of the sequence of tone units which make up this little passage. We ask what is the meaning of each of the tone units, and what relationships do we find set up among them.

The microtext 'Prince Lazarus' is a fragment of a radio talk show in which Mary Lou Finlay interviews Howard Turney. This type of program is designed to inform hearers on a variety of topics, but also to entertain them. This episode was aired on the Canadian Broadcasting Company on December 10, 1998. Before the microtext, Mary Lou has given a 'backgrounder': the information that Turney plans to establish a modern Utopia on a coral reef in the Caribbean, and that it will be a very, very, expensive project. In our discussion we construct a number of sentences using the name 'Howard Turney'. These are, of course, entirely our own invention, designed to bring out the meaning of a tone unit by contrasting it with other possibilities. They contain no reference to any living person.

Mary Lou:	We reached Howard Turney, a.k.a. His Royal Highness, Prince Lazarus Long, in Tulsa Oklahoma. Prince Lazarus?
Howard Turney:	Yes, this Lazarus is fine. How are you?
Mary Lou:	I'm very fine. How are you?
Howard Turney:	Very good.
Mary Lou:	How are you coming along with your plans for Utopia?
Howard Turney:	It's coming along nicely. The only — er...we have a little holdup, that — er — happened as a result of the — er — hurricane.

Mary Lou: // 4 ∧ we / reached / Howard */**Tur**ney // 3 a. k */ **a //** 5 ∧ his */ **Roy**al
/ Highness // 5 ∧ Prince */ **Laz**arus / Long // 1 ∧ in / Tulsa Okla*/**ho**ma //

`PLAY` ◀Sound 6.1.1a

Mary Lou: // 2 Prince */ **Laz**arus //
`PLAY` ◀Sound 6.1.1b

Turney: *// 1 yes this / Lazarus is */ **fine** // 1 how */ **are** you //
`PLAY` ◀Sound 6.1.1c

Mary Lou: // 3 ∧ I'm /very */ **fine** // 2 how are */ **you** //
`PLAY` ◀Sound 6.1.1d

Turney: // 1 very */ **good** //
`PLAY` ◀Sound 6.1.1e

Mary Lou: // 2 how are you coming a/long with your / plans for U*/**to**pia //
`PLAY` ◀Sound 6.1.1f

Turney: // 3 it's / coming a/long */ **nice**ly // // ∧ the / only / ∧ er ... // 4 ∧ we have a little
*/ **hold**up that er // 5 happened as a re/sult of the er*/**hur**ricane //

`PLAY` ◀Sound 6.1.1g

The microtext follows a short 'backgrounder'. Here they are together:
`PLAY` ◀Sound 6.1.1h

6.1.2 Representation of wave forms

Using a Praat TextGrid, the utterance is transcribed using ordinary orthography and division into words. Upper case is used for *I* and for the initial letters of proper names.

Units are specified to the right of the TextGrid, and the TextGrid unit boundaries line up with the waveform and frequency line. There is no attempt to align orthographic letters with phonemes (unless, of course, the unit in question is itself a phoneme).

As in our prosodic transcription, foot boundaries are shown by a single slash and tone unit boundaries by a double slash; tonic syllables are upper case and are preceded by an asterisk (but not shown up in bold type), and silent Ictus is shown as usual by a caret.

Figure 6.1a segments in FEET and shows that *reached*, *Howard* and *Turney* each begin with a salient syllable, and that these syllables occur at roughly regular intervals.

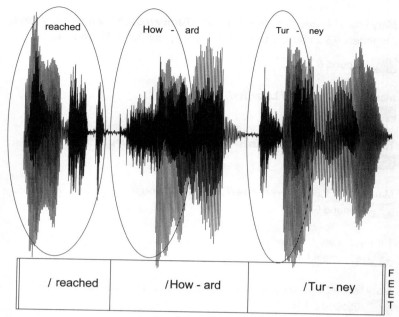

Figure 6.1a PLAY 🔊

Figure 6.1b shows the full waveform, including the initial proclitic syllable *we*. The first foot has a silent Ictus, the symbol ∧ appearing in its appropriate place as determined by the rhythm of what follows.

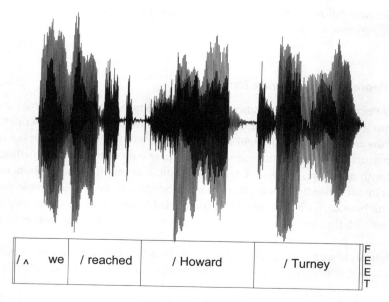

Figure 6.1b PLAY 🔊

In Figure 6.1c the foot boundaries are shown at the bottom, and foot structure is shown at the top.

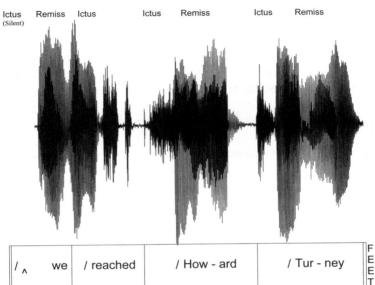

Figure 6.1c PLAY ◀

Figure 6.1d shows both the frequency trace and the waveform for the full tone unit. It can be seen that the tonic foot *Turney* displays the fall-rising pitch contour that is characteristic of tone 4.

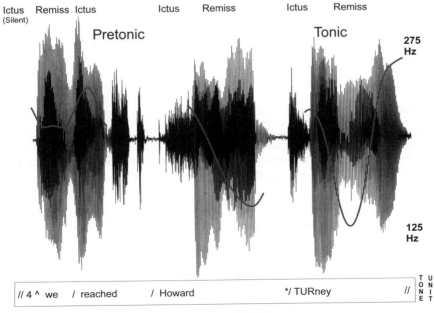

Figure 6.1d PLAY ◀

6.2   Structure and context of the text

6.2.1 Structure

The text 'An interview with Prince Lazarus' contains the introductory 'backgrounder' by the interviewer, followed by the interview proper. Our microtext contains just the first few moments of the interview, consisting of the three parts:

(a) transition (from backgrounder into interview)
(b) making contact
(c) first exchange (in the interview proper)

Here is the text again, showing these stages:

(a) transition

Mary Lou:	We reached Howard Turney, a.k.a. His Royal Highness, Prince Lazarus Long, in Tulsa Oklahoma.

(b) making contact

	Prince Lazarus?
Howard Turney:	Yes, this Lazarus is fine. How are you?
Mary Lou:	I'm very fine. How are you?
Howard Turney:	Very good.

(c) first exchange

Mary Lou:	How are you coming along with your plans for Utopia?
Howard Turney:	It's coming along nicely. The only — er...we have a little holdup, that — er — happened as a result of the — er — hurricane.

6.2.2 Context

We could contextualize the interview text as follows:

Context: overview. The backgrounder, and the text itself, are there to entertain a radio audience through the witty presentation of information.

Field: First order: entertainment: radio interviewing.

Second order: social engineering: building a modern Utopia.

Mode: Spoken spontaneous or, initially, non-spontaneous: reading from a script or full notes. Radio audience: no feedback. Monologue.

Tenor: The backgrounder sustains the relationship between Mary Lou and her audience which was established from the beginning of the program. The tenor dimensions are formality, affect, intimacy and power.

Formality: neutral.

Affect: amused irony.

Intimacy: distant.

Power: shared (Mary Lou has control over the whole discourse, but the audience can always switch stations).

6.2.3 Backgrounder

The text of Mary Lou's introductory backgrounder is as follows:

Mary Lou: In the 16th century Sir Thomas More invented Utopia, a perfect society on an island paradise. Lazarus Long plans to go a step further. He wants to build a genuine new Utopia on a coral reef in the Caribbean. But first he has to clear a few hurdles. He has to secure the permission of the Honduran government, which could lay claim to the reefs, and then there's the matter of the two hundred and sixteen billion dollars (US) he needs to transform this Utopian dream into reality.

PLAY Sound 6.2.3

6.3 Transition

Mary Lou: // 4 ∧ we / reached / Howard **Tur**ney // 3 a. k */ **a** // 5 ∧ his */ **roy**al / highness // 5 ∧ Prince */ **Laz**arus / Long // 1 ∧ in / Tulsa Okla*/**ho**ma //

PLAY Sound 6.1.1a

With this clause the interviewer makes the transition from her introductory background narrative to the dialogic mode required by the interview proper. The initial wording *we reached*, beginning with the Given element *we* as Theme and moving to the New on *reached,* locates the text within the primary field which is that of the radio interview; the remainder of the clause, identifying the person to be interviewed, bridges into the secondary field, which is that of social engineering as manifested in the interviewee's plans for the future. The clause-final focus on *Tulsa Oklahoma* locates Howard Turney in relation to his role in both fields — both as social engineer and as person about to be interviewed.

The transition in fact consists of a single clause, realizing a statement in declarative mood. On the basis of neutral, or 'unmarked', intonation choices, we would predict that it would consist of one tone unit (neutral tonality), with focus on the final item (neutral tonicity), and that its tone would be a falling tone, tone 1. If we leave out the elaborating segments following *Howard Turney*, we can imagine a court room dialogue in which a very deliberate witness is responding to a lawyer's question:

wsg: // 1 where did you /reach Howard */**Tur**ney //

makh: // 1 ∧ we /reached /Howard /Turney in /Tulsa Okla*/**ho**ma //

PLAY 🔊 Sound 6.3

In fact, however, the intonation pattern used by the interviewer is not neutral. She divides the clause into a number of tone units, five in all (marked tonality); two of these have focus elsewhere than on the final lexical item (marked tonicity), and there is considerable variety in the choice of tone.

To bring out the meaning that is carried by these intonation features, we will introduce a few variations along the way, illustrating with sound icons performed and recorded by ourselves. For the first part of these we will continue to use the shortened version of the text.

6.3.1 Marked tonality: grammatical system of INFORMATION DISTRIBUTION

Here is the clause divided into two information units, each of them selecting tone 1:

// 1 ∧ we / reached / Howard */**Tur**ney in // 1 Tulsa Okla*/**ho**ma //
PLAY 🔊 Sound 6.3.1

The tonality means 'here are two separate quanta of information to be attended to, each with its own component of New'.

By breaking the clause into two information units at this point, the speaker treats the fact of reaching Howard Turney and the fact of where he was located when he was reached as different messages each with its own significance to the listener.

6.3.2 Tone sequence: grammatical system of STATUS

If both information units have tone 1, as here, this means 'these two propositions are independent of each other, and each carries its own weight'. If there is exact tone concord, so that the second can be heard as a repetition of the same tone pattern as the first, this means 'the second unit is in some respect an elaboration of the first'.

But the two units might be on different tones. There are two other possible sequences that are in systemic contrast with this one: tone 3 + tone 1, and tone 4 + tone 1. Both these mean 'these two units are interconnected'; but the relative status of the two will differ.

A 3 ∧ 1 sequence means 'the two units are of equal status'. Here is the clause spoken on this 3∧1 tone pattern:

// 3 ∧ we / reached / Howard */**Tur**ney in // 1 Tulsa /Okla */**ho**ma //

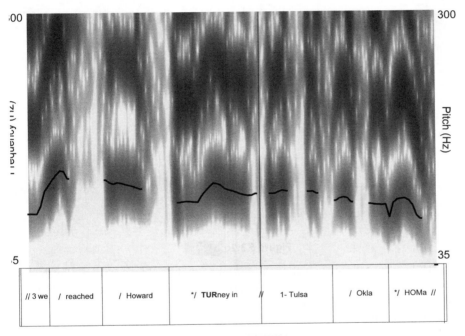

Figure 6.3.2a PLAY ◀

A 4 ∧ 1 sequence means 'the two units are of unequal status; the significance of the first is contingent on that of the second'. Here is the clause spoken on this 4 ∧ 1 tone pattern:

// 4 ∧ we / reached Howard */**Tur**ney in // 1 Tulsa Okla*/**ho**ma //

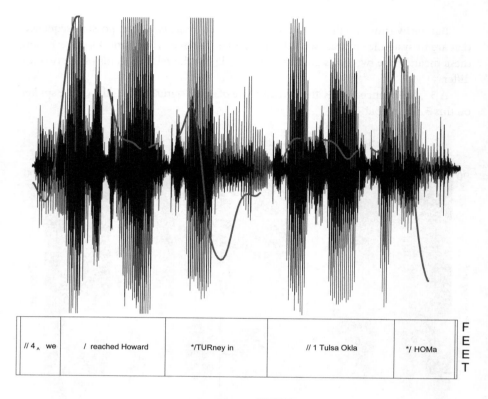

| // 4 ⌄ we | / reached Howard | */TURney in | // 1 Tulsa Okla | */ HOMa | F E E T |

Figure 6.3.2b PLAY 🔊

Thus while in a 3 ^ 1 sequence the tone 3 means simply 'hold on; I haven't finished', in the 4 ^ 1 sequence the tone 4 means 'I'm starting with something which has to be taken in conjunction with what follows'.

Listening to these in sequence (independent, equal status and unequal status) makes the differences in tone and in meaning more evident.

PLAY 🔊 Sound 6.3.2c

6.3.3 Mapping status onto Theme ^ Rheme

One typical context for such sequences is that where the 3 ^ 1 or 4 ^ 1 is conflated with the grammatical structure of Theme ^ Rheme; the first tone unit enunciates the Theme. The Theme provides the orientation of the clause, the point from which the speaker takes off; this often makes a linkage to the previous discourse, with the Theme being something that is familiar to or easily retrievable by the listener but is marked out by having its own focus, as something the listener should attend to: '*this* is what I'm on about'. This context particularly favours 4 ^ 1, since the tone 4, while showing that the significance depends on what is to follow, adds its usual prosody of uniqueness and even contrast.

The interviewer puts the focus on *Howard Turney,* who has already been introduced; the tone 4 highlights his identity, perhaps in a rather pointed contrast to what is going to follow. Here *Howard Turney* is not marked out as Theme — the Theme is *we,* the broadcaster; but we could illustrate the general principle by switching the Locative into thematic position in the clause.

// 4 ∧ in Chi*/**ca**go we // 1 located /Daniel */ **Rob**erts //

// 4 ∧ in / Tulsa Okla*/**ho**ma we // 1 reached / Howard */ **Tur**ney //

// 4.∧ in Los */**An**geles //1∧we...

PLAY ◀ Sound 6.3.3

The effect would be to give the main prominence to the achievement of reaching these individuals. But it would be inappropriate in this case, because this would make *Howard Turney* the focus of the New information, whereas by now the listeners already know all about him.

6.3.4 Tone concord: grammatical feature of elaboration, in system of LOGICAL
SEMANTIC RELATIONS: EXPANSION

We saw in Chapter 5 that, while the informational system of STATUS is in unmarked association with the clausal (clause nexus) system of INTERDEPENDENCY, or TAXIS (equal status goes with parataxis, unequal with hypotaxis), there is another principle cutting across this one, which is that the logical semantic feature of elaboration is typically associated with tone concord. In tone concord, the tone of the first part, for whatever reason it is selected, is quite precisely echoed by the tone of the second.

We can illustrate this by elaborating on *Howard Turney* with his adopted name *Prince Lazarus Long:*

// 1 Howard */ **Tur**ney // 1 Prince / Lazarus */ **Long** //

// 2 Howard */ **Tur**ney // 2 Prince / Lazarus */ **Long** //

// 4 Howard */ **Tur**ney // 4 Prince / Lazarus */ **Long** //

PLAY ◀ Sound 6.3.4

Building this into the clause, we might have had the tone sequence 3 ^ 3 ^ 1:

// 3 ∧ we / reached / Howard */ **Tur**ney // 3 ∧ Prince /Lazarus */ **Long** in // 1 Tulsa Okla*/ **ho**ma //

PLAY ◀ Sound 6.3.4a

Or, treating the two parts of the clause as unrelated in status, so that each operates as an independent piece of information on tone 1, and then combining this with the tone concord between the two names, we would end up with the sequence 1 ^ 1 ^ 1:

// 1 ∧ we / reached /Howard */ **Tur**ney Prince // 1 Lazarus */ **Long** in // 1 Tulsa Okla*/
homa //
PLAY Sound 6.3.4b

But Mary Lou does not use this tone concord pattern — not, at least, at this point.

6.3.5 Marking elaboration by other means

Unlike the other categories of expansion, namely extending and enhancing, the elaborating relationship is usually not marked by any form of wording. Typically, tone concord
functions as its only explicit sign — as the realization of it, in fact. There are symbols
for elaboration in writing, such as *i.e., viz., e.g.;* and a few expressions in words such as
namely and *that is to say,* but these are fairly restricted in their use.

For elaborations of personal names, in legal contexts, *alias* came to be used, from
Latin *alias* 'otherwise'; this was taken over by the police in various countries, but has
since tended to be overtaken by *a.k.a.* standing for 'also known as'. Mary Lou uses *a.k.a.*
here, reading it out as a string of initials, not as an acronym. Using *a.k.a.* does not rule
out tone concord, but it does make it redundant. Normally *a.k.a* is attached proclitically
to the following tone unit. What Mary Lou does, however, is to make *a.k.a.* a separate
tone unit, and then return to *Prince Lazarus Long* on a different tone.

For the listener, interpolating the *a.k.a.* lowers the expectation of tone concord,
although it would still be heard as appropriate; and it does sound for a short instant as
if Mary Lou was returning to tone 4. In the event, however, she changes direction and
moves into tone 1.

It would have been possible to incorporate the *a.k.a.* and still return to tone 4, either
with *a.k.a.* in the Pretonic:

*// 1 **Oh** we // 4 reached / Howard */ **Tur**ney // 4 a.k./a. Prince /Lazarus */ **Long** in // 1
Tulsa Okla*/**ho**ma //.
PLAY Sound 6.3.5

or with *a.k.a.* as a separate tone unit:

// 4 ∧ we / reached / Howard */ **Tur**ney // 3 a.k.*/a // 4 Prince / Lazarus */ **Long** in // 1
Tulsa Okla*/**ho**ma //.
PLAY Sound 6.3.5a

The sequence of tones is now 4 ∧ 3 ∧ 4 ∧ 1. In this version the two fall rising tones (tone 4)
by their tone concord, show the elaborating relationship between the two names: 'these two
refer to the same person'. The choice of tone 4 shows the status: 'it is not the reaching I'm
focusing on, so much as the location'. The final tone 1 shows that this is a straightforward
statement of fact; while the tone 3 on *a.k.a.*, since it is isolated in its place between the two
tone 4's, seems to be signaling not so much a non-final status (it has no content of its own
anyway) but rather a lack of commitment to the name that follows. The effect of this is
to introduce a note of playfulness, part of the relationship the interviewer is maintaining
with the radio audience: 'this is a bit of fun — I don't necessarily believe in it myself'.

6.3.6 Names and titles

We saw in Chapter 5 that the relationship that is construed by tone concord in the clause nexus covers a range of meanings within the general category of elaborating: repeating — using exactly the same wording; paraphrasing — saying the same thing in different words; clarifying — giving a gloss on the meaning; specifying — making the meaning more specific; exemplifying — giving examples of what is meant. All these can be construed by the TONE system as 'is the same as' or 'equals'.

When the same pattern of tone concord is used to relate nominal groups, it construes what in the clause grammar is a relationship of identity, between two characterizations of some person or some thing, like *the Smithsons, the family next door* or *the Canadian capital, Ottawa*. Since the relationship is one of identity, the two parts can appear in either order. We can also construe this relationship as a predication, by making it into a clause with the verb *be*: *the family next door are the Smithsons / the Smithsons are the family next door*. A number of other verbs occur which foreground different aspects of this identifying relationship, like *represent, stand for, be called, serve as, constitute*; for example *Ottawa serves as the Canadian capital*.

So we could say *Howard Turney is Prince Lazarus Long*, or *Prince Lazarus Long is Howard Turney*; and it is this relationship of identity that we heard expressed in the last two sound icons. But there is still one further piece of wording in Mary Lou's transition, namely *His Royal Highness*. We would expect this to be incorporated into the clause as a pretonic to the name that follows:

> // 4 ˄ we / reached / Howard */ **Tur**ney // 3 a.k.*/**a**. // 4 His / Royal / Highness Prince / Lazarus */ **Long** in // 1 Tulsa Okla*/**ho**ma //.
> PLAY ◀ Sound 6.3.6

But in fact she makes *His Royal Highness* into a separate tone unit, giving a very different interpretation to the alternative version of Howard Turney's name. If we continued with the same pattern of tone choices what we would hear is something like the following:

> // 4 ˄we / reached / Howard */**Tur**ney // 3 a.k.*/**a**. // 4 His / Royal */ **High**ness // 4 Prince / Lazarus */ **Long** in //1 Tulsa Okla*/**ho**ma //.
> PLAY ◀ Sound 6.3.6b

Here there is tone concord not only between *Howard Turney* and his adopted name but also between the two parts of the adopted name itself. *His Royal Highness* is being presented as if it was not a title but another name. This is rather as if we were to say *Mr. Howard Turney* on two tone units, one for *Howard Turney* and one for the *mister*.

> // 4 ˄ we / reached */ **Mis**ter // 4 Howard */**Tur**ney //
> PLAY ◀Sound 6.3.6c

We would be unlikely to hear this in an ordinary introduction!

6.3.7 . . . And as Mary Lou says it

Let us now compare the predicted version of this clause — unmarked in respect of all systems except the unmarked tonality, since that would clash with the requirement of tone concord — with what Mary Lou actually says. We give the predicted version first.

> // 4 ∧ we / reached / Howard */ **Tur**ney // 4 ∧ a.k. a. his / Royal / Highness Prince / Lazarus */ **Long** // 1 ∧ in / Tulsa Okla */**ho**ma //
> `PLAY` ◀Sound 6.3.7

Now here once again is Mary Lou's own voice:

> Mary Lou: // 4 ∧ we / reached / Howard */**Tur**ney // 3 a. k */ **a //** 5 ∧ his */ **Roy**al / Highness // 5 ∧ Prince */ **Laz**arus / Long // 1 ∧ in / Tulsa Okla*/**ho**ma //
> `PLAY` ◀Sound 6.1.1a

Mary Lou is a professional radio personality and naturally puts her own individual stamp on things. One way she does this is by manipulating the English intonation system. The effect is to distance her talk somewhat from ordinary conversation, and to highlight the special rhetorical flavours of the message.

She starts with a tone unit that is not at all out of the ordinary. Howard Turney has been mentioned already. He needs a tonic focus, because his identity is going to be further specified and this allows for the possibility of tone concord; but this tone unit can be given a lower status than what follows, and so the tone will be tone 4. The Tonic will occur in its unmarked place at the end of the name — i.e. on the surname; but the Pretonic will be boosted to a higher pitch on *reached* because that is the beginning of the New.

> // 4 ∧ we / reached / Howard */ **Tur**ney //
> `PLAY` ◀Sound 6.3.7a

From here on things begin to depart from the pattern that would be expected.

She maps *a.k.a.*, which would normally be not even salient, onto a separate tone unit. The listener thus processes it separately; and this gives an effect of amused irony, perhaps enhanced by the tone 3 'now wait for it!' and the drop in pitch which makes it sound like a conspiratorial 'aside'.

> // 3 a.k.*/a //
> `PLAY` ◀Sound 6.3.7b

But the expectation of tone concord set up by the *a.k.a* has already been sabotaged by her giving this a separate tone unit; it is now thoroughly frustrated when she switches to a tone 1, on *his royal highness*. And there are two further surprises here, apart from just the tone: first, that the title also, as well as the *a.k.a*, is given a separate tone unit; and secondly, that the tonic is in the 'wrong place' — it comes on *royal*, instead of on the final lexical item *highness*.

// 5 ∧ his */ **Ro**yal / Highness //
PLAY 🔊Sound 6.3.7c

We detect a slight shift of direction here, as if she had been moving into a tone 4 but the marked tonic at *royal* then imposed its own assertive tone 5. This heightened emphasis on *royal* makes it seem even more as if she is 'sending up' the whole project; and it 'marks' the following *highness* as if it was Given — this is no mere highness, but a *royal* highness.

This is followed by *prince lazarus long*, also on tone 5, and with the impression of tone concord strongly reinforced by the same marked tonicity: the tonic is on *lazarus*, not on *long*. This adds further to the impression of a sendup, because while *long* is an entirely ordinary surname, *lazarus* is far from ordinary and carries a significant semantic load.

// 5 ∧ Prince */ **Laz**arus /Long //
PLAY 🔊Sound 6.3.7d

Moreover there is a very slight pause before the *lazarus*, which frames the name as if the speaker was putting 'scare quotes' around it, thus foregrounding the rather bathetic collocation that follows.

So the entire sequence of title plus name is made strange by Mary Lou's choices of intonation. The final tone unit *in Tulsa Oklahoma*, however, returns the listener to the expected tonal pattern. There is one tone unit, the tone is tone 1, and the tonic falls in its regular place, on the accented syllable of the final word.

// 1 ∧ in / Tulsa Okla*/**ho**ma //
PLAY 🔊Sound 6.3.7e

And yet Mary Lou is still playing with the system, although this time more at the phonetic level. There is a striking regularity in the tempo of the syllables; and an exaggeratedly clear articulation of the individual phonemes, together with perhaps a slight burlesque of the vowel of the tonic syllable. This is, after all, a Canadian speech event, where 'Tulsa Oklahoma' can sound every bit as exotic as 'Prince Lazarus Long'.

Here once again is Mary Lou's complete utterance, together with its representation in terms of pitch contour and soundwave:

Mary Lou: // 4 ∧ we / reached / Howard */**Tur**ney // 3 a. k */ **a** // 5 ∧ his */ **Ro**yal / Highness // 5 ∧ Prince */ **Laz**arus / Long // 1 ∧ in / Tulsa Okla*/**ho**ma //

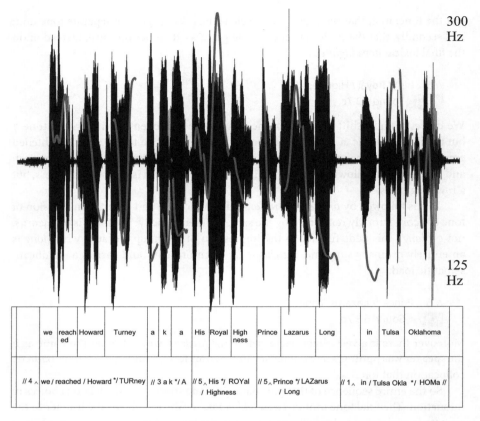

	we	reach ed	Howard	Turney	a	k	a	His	Royal	High ness	Prince	Lazarus	Long		in	Tulsa	Oklahoma
	// 4 ∧ we / reached / Howard */ TURney				// 3 a k */ A			// 5 ∧ His */ ROYal / Highness			// 5 ∧ Prince */ LAZarus / Long			// 1 ∧ in / Tulsa Okla */ HOMa //		

Figure 6.3.7 and Sound 6.1.1a PLAY

6.4 Making contact

Mary Lou: Prince Lazarus?
Howard Turney: Yes, this Lazarus is fine. How are you?
Mary Lou: I'm very fine. How are you?
Howard Turney: Very good.

PLAY Sound 6.4

Here is the transcription, sound icon, and waveform of the first two turns.

// 2 Prince */ **Laz**arus *// 1 yes this / Lazarus is */ **fine** // 1 how */ **are** you //

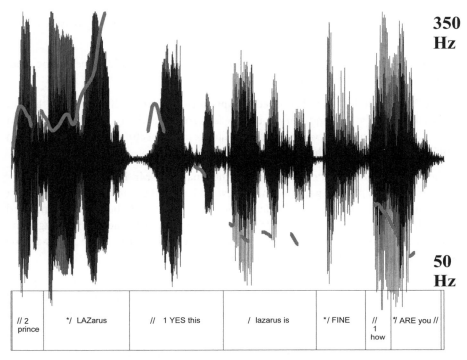

350 Hz

50 Hz

// 2 prince	*/ LAZarus	// 1 YES this	/ lazarus is	*/ FINE	// 1 how	*/ ARE you //

Figure 6.4 and Sound 6.4a PLAY

6.4.1 'Prince Lazarus?'

// 2 Prince */ **Laz**arus //
PLAY Sound 6.4.1

Let us fill out the earlier summary of the context.

Field. What's 'going on' is a continuation of the secondary field introduced in the 'back-grounder' and linked to 'Howard Turney' in the transition. This reiteration of Turney's Utopian name shows that the discourse has now moved firmly into that world.

Mode. The primary relationship between the radio program and its audience remains in effect, but there is now a secondary mode, spoken spontaneous dialogue. With the combination of minor clause and tone 2, Mary Lou checks the identity of the person she has reached on the telephone. But the interactive role relationship of the second order mode is in interplay with the one way primary communication with the radio audience. What is a question in the second order, a demand for information from Howard (who is put into the role of answerer), is at the same time a first order statement, the presentation of information to the radio audience, which has been put into a 'receive only' mode by the situation.

Tenor. This is beginning of the building of an interpersonal relationship between Mary Lou and Howard.

Formality. This is slightly formal, shown by the choice of the addressee's name as an opener, rather than, for example, 'Hi.'

Affect. This might be termed 'amused conspiratorial'. Voice quality, the slight hint of irony, contributes to this, and Mary Lou's tone is warm rather than cold. Friendliness and warmth are important, of course: success or failure in connecting along this dimension will have a lot to do with the smooth flow of the interview.

Intimacy. The choice of 'Prince Lazarus' rather than, say 'Mr. Long' shows that Mary Lou has agreed to play the game in which Howard Long has become a Prince. The effect of this on intimacy is complex. By definition there is great gulf between a prince and someone who is not royalty — but at the same time Mary Lou, by the very act of agreeing to play the role of someone addressing royalty, has established a certain intimacy. She is in the game with Long, rather than on the outside.

Power. This is the dimension most clearly established here by intonation. Mary Lou could have used tone 1; but this would be to assert that she had reached him, and would tend to limit the options for his response, more or less to a bare acknowledgement of his identity.

Figure 6.4.1 illustrates the difference between tone 1 and tone 2 as variants for this enquiry. You can hear them together in Sound 6.4.1a (*overleaf*).

> // 1 Prince */ **Laz**arus / ∧ or // 2 Prince */ **Laz**arus //

Mary Lou, of course, did not produce a tone 1 here. The tone 2 which Mary Lou does select, however, still exerts some power. In demanding yes/no confirmation she remains in control of the interaction, and Turney's response is restricted to polar rather than lexical information. But it is 'social': Mary Lou is *asking* whether they have established connection, rather than *asserting* that they have, and she thus draws Howard into shared participation right from the beginning.

> // 2 Prince */ **Laz**arus //
> PLAY ◀ Sound 6.4.1

6.4.2 'Yes, this Lazarus is fine.'

Howard Turney's *yes* itself is quite straightforward.

> *// 1 **yes** ...//
> PLAY ◀ Sound 6.4.2

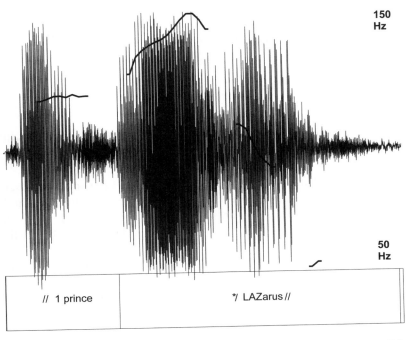

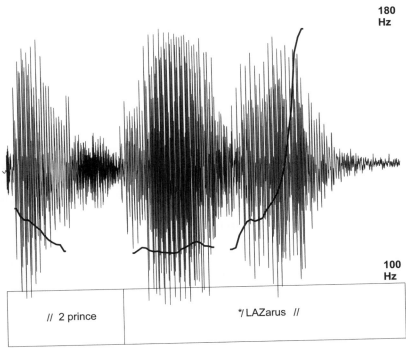

Figure 6.4.1 and Sound 6.4.1a PLAY 🔊

It actually sounds like the beginning of 'Yes, this is Lazarus', which is what we would expect in the context. But what follows instead is a smooth transition, in the same foot, to 'this Lazarus is fine'.

// 1. . . . this / Lazarus is */ **fine** //

PLAY ◀Sound 6.4.2a

At this point the ideational metafunction seems to have operated out of phase with the interpersonal: Turney has provided the information which it is not Mary Lou's role to demand until later in the ritual.

One possible explanation, suggested by the jump up to a high pitch on *this*, is that Turney did start out to acknowledge *yes, this is Lazarus*, but then telescoped this into a response to an expected greeting *how are you?* No such greeting had in fact been offered; but he might have anticipated it, or even thought he heard it. But we will take the text at its face value: *yes, this Lazarus is fine*.

Mary Lou is 'in charge' at this point, having posed a question through her intonation, and Turney is playing his role by answering. The polar certainty of his tone 1 choice is the complementary fit to the polar uncertainty of her tone 2.

He sounds friendly, with a jovial voice quality, and the steadily descending pitch of his Pretonic suggests that he is confident and relaxed.

Again, let us consider an alternative scenario. Suppose Turney had been less self-assured, less confident of his ability to handle the interviewer and successfully put his message over to the radio audience.

// 2 ∧ Prince */ **Laz**arus //
PLAY ◀Sound 6.4.1

*// 1 **yes** // 1 this is */**Laz**arus //
PLAY ◀Sound 6.4.2b

Something like this would be more formal and less friendly. Its falling tone would mark it squarely as an information giving answer to a question. It would be like an assertion of power, a way of not yielding control of the dialogue to the person operating in the interviewer role.

Turney's actual response, for all its friendly informality, is quite complex.

Phonologically, the syllable *this* is a Remiss (non-salient) syllable rounding off the foot beginning with *yes*. In terms of information units, however, it goes with what follows: the elliptical response *yes* is mapped into one information unit and the declarative statement *this Lazarus is fine* into another. Here the salient syllables are *Laz* and *fine*.

But *yes this* is not a typical foot. *This* is an interesting demonstration of the interaction between salience and rhythm in establishing Ictus ∧ Remiss patterning. In order to look at *this* we have to place it in its rhythmic context:

*// 1 **yes** this // 1- Lazarus is */ **fine** //
PLAY ◀Sound 6.4.2c

In terms of the three characteristics often associated with salience, namely length, loudness and pitch change, two syllables are clearly non salient: 1) *rus* in *Lazarus*, and 2) *is*. They both have less amplitude than *Laz*, they both are much shorter than *Laz*, and they both have less pitch change than *Laz*. See Figure 6.4.2a.

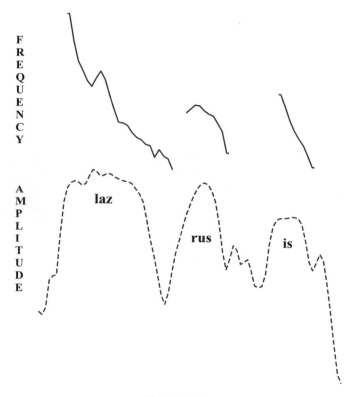

Figure 6.4.2a

By the same three characteristics three syllables clearly stand out as salient: 1) *yes*, 2) *Laz* and 3) *fine*. But *this* in *yes this Lazarus* is harder to classify. In terms of length and amplitude it is like *rus* and *is*, but in terms of pitch change it has a reasonable claim to salience: it jumps up from the end of *yes* (and the jump is particularly noticeable because the falling contour with which *yes* ends is clearly heading down through the voiceless sound with which the syllable ends). And the range of the fall on the syllable *this* is respectable. In addition, it initiates a long falling contour culminating in *fine*.

We need to make a comment on the syllable *this*. In terms of pitch, it sounds as though it was Ictus, and it takes its place in the contour line of the tone that is followed up by *Lazarus is fine*. But in terms of loudness and length, and of its location in the rhythm pattern, *this* remains non-salient and Remiss.

The reference of *this* clearly operates within the secondary field, not the primary. Mary Lou and her audience no doubt share a general North American awareness of things Biblical. Literary concordances continue to turn up citations of Lazarus. What *this* does is to distinguish the 'Lazarus' of the Utopian social engineering world from the 'other' Lazarus — but, through the very process of distinguishing, making firm contact with the Biblical world and importing some of that meaning into his name. Life in the new Utopian world on the reef would, we may surmise, be laced with Old Testament values.

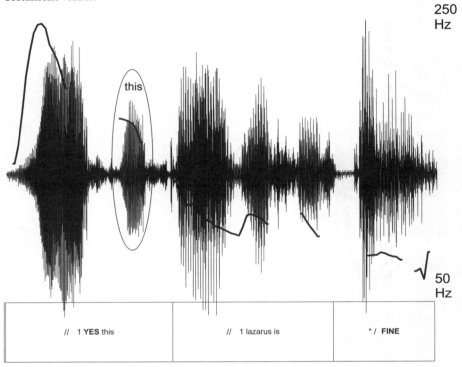

Figure 6.4.2b and Sound 6.4.2c PLAY

What is going on here is the little dance we all do in the process of making or renewing acquaintance. 'I'm fine, thank you' is an obligatory answer — even if you have a violent cold and a bad headache, 'I'm fine' is likely to come tripping out, because the field is not really health at all. We do this so often that it generally goes very smoothly: bow and turn, nod and step back, all without thinking about it. In this case, however, Turney disturbs the measure: he has volunteered the state of his health before he's been asked.

6.4.3 'How are you?'

Turney now puts into words the formula which was inspired by his previous response, namely *how are you?* But he does so in a way that is not reciprocating, but initiating, as we can tell by the location of the Tonic.

You, the final item, is a pronoun, and 'phoric'; that is, it is referential in terms of the time and place of the act of speaking. As a phoric item it should not take the tonic, 'other things being equal'. The tonic syllable should fall on *are*, the process of being in some state of health or other — which is precisely where it does fall.

If this were a smooth opening of this stage in the dialogue, it would sound perfectly natural. But, as we have seen, the dialogue is not smooth. Other things are not equal. The process of 'being in a state of health' has already been blurted out by Turney, and therefore *are*, the Process, is most definitely 'given' information. In this situation, *you* should indeed be marked as New, as in the following example:

// 13 how */ **are** you Lieu*/**ten**ant //

// 1 oh / this old / soldier's */ **fine** // 1 how are */ **you** //
PLAY ◀ Sound 6.4.3a

If Turney had put the tonic on *you*, Mary Lou would have been given a signal that the 'state of health' ritual would be completed with her reply, and that it would then be time to move on to another topic.

Her mild confusion, and her amusement at the turn in the discourse, are shown by the slightly humorous voice quality of her answer, and also by the slight fluff in the articulation of the 'f' in *fine*. Her answer trumps his answering a question before it has been asked by her own asking a question when it has already been answered:

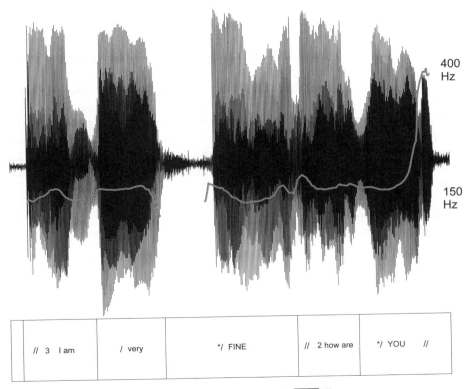

// 3 I am	/ very	*/ FINE	// 2 how are	*/ YOU //

Figure 6.4.3 and Sound 6.4.3b PLAY ◀

6.4.4 'I'm very fine.'

PLAY Sound 6.4.4a

This utterance is neutral in tonality and tonicity, and also in the alignment between information distribution and tone. One clause is mapped onto one information unit, which is realized through one tone unit. The rhythm is not forcing any of the syllables into a previous tone unit, nor picking up any syllables at the end from one that follows. 'Very fine' is the last lexical item in the clause, so it contains the tonic syllable, which is located on the final word.

The tone, on the other hand, is marked. This is a declarative statement where the unmarked tone is tone 1. The choice of tone 3 realizes a combination of two features, one interpersonal (confirmatory), the other logical (non-final, equal status). The first is backward-facing, meaning 'I'm responding, in a cooperative manner, to what you asked'; the second is forward-facing, meaning 'and I'm going on to say something connected with this to you'. We would expect this to be followed by an unmarked tone 1.

> // 3 ∧ I'm very */ **fine** and // 1 how are */ **you** //
> PLAY Sound 6.4.4b

6.4.5 'How are you?'

But in fact Mary Lou does not use tone 1; she uses tone 2. Her choice of tone 2 has precisely the effect of downplaying the ideational component in the meaning of the question. At the same time it carries the modest interpersonal flavour of 'if I may ask' that is a feature of tone 2 wh- interrogatives.

Since this is a response to Turney's initiating enquiry *how are you?* (where the focus came, as expected, on the *are*), Mary Lou has to put the focus on the *you*. This is again as would be expected; but, combined with the 'request for permission' contained in the choice of tone 2, it foregrounds the need for Turney to respond. Which he does — albeit with much lower amplitude, pitch range, and paralinguistic enthusiasm than when he produced it the first time around. The difference in amplitude is particularly noticeable when the question and answer are played together:

> Mary Lou: // 2 how are */**you** //
> PLAY Sound 6.4.5a

> Turney: // 1 very */**good** //
> PLAY Sound 6.4.5b

6.4.6 'Very good.'

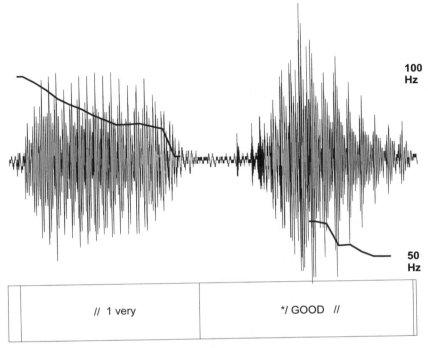

// 1 very	*/ GOOD //

Figure 6.4.6 PLAY 🔊

The 'dance' is now completely back in synchronization. Turney has played his complementary role faultlessly, giving back the elicited attribute *good*; the ellipsis in his clause shows maximum cohesion with his dialogic partner, and his choice of tone 1 on this jointly constructed clause is perfectly in accord with what is expected.

The falling tone 1 allows Mary Lou to interpret Turney's *very good* as a closure, putting an end to this phase of the interview. She constructs it as a signal to her that she can now move straight into the crucial question about his 'plans for Utopia'. If Turney had used a tone 3, which would be unproblematic as a response to *how are you?*, it could have suggested that some further exchange was needed before moving on to the next phase.

6.5   First exchange

Mary Lou: How are you coming along with your plans for Utopia?
Howard: It's coming along nicely.
                   The only — er...we have a little holdup, that — er — happened as a
                   result of the — er — hurricane.

PLAY ◀ Sound 6.5

6.5.1   First move: 'how are you coming along with your plans for utopia?'

// 2 how are you coming a/long with your / plans for U*/topia //

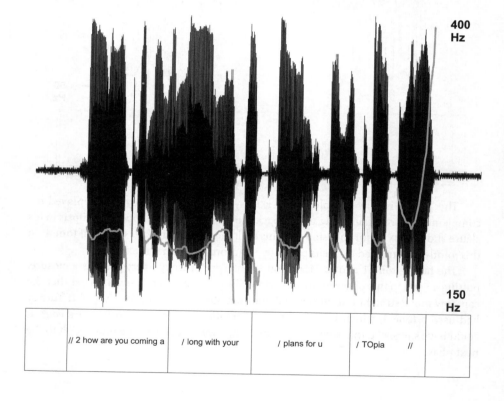

// 2 how are you coming a	/ long with your	/ plans for u	/ TOpia //	

Figure 6.5.1a PLAY ◀

The tonality is neutral: One clause is mapped onto one information unit which is realized as one tone unit.

The tonicity is also neutral. The last lexical item is the noun *Utopia*, which is where the tonic foot is located. This is in fact the final element in a complex prepositional phrase *with [your plans [for [Utopia]]]*, all of which therefore falls within the focus of the information unit. The whole of the information unit functions as the New.

Note how the rhythm in the Pretonic would allow two possible metric interpretations: either with three feet as shown, or with six, recognizing the secondary beat within each:

// how are you ′ coming a/long ′ with your / plans ′ for U/topia //

The tone, however, is marked. This is an interrogative lexical question. It is the Circumstance of manner, 'how', which is at issue, not the polarity of the process 'getting along'. The neutral key and tone combination for a clause of this Wh- interrogative mood would be a falling tone, tone 1. Here, however, Mary Lou uses the 'mild' variant tone 2. This softens the force of the speaker's request for an answer; it is more like a request for permission to ask the question, as if she had added *may I ask?* — and has the same effect, that it could be heard as somewhat patronizing or ironic.

For a note on the low Pretonic to tone 2 see Chapter 7 section 7.5 below. Here is Halliday's rendition of the neutral tone 1 form of the utterance:

// 1 how are you /coming a/long with your /plans for U*/**to**pia //

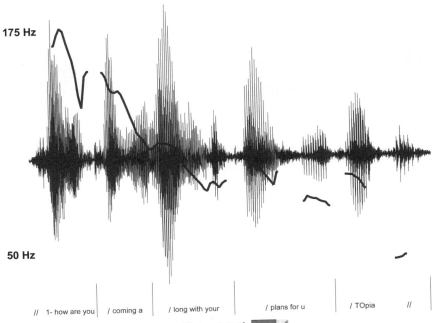

175 Hz

50 Hz

// 1- how are you | / coming a | / long with your | / plans for u | / TOpia | //

Figure 6.5.1b PLAY

6.5.2 Second move: 'it's coming along nicely.'

The tonality is neutral: one clause mapped onto one information unit realized as one tone unit.

The tonicity is also neutral: the last lexical item is the word *nicely*, which is where the tonic foot is located.

The key, however, is marked. This is a declarative statement, and tone 1 would signal a simple positive polar 'yes' about the proposition, with Turney in full interpersonal control, but not asserting himself particularly strongly. But the interpersonal situation is a bit charged. Mary Lou's question not only demands a response: it brings forward a bit of the 'everything is well' expectation of the previous phatic communion. And Turney's choice of tone 3 is the KEY system's way of showing that he is acceding to what is expected. But it does suggest, through the other, 'non-final' component in its meaning, that there is something more to be said.

If Turney had used tone 4, this would have injected a more explicit note of reservation: it would have suggested that the 'something more' was less nice and even quite nasty. At the other extreme, a tone 5 would have signalled that, whatever might have been suggested to the contrary, the future was sunny and assured.

// 3 It's / coming a/long */ **nice**ly //

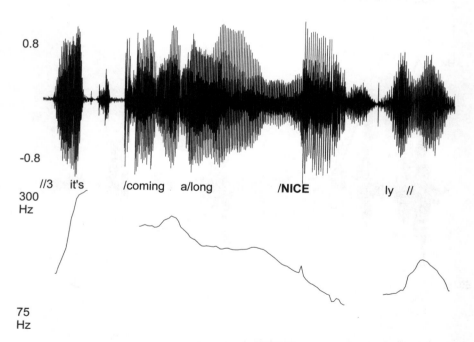

Figure 6.5.2 PLAY

6.5.3 Third move: 'the only, er, we have a little holdup that, er, happened as a result of the, er, hurricane.'

Turney: // ∧ the / only / ∧ er . . . // 4 ∧ we have a little */ **hold**up that er // 5 happened as a re/sult of the er*/**hur**ricane //

PLAY ◀ Sound 6.5.3

Having given this reassurance, Turney goes on to acknowledge that not everything is as it should be. He starts with a nominal group *the only . . .*, perhaps on the way to *the only holdup*, but stops short and changes direction. We can only guess where he was heading; but if we consider a plausible wording such as *the only holdup has been the effect of the hurricane*, he might well have chosen to avoid a formulation that would give 'the holdup' too much thematic prominence. In any case he switches from what would have been an identifying clause to one that is possessive attributive and has *we* as the Theme.

The Attribute is then *a little holdup that happened as a result of the hurricane*. In principle the *that . . .* clause could be an embedded 'defining relative' clause, which would have made this a single nominal group with the *that . . .* clause as Qualifier. But there are several reasons for doubting this, and for interpreting it rather as a hypotactic 'descriptive' clause: (i) the antecedent is *a holdup*, not *the holdup*; (ii) there is a hesitation sound *er* which masks a silent Ictus, something that is typical of the hypotactic type but unusual with the embedded; (iii) the two clauses take up two information units, which is normal (unmarked tonality) with the hypotactic type but with the embedded would constitute a marked and less probable option. It seems more plausible — it makes more sense, in fact — to understand this as two information units conflating with two ranking (i.e. non-embedded) clauses, and hence as having the tonality unmarked. The tonicity is unmarked in either case.

The tone pattern is tone 4 followed by tone 5. Since the first clause is a declarative, tone 4 is a marked choice; but while globally marked, so to speak, locally it is quite predictable, as it constitutes a qualification to what has gone just before: the sense is 'all is well — except . . .'. The next clause is an elaboration of the first one, and might have repeated the same tone with tone concord; in fact it starts by sounding as if it is going to do this but then gets deflected, the switch being facilitated by the hesitation sound coming just before the Tonic. Whether or not that is how the speaker arrived there, in the event he ends on a tone 5; this gives the hurricane the standing of being not merely new but also unexpected, and therefore justifiably the cause of a little holdup.

We leave the analysis of the interview with Prince Lazarus here. Our aim has been to suggest how much meaning is construed by these prosodic resources, and how they are closely integrated with the other systems of English grammar. The listener is always processing at all strata at once, and it seems to us desirable for the analyst to do the same.

7 The secondary tones

7.1 Primary and secondary tones

We refer to the tones that have been discussed so far — the five simple and two compound tones 1 2 3 4 5 13 53 — as the 'primary tones' of spoken English.

This set of seven primary tones is exhaustive, in the sense that this is all there are. Every instance of a tone unit can be assigned to one or other of these seven tone categories.

But this categorization is still fairly gross, and it is obvious that there is a great deal of variability within each one of these primary tones. The question that arises, therefore, is whether we can show that at least some of this variation is systemic: that is, whether there are further consistent distinctions in meaning made by more subtle differences in tone.

And the answer is that there are. That is to say, we can recognize sets of finer, more 'delicate' tonal categories that occur systematically in spoken English, and serve to make meaningful distinctions within the general meanings construed by the primary tones. We refer to these as 'secondary' tones.

Secondary tones are of two kinds.

(1) One kind is a simple subdivision, or subcategorization, of each of the primary tones. For example a falling tone, tone 1, may be high falling, mid falling or low falling according to where it starts. Since all these variants end low, and all take the same amount of time (of course, the actual duration over which the fall takes place is highly variable; but the variation is determined by other factors — it does not relate to the height of the fall), the movement in pitch with the high falling is steeper than that with the low. Schematically we could represent the three variants as

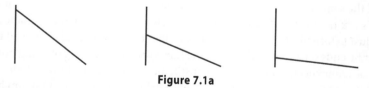

Figure 7.1a

In fact the choice is not one of absolute pitch range, but of the pitch of the onset relative to what has gone before. We shall return to these details below; here we are just illustrating the principle behind this kind of secondary tone. We call these the 'direct' secondary tones, since they are directly related to the primary ones: they are just more finely specified variants within the given primary tone.

(2) The other kind of secondary tone is called 'indirect', because it is sited not in the Tonic but in the Pretonic segment of the tone unit. For example: a falling tone, tone 1, is 'falling' by virtue of the pitch movement in the Tonic segment.

But there may also be a Pretonic segment; and if there is this allows for further secondary variation. In the case of tone 1, the pretonic has three variants: it may be steady, bouncing or listing. We can represent the movement schematically as

Figure 7.1b

Again, we shall discuss these in greater detail below. The point to be made here is that, like the direct secondary tones, these indirect secondary tones create more subtle differences in meaning within the semantic space defined by the particular primary tone with which they are associated.

For example, in the Lawyer text C says

// .1+ that / sounds more / like my */ **aunt** //
PLAY Sound 7.1

with the 'high' direct secondary tone on *aunt*. This heightens the 'newness' of the aunt, foregrounding the contrast between the aunt and the lawyer and drawing attention to the absurdity — and the lawyer laughs in response. Suppose instead C had said

// .1- that / sounds more / like my */ **aunt** //
PLAY Sound 7.1a

with *aunt* downplayed, low falling instead of high falling, and probably a descending pretonic: it would have sounded serious instead of joky, as if it was to be expected that a lawyer's advice should resemble that of an aunt — perhaps the comparison had already been made. Now suppose a mid fall:

// .1. that / sounds more / like my */ **aunt** //
PLAY Sound 7.1b

This is somewhere in between the other two — what we might feel to be the unmarked variant, in which my aunt is being picked out rather than, say, my teacher, but without any overtone of absurdity or even unexpectedness.

This particular set of alternatives (shown in the notation as 1+ 1. 1-) is known as the system of DECLARATIVE KEY, having the three terms 'strong', 'neutral' and 'mild'. This system forms part of the grammar of spoken English. In this respect the systems realized by the secondary tones are no different from those realized by the primary tones: they are all grammatical systems, their meanings being defined within the overall lexicogrammar of the language. Of course, the exact meaning of any one instance will be determined by its environment; but that is true of all grammatical systems, whether realized by intonation or by anything else. For example, the exact meaning of 'first person possessive', realized by the possessive determiner *my*, varies not only according to who the speaker is (that is a general feature of deictic expressions) but also as between, say, *my aunt, my ideas* and *my pyjamas*; but all share the common property of being associated with *I / me* and contrasting with *your, her, his, its, our* and *their*. Likewise the meaning of 'strong key' varies as between different discursive environments; we may compare the joky sense conveyed in the example of *my aunt* with the simple highlighting of the noun *stress* in Thwaite's Doctor and Patient text:

// 1+3 ∧ I / want to know / how / ∧ how to / cope with / ∧ */ **stress** */ **real**ly //
PLAY ◀ Sound 7.1c

where the silent foot coming before the word *stress* serves to create suspense which further shows up the choice of the strong key. But all instances share the feature of an additional beefing up, a calling to attention which heightens the interpersonal meaning of the message. Like all grammatical labels, names like 'KEY: strong / neutral / mild' attempt to represent such shared features, either by identifying some core meaning of the category or by having recourse to very general semantic terms.

7.2   The 'line of arbitrariness'

If we were writing a grammar of spoken English, those systems that happened to be realized by intonation would be interspersed with all the other systems according to their location in the grammatical network. But we are not. We are writing a book about intonation, and specifically about the part played by intonation in the grammar of spoken English.

This means that, since intonation is a phonological feature, we need to show how these resources are organized at the phonological level. All the contrasts that we are recognizing here are those which function grammatically; that is the criterion for including them. But the systems into which they are organized in the phonology do not stand in a one-to-one relation with systems in the lexicogrammar. There is no general pattern of correspondence between systems at these two strata.

We might well ask why there should be any correspondence at all. After all, there are no grammatical systems mapping directly into the vowels and consonants of the articulatory system; we do not expect to find correspondences across what is called (for that very reason) the 'line of arbitrariness' in language. The resources of articulation are scattered all around the lexicogrammar to do their work. Why should it be otherwise with the prosodic resources — those of rhythm/stress and intonation?

We should note that many languages seem to have a few systems which can be set up in matching phonological and lexicogrammatical terms. English, for example, pairs voiced and voiceless fricatives with verbs and nouns, in words like *use/use, grease/grease, halve/half, breathe/breath*. Sometimes these matches suggest that the relationship may be not quite arbitrary, for example when the opposition of masculine and feminine is matched with that between back and front vowels (e.g. in Latin, as back/non-back, or in Urdu as non-front/front): front vowels carry higher-pitched resonance than back vowels, women have higher-pitched voices than men.

These are, at best, minor motifs in the articulatory systems; but as one moves from the articulatory to the prosodic there is more likelihood of matching between systems at the two strata. An obvious example in English is the rhythmic opposition, in the latinate part of the vocabulary, between nouns and verbs in two-syllable words that in Latin consisted (or would have consisted) of a derivational prefix plus stem: pairs like *suspect (**sus**pect/su**spect**), contest, subject, combine, export, progress (**con**test/con**test*** and so on). There are many hundreds of these; and new formations generally continue to follow this pattern, at least in the 'inner circle' of English-speaking communities (for whom exceptions will tend to stand out, e.g. if someone says

// ∧ I / will */ **ab**sent my/self for a / minute //
PLAY ◀ Sound 7.2

instead of *absent*). Here we can say that, for a demarcable section of the lexicon, there is a phonological system of ACCENT, with opposition of two terms 'descending/ascending', which realizes a grammatical system of WORD CLASS ASSIGNMENT where the terms are 'nominal/verbal'. ('Nominal' includes noun and adjective, and their derivations and inflections: *export market, highly suspect behaviour, subjecthood, absently*; 'verbal' includes verb and preposition, and their derivations and inflections: *unsuspectingly, disconcerted, instantiate, despite*). But, overall, the phonological patterns of rhythm and stress serve to map word accent into the total flow of the discourse, rather than directly realizing systems at the lexicogrammatical stratum.

What about systems of intonation? As we have seen, the underlying system of five tones is a highly general resource which makes meanings all around the grammar. It would be possible to derive all the meanings of the tones from a simple phonological opposition between falling and rising, and then to map these on to a (proto-)grammatical system of certain / uncertain, with polarity as the fulcrum — a system of 'polarity known / polarity unknown'. But while such an observation has a place in the total chain of explanations, including historical explanations (phylogenetic and perhaps ontogenetic), it is doubtful whether a generalized system along these lines has a place in an analytic account of the (post-infancy) spoken language. The system of TONE in the phonology is not the realization of any single system in the lexicogrammar.

When we came to the systems of TONALITY and TONICITY, where intonation and rhythm combine, there we do find that these systems make grammatical meaning in a consistent overall fashion. Within the textual metafunction, they construe a distinct grammatical unit, the information unit, and map it on to a unit of the clause-based rank scale, with a default condition whereby one information unit is mapped on to one ranking (non-embedded) clause. This turns out to be a fundamental semogenic device for all discourse in spoken English — and in fact in written English also, since both writers and readers typically construe the text as a sequence of structured information units.

7.3 Phonaesthesia

We need to take one further step in the general discussion, before getting down to the details of the secondary tones. This concerns phonaesthesia, or sound symbolism — the universal tendency to rebel against the principle of arbitrariness.

More than anything else, the one thing that made human language possible was the decoupling of the content from the expression, so that there need be no natural, iconic connection between the sound and the meaning. Once language is freed from the constraint of iconicity it can take off and mean anything that can be organized semiotically (which simply means anything that can be meant). There is nothing wrong with Saussure's principle of the arbitrariness of the linguistic sign — except perhaps the name 'arbitrariness', which carries too much of a negative interpersonal loading (we remarked earlier that 'conventionality' is a better term from this point of view).

But, throughout the history of language, there has always been a contrary motif — a kind of resistance to totally severing the phono-semantic bond. At the level of perception, of course, there are expressions where the meaning is itself a kind of sound, or a source from which a sound is heard to come forth: hence onomatopoeia, or sound imitation, like English *quack, buzz, cuckoo, tinkle*. These are the most clearcut cases of non-arbitrariness, where the patterns of articulation — consonants and vowels organized in syllables — are mimicking what is perceived by the ear; and they can override the general direction of sound change if this is undermining the effect — for example, when <u>mew</u> 'sound made by cats' changed from [mɛː ʷ] to [mju:] it was rephonologized as <u>miaow</u> [mɪaʷ]). If we start from these we can go on to recognize, in English, a steady cline of sound patterns which, as we proceed, are hardly imitations any more and yet seem to retain some degree of sound symbolism: words like <u>creak</u>, <u>rumble</u>, <u>spatter</u>, <u>crash</u>, <u>clang</u>. We may think of these first as individual words; but in fact this kind of sound symbolism, in English, engenders very many groups of words which form what are called 'phonaesthetic series'. Here are a few such series as illustration.

>   rump lump bump hump clump sump dump ... (rounded protrusions or hollows)
>   curl twirl swirl whirl whorl furl ... (circular movements or shapes)
>   sniff sneeze snort snarl snigger sneer ... (facial emission or gesture)
>   ash trash hash mash smash ... ((make) shapeless and valueless)

There are large numbers of these, usually characterized by having a syllable onset or a syllable rhyme in common. Not all those cited (for example in websites devoted to sound symbolism) are equally convincing; but there are enough clear cases to demonstrate that there is this strong undercurrent of non-arbitrariness in the relationship of sound to meaning. To what extent, or in what sense, this relationship is a natural, iconic one in each case is debatable (and has been much debated): a few could be imitations, like the *sn-* in *snore, snarl*; while at the other end there are some where the form of expression seems arbitrary (why *gl-* for small or diffuse manifestations of light, as in *gleam glint glimmer glisten glow*?), and in some instances there are two distinct series with the same sound (*sl-* as both 'slender' and 'slippery'). At the least, there is a non-random association between certain sounds and certain meanings; and at least some speakers perceive at least some instances as natural.

In other words, even in the articulatory section of the phonology there is at least in some languages a constraint on total arbitrariness, and that even in the experiential regions of the meaning potential. These manifestations of non-arbitrariness take different forms in different languages (see e.g. Kakehi's studies of Japanese); but it is not an exceptional or isolated phenomenon. Given this, it is much more to be expected that in the prosodic regions of the phonology we shall find non-arbitrary relations between the phonology and the lexicogrammar.

It is in this context that we can return to the features referred to at the end of the last section. The systems of 'tonicity' (tonic prominence, in phonology, construing the focal point of New information in the grammar) and 'tonality' (one line of melody, or tone unit, in phonology construing one item of information in the grammar) both seem non-arbitrary in their relation between sound and meaning. We might even extend this to the system of tone, at the most abstract level: falling tone in phonology construing certainty in the grammar, rising tone construing uncertainty — and if these are felt to be natural, then the same principle extends also to the other tones: level, either opting out of or postponing the choice; falling-rising, certainty overtaken by uncertainty ('there's a 'but' about it'), and rising-falling, uncertainty overtaken by certainty ('see? there's no doubt').

All these features are being located at a high level of generality; they represent the primary 'moment' in delicacy of the prosodic part of the phonology. The question arises whether the same sense of naturalness will be felt when we come to more specific distinctions, the secondary tones that are the subject of the present chapter. Let us return to the example already given, of the DECLARATIVE KEY system operating as a sub-system of tone 1.

It is no surprise to find that tone 1+ (a wide fall) expresses 'strong key', while tone 1- (a narrow fall) expresses 'mild key', and the median term tone 1. (mid fall) is the neutral term in the system. The high onset, with upjump, and steep fall from high to low could be said to 'sound more forceful', and it seems unlikely that anyone given the meanings and asked to match them with the sounds would do so in any other way.

7.4   Secondary tone systems: tone 1

(1) Direct secondary system: DECLARATIVE KEY

strong 1+   neutral 1.   mild 1-

When in the course of his interview with the lawyer, the client says

// 1+ that / sounds more / like my */ **aunt** //
PLAY 🔊 Sound 7.4

the meaning is 'more than like my lawyer': the tone is contrastive, forceful, underlining the point. This 'strong' variant of tone 1 merges into the high rise-fall of tone 5, which has an even more exclamatory flavour; it is often difficult to decide between the two, especially since the neutral pretonic to tone 1 (see system (2) below) tends to move up towards the onset of the tonic. But the tone 5 has a rise within the tonic itself, and this pattern may be perceived also in each foot within the pretonic segment. Thus:

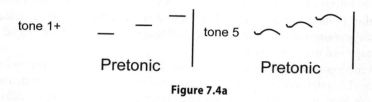

Figure 7.4a

By contrast, the 'mild key' variant tone 1- de-emphasizes the newness of the tonic; the tonic is still the focal point of the information unit, but there is nothing really unexpected about it. For example,

> // .1- had any de/pression or an/xiety in the */ **past** //
> PLAY ◀ Sound 7.4a

> // .1- ∧ and / any medi*/**ca**tions that you're / taking at the / moment //
> PLAY ◀ Sound 7.4b

By using the mild key, the doctor is saying 'well I have to get this information; but I don't want to turn it into a major issue'. Here the pretonic tends to drift downwards:

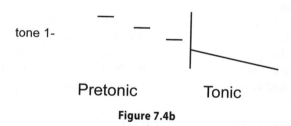

Figure 7.4b

When the doctor wants to confirm a point that is new information, she uses the neutral tone 1.. The patient has mentioned tonsils, but without further specification; the doctor draws the inference:

> // .1. had your / tonsils */ **out** //
> PLAY ◀ Sound 7.4c

where tonsils is now Given and the New falls on the grammatical adverb *out*; otherwise it would have been on the final lexical item *tonsils*:

> // .1. ∧ I've/ had my */ **ton**sils / out //
> PLAY ◀ Sound 7.4d

Similarly the lawyer uses the neutral tone 1. in discussing the making of the will:

> // 4 ∧ but / every so */ **oft**en you // .1. might just / want to / think about ...
> / whether you're */ **hap**py with it //
> PLAY ◀ Sound 7.4e

Typically, here the pretonic remains fairly level throughout.

Clearly the three terms 1+ 1. 1- make up a continuous system; but there are reasons for considering it a choice among three distinct options. Phonologically, provided there is a pretonic the distinction appears rather clearly. In the neutral tone 1. the tonic starts at the same pitch as the end of the pretonic, without jumping up or down; while in the marked options there is a jump in pitch at this point, upjump with 1+, downjump with 1- . If there is no pretonic, of course, this does not apply; in such cases a judgment has to be made on grounds of the pitch gradient alone — height of onset and steepness of fall. This can be heard for example in

> // 1+ ∧ you */ **love** / ginger / nuts //
> PLAY ◀ Sound 7.4f

But of course the judgment is also being made on grounds of meaning. Grammatically there is a median value, and there are two outer values, a toning up, so to speak, and a toning down. This is a common feature of interpersonal systems, with modality perhaps as the prototypical case; and in assigning doubtful instances, as one has to do if compiling a quantitatively-based grammar, the evidence from the flow of meaning in the discourse is balanced alongside the evidence from the flow of sound.

Here are the final three turns from the Lawyer text:

> L. *// 1. **good** // 3 all */ **right** then //
> C. *// 3 ∧ o*/**kay** / ∧ well // 1. thanks very */ **much** //
> L. // 1+ no */ **prob**lem //
>
> PLAY ◀ Sound 7.4g

— where the lawyer's final turn may be a tone 5; the two authors came up with different interpretations of this one!

(2) Indirect secondary system: FORCE

> insistent -1 neutral .1

The 'insistent' term is phonologically very distinctive, because each foot displays a particular movement: a bouncing movement starting from a low, dipping tone and going rapidly up to about mud-high. (It is therefore very useful for investigating rhythm: change any tone 1 pretonic to -1 and you will hear each foot standing out clearly as a distinct unit.)

Figure 7.4c

The force of this 'insistent' pretonic is somewhat argumentative, so it naturally tends to associate with the 'strong' term in the KEY system.

> *// -1+ ∧ l / can't see / what you're com*/**plain**ing a/bout //
> PLAY ◀ Sound 7.4gg

(3) Indirect secondary system: CO-ORDINATION

> listing ...1   neutral .1

The 'listing' pretonic is actually a succession of two or more rising movements enumerating the non-final items in a list. It is clearly related to a sequence of tone 3 tone units; but here the pitch is usually higher (high rising rather than low rising), and the grammatical unit that is typically mapped into each rising segment is a word, group or phrase rather than a clause. Each item in the list may be either of one or of more than one foot, but they are usually kept fairly short. An example from the 'Hailstone' text:

> // 4 ∧ and / you know the / major */ **foods** in those / south pacific / islands are
> // ...1. ∧ things like / breadfruit / taro and // 4 those kinds of in/credibly
> */ **bor**ing // 1 horrible */ **things** //
>
> PLAY ◀ Sound 7.4h

Here the speaker injected an attitudinal Epithet of APPRAISAL into the general category with which she closed the list; hence the 'included' tone unit with tone 4.

This listing pretonic can also occur, less frequently, with tone 2, where it resembles a succession of tone 2 tone units but (unlike a true tone 2 sequence) the items in the list do not rise to the same pitch as the final tonic. The doctor is probing the patient's medical history:

> // -2 had any / oper*/**ations** // ...2 asthma / eczema / hayfever / anything like */ **that** //
> PLAY ◀ Sound 7.4i

The effect of the "listing" pretonic is that the sequence sounds like a list of items in a single question rather than a succession of separate questions.

In both these systems, FORCE and CO-ORDINATION, the 'neutral' term is the same. Phonologically, the three pretonic contours .1 -1 and ...1 form a single system; but grammatically the opposition of listing versus neutral is quite distinct from that of insistent versus neutral.

The neutral pretonic tends to follow a fairly steady course, which may either stay level or else drift up or drift down. Although the range of its variation is considerable, we are not convinced that there is a systematic difference in meaning among these variants, and so we have not attempted to distinguish them grammatically.

One feature that does occur within the pretonic segment is a 'boosting' of some non-initial foot. It is important to note that the pretonic system is entered only at the first salient syllable in the tone unit (that is, at the first filled foot); any proclitic syllables before this point cannot select in any pretonic secondary system. This is simply one manifestation of the principle that all intonation systems are realized through the Ictus element in the foot structure. So in an example such as

> // 1 ^ and there've been / quite a few / things going */ **on** //
> PLAY ◀ Sound 7.4j

the upjump at *quite* is not a booster, because the previous matter is all proclitic. Likewise the upjump at *lush*:

> // 1 ‸ it's that / lush */ **trop**ical / ^ kind of / stuff //
> PLAY ◀ Sound 7.4k

On the other hand, in

> // 1+3 ‸ I / want to know / how to / ‸ how to / cope with */ **stress** */ **real**ly //
> PLAY ◀ Sound 7.4l

there is an upjump on *cope*, which serves to boost this foot — and in this way show that this is where the New element begins. Since the patient has come to consult the doctor, she treats the foregoing *I want to know how* as Given. The repeat of *how to* without the Ictus has the effect of further foregrounding the prominence given to *cope*.

It is this boosting at some point within the neutral pretonic to tone 1 that typically realizes the shift from Given to New. The marked pretonics -1 and ...1 are typically all part of the New: items enumerated as a list are usually being presented as fresh information, while the bouncing pretonic -1 is used precisely to signal that what is being said is being insisted on as in some sense contrastive (to what has been said or is to be expected). But the unmarked, neutral pretonic may contain both Given and New material; often there is no clear boundary between them, but if the speaker does want to make a definite move from what is being presented as Given to what is being presented as New, then disrupting the relatively steady flow of the melody by shifting to a higher pitch has exactly the required effect on the listener. (When we use expressions like 'the speaker wants to ...', we are of course not suggesting any conscious awareness on the speaker's part.)

In all these secondary tone systems, direct and indirect, where there is a 'neutral' term this is typically the most frequent variant occurring in natural speech. Our use of the dot (full stop, period) to symbolize these neutral options is meant to suggest this pattern. The neutral is a kind of default choice, based on the good reason principle:

choose this option unless there is good reason for choosing something else. It is not *defined* by frequency, and there will often be particular registers (functionally defined sub-systems), or particular text fragments (related groups of instances), where a marked term comes to the fore and perhaps becomes the localized default choice (for example, certain types of discourse which require a lot of things to be enumerated). But as a general rule the neutral term will also be the one that stands out as being the most frequent choice in the system.

7.5   Secondary tone systems: tone 2

(4) Direct secondary system: SPECIFICATION OF QUERY (INTERROGATION POINT)

    unspecified 2.   specified 2

With tone 2. the tonic is a straightforward rising tone. Here what is at issue is the whole of the information unit, and the tonic will often be in its unmarked location, on the final lexical element in the tone unit. For example

    // .2. ∧ have you / been in */ **hos**pital for / anything //
    PLAY ◀ Sound 7.5

This is a straightforward query by the doctor in the context of a preliminary discussion with a new patient. 'Medical problems' had just been referred to, so this represents a move towards a more detailed investigation.

As the doctor's enquiry progresses, the moment arrives when the patient, asked about her allergic reaction to medication of any kind, mentions penicillin. The doctor picks this up:

    // .2 ∧ what / happens when you / take peni/**cil**lin //
    PLAY ◀ Sound 7.5a

Here the tonic is a sharp fall-rise, distributed over the final foot (the last two syllables of penicillin). This marks out penicillin as the focal point of the query; it gives a clear specification that this is what the question is about, and the patient responds with an appropriately informative answer: 'Well, it's so long ago, but, em, when I was a child I broke out in red rash'.

This sharp fall-rise is, in fact, a combination of a falling tone 1 with a rising tone 2; the fall-rise signals something like 'I'm telling you: this is what I want to know'. This fall-rise may be spread over more than one foot, in which case it could be interpreted as two tone units, a tone 1 followed by a tone 2, as in

    // .2 ∧ so you / drink most */ **nights** do you */ **then** //
    PLAY ◀ Sound 7.5b

    // .2 did you bring / home some */ **vid**eo */ **did** you //
    PLAY ◀ Sound 7.5c

(i.e. with tone 1 tonic on *nights* and *video*, and tone 2 on *then* and *did you*). In such cases the fall may sound like a completed tone 1; it is interesting to cut at this point and listen. However, there are reasons for interpreting this as a variety of tone 2. First, the fall and rise may be on a single foot, as in the *penicillin* example above; or even on a single syllable, in the case of a monosyllabic tonic foot, as in

// 2 ∧ was it in the */**car** //
PLAY ◄ Sound 7.5d

Second, and more critically perhaps, the pretonic options available to tone 2 are those of tone 2. (see system (5) below) and not those of tone 1. Third, even where the fall and the rise are separated, the whole usually forms a single information unit, as in the previous two examples. As always, there are borderline cases, where either interpretation could be justified; but it seems clear from their function in the discourse that there is a systemic opposition between these two variants 2. and 2. The simple rise, tone 2., is the unmarked option; the fall-rise, tone 2, adds a further specification of the focal point of the query.

(5) Indirect secondary system: INVOLVEMENT (INTERROGATIVE)

neutral .2   involved –2

The neutral variant is high and tends to be fairly level, as in

// .2. does the / Wallace line go / round the whole */ **globe** //
PLAY ◄ Sound 7.5e

This is the most unmarked form of a yes/ no interrogative, both tonic and pretonic being neutral. Contrast this with

// -2. ∧ was / that when you / newly moved / into the */ **area** //
PLAY ◄ Sound 7.5f

where the pretonic is marked, as what we are calling the 'involved' variant. This is also fairly level, but maintained at a low pitch. Roughly speaking, the pitches of these two pretonics correspond to the two terminals of the rising tonic:

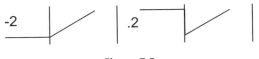

Figure 7.5

This gives to both of them a feeling of solidarity with the tonic; but the 'involved' tone -2 is, well, more involved. The questioner adds a feature of urgency, perhaps, or wonder, or simple disbelief. In this last example, the doctor has been probing the patient's feeling of stress, and has just been told that her sense of having a brick pressing on her chest began about one month earlier; this suggests one factor which may have been significant, and which the doctor immediately checks out. In this way the patient's response is framed by an aura of importance which would have been lacking if the doctor had simply used the neutral (high) pretonic tone .2 .

Another example of the prosody of 'involvement' that comes with the low pretonic -2 is the patient's somewhat conspiratorial response to being told she should restrict her intake of alcohol to just so much in a week:

// -2. ∧ can I / save it / up and / take it / all on * / **Sat**urday //
PLAY 🔊 Sound 7.5g

Both she and the doctor laugh at this point. Had the patient used the unmarked pretonic here, it would have been meant (and interpreted) as a straightforward question to be answered.

In both these examples, the marked pretonic has been combined with the unmarked tonic 2. . What about the marked, fall-rise tonic 2? Is it possible to have both tonic and pretonic marked, tone -2? This combination, with its notable upjump from pretonic to tonic, is doubly marked, and certainly the least frequent of the four (an expected distribution of marked and unmarked variants would predict about 1% of all occurrences). There are none in the small set of texts being used for illustration in this chapter. But it is a possible choice. Suppose, for example, the patient had said

// -2 ∧ can I / save it / up and / take it / all on */ **Sat**urday //
PLAY 🔊 Sound 7.5h

this would have made Saturday a very specific point of the enquiry: not just a question of taking it all at once, but explicitly on Saturday — perhaps even one particular Saturday, the one that is just coming up. But this forces attention to two quite different aspects of the question, and it would be rather more likely to find this split up into two information units.

We referred in Chapter 1 to the phenomenon known to linguists as HRT — standing for 'high rising tone', but used only to refer to a particular function of this tone: its use in declarative clauses to give information, often elliptically in answer to a question, and to build up narrative monologue, especially in personal experience recounts, jokes and the like. Phonetically it is indistinguishable from the straight rising tonic variant of tone 2; but the pretonic, if there is one, is generally the marked, low variety -2. The doctor asks the question, 'How much alcohol do you drink on average in a week?'; and after some prevarication the patient answers

// -2. ∧ em / probably a/bout er / ∧ / ∧ / three */ **bot**tles //
PLAY 🔊 Sound 7.5hh

This is a typical example of the HRT used to answer an information-seeking question. The doctor then continues with the HRT in her own follow-up, this time on an imperative clause, meaning 'that's what I want you to take notice of':

// 4 try and / limit / if you */ **can** // -2. ^ to about / two / standard
/ drinks a */ **night** // -2. ^ that's worth / two / glasses of */ **wine** //

PLAY 🔊 Sound 7.5i

There has been much attention paid to the HRT, especially in Australia, which seems to have been where it first began, or at least where it was first noticed and recorded. It is even brought up from time to time in the media, in correspondence columns and talkback radio, where it attracts the same kind of disapproval as grammatical errors and spelling mistakes, being associated in particular with the discourse of 'the younger generation'. The rising tonic carries a prosody of 'get it?' or 'is that what you wanted to know?'; and probably the choice of low rather than high pretonic avoids the strongly interrogative flavour of the sequence high level plus high rising. In North American English the low pretonic to tone 2 is noticeably more frequent, with tone 2 as a whole, than in British or Australian; this might well have had some influence on younger Australians of a generation or so ago — it is hard to say.

It may be useful here to recall the primary system with WH- type (lexical) inter-rogatives already introduced in Chapter 1. Since these interrogatives do not raise the question of polarity, their unmarked tone is tone 1, exactly like that with declaratives; but there is a marked option by which they take tone 2 — two such marked options, in fact, though with different forms and different contrasts in meaning attached to the choice. The first is the system of LEXICAL INTERROGATIVE KEY, with terms 'neutral' and 'mild'. When the doctor asked the question about the patient's alcohol consumption, what she actually said was

// .2. how much / alcohol do you / drink on */ **av**erage in a / week //
PLAY 🔊 Sound 7.5j

Here the doctor selected the 'mild' option in the KEY system, and this has a significant effect: it makes the WH- question sound much less accusing. In this system the tonicity remains unmarked: in both variants the focus falls at the end of the information unit; and the usual pretonic, with the 'mild' (tone 2) variant, is the high, unmarked one tone .2 .

The second system is called RELATION TO PREVIOUS UTTERANCE, with the two terms 'neutral' and 'echo question'. Here, in the 'echo' variant, the tone is tone 2 but the tonicity is marked: the focus typically falls on the WH- item itself, and therefore at the beginning of the information unit. This tone 2 option came to be called an echo question because it typically occurred as the request for a reminder: the speaker hadn't heard, or had forgotten, or didn't believe what was said; but the query is often simply self-addressed, as it seems to have been here:

*// -2. **what's** that / one a/gain //
PLAY 🔊 Sound 7.5k

(Where there are a number of feet, as here, the rise is steady, with perhaps more move-ment in pitch towards the end; but the tonic is still at the beginning — as you can hear if you try repeating with the tonic at the end.)

7.6   Secondary tone systems: tone 3

With tone 3, which is phonologically a level tone (that is, neither falling nor rising) although always realized phonetically as a low rising contour, there are no secondary distinctions of a 'direct' kind. While the range of phonetic variation is considerable, from a barely perceptible rise which may be audible only when the sound is slowed down to one that is indistinguishable from a tone 2, there is no systemic difference among the variants. There is however an 'indirect' secondary tone system, with two terms realized by distinct types of pretonic.

(6)   Indirect secondary system:

  unmarked (mid level) **.3**   marked (low level) **-3**

Like the pretonic variants of tone 2, these tend to remain fairly steady in pitch, and they correspond in principle to the two end points of the tonic.

   However, as pointed out in Chapter 5, tone 3 has a number of different functions in the grammar, though all are derived from its opting out of the basic opposition of fall versus rise. It may mean 'I haven't finished', as in sequences of 3 (...) 1; it may mean 'this is an additional, minor point', as in compound tones 13 and 53; or, taken by itself, it may mean 'I'm uncommitted', 'I don't consider this important' — some disclaimer of that kind. The fact that it rises puts it on the side of uncertainty, as opposed to the certainty implied by a fall; in other words, although it is neutral as between tone 1 and tone 2, it is marginally closer to tone 2, with which it sometimes overlaps. But the secondary variants, .3 and -3, tend to occur in different systemic environments; they seldom appear as in simple opposition one to the other.

   So while these two pretonic variants do constitute a system at the phonological level, in our initial analysis we had not recognized any one grammatical system for which they served as the realization. They were seen as functioning separately in various different primary systems. However, they could perhaps be shown to contrast with each other in the imperative, because here, while tone 1 is always possible, it is marked as being rather peremptory, and tone 3 can be regarded as the norm, at least in dialogue; and here there may be a systemic contrast between these two secondary variants. Consider this turn by the lawyer:

   // .3 once you've / ∧ had a / look at the */ **will** and // .3 made the
   */ **change**s / to it // .3 send it back */ **in** because it // .3 will need a*/**mend**ments //

   PLAY ◀ Sound 7.6

Here, the first two tone units are tone 3 because the clauses are dependent and non-final; the speaker could have continued with tone 1:

   // .1. send it back */ **in** because it // .1. will need a*/**mend**ments //
   PLAY ◀ Sound 7.6a

But in fact she continues with tone 3, on both the imperative clause and the following hypotactic causal clause, showing that this is in fact the overall key of the proposal. Now supposing she had used the low pretonic:

> // -3 send it back */ **in** because it // -3 will need a */**mend**ments //
> PLAY ◀ Sound 7.6b

this would have carried a marked prosody of warning, drawing attention to the serious-ness of what was being requested. This contrast can be felt with an imperative that has an inherent warning in itself, such as *make sure you keep your eyes closed!*, where the mid-level .3 version would sound almost jaunty, certainly not serious or life-threatening.

In the declarative, on the other hand, the low tone -3 has what seems to be quite the opposite effect: it imports an air of casualness. Note the patient's answer:

> // .1- had any de/pression or an/xiety in the */ **past** //
> — *// 1. **no** // -3 only the / usual when you / break up with a */ **boy**friend //
>
> PLAY ◀ Sound 7.6c

to which the doctor then responds on the same tone,

> // -3 fair e*/**nough** //
> PLAY ◀ Sound 7.6d

You can get this effect in the imperative, if you use tone -3 on a clause such as *do whatever you like!* ('I don't care'); and this gives a feeling of ambiguity to a clause such as

> // -3 better keep / out of the */ **way** //
> PLAY ◀ Sound 7.6e

which could be either lighthearted, almost joky ('let's not get involved — there's an argument going on'), or else a serious warning if a heavy truck is backing out in front of you.

In general wherever tone 3 is used as a separate tone unit, if there is a pretonic then tone -3 can function as a marked variant. When tone 3 occurs as a minor tonic in tones 13 and 53, no pretonic options are available (this is why these are considered as compound tones, and not as a succession of two tone units).

7.7   Secondary tone systems: tones 4 and 5

The complex tones 4 (falling-rising) and 5 (rising-falling) each has one secondary tone system, having an unmarked term which is mid to high (4., 5.) and a marked term which is low (4, 5). In both cases the distinction is a gradual one, affecting mainly the tonic but also the pretonic profile. We might represent the difference schematically as follows:

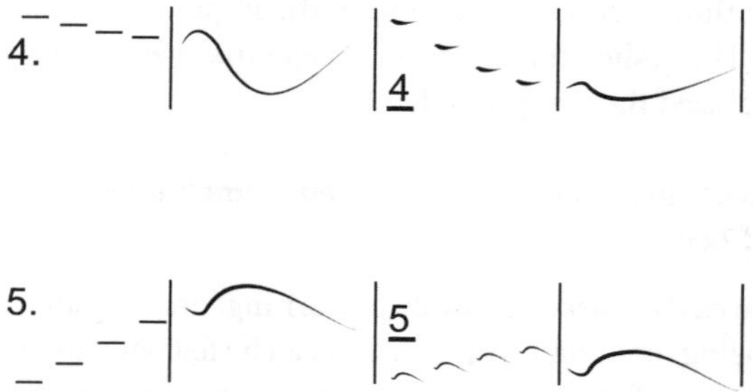

Figure 7.7

In the low variety each pretonic foot tends to foreshadow the tonic by mimicking its basic outline. In addition the low 5 (but not the low 4) tends to have a breathy quality associated with it.

Each marked term functions as in some sense a souped-up version of the unmarked, exaggerating the meaning created by the tension between the two halves of the tonic movement, the fall and the rise.

In their discourse functions, tones 4 and 5 are very different. Tone 5, which (like tone 1) ends on a fall, tends to be independent and final. Tone 4, which (like tone 2) ends on a rise, tends to be dependent and non-final. The effect of the souping up is therefore different in the two cases. We will take tone 4 first.

(7) Tone 4: secondary system DEPENDENCY TYPE

unmarked (high) 4. contrastive (low) 4

The lawyer speaks largely in clause complexes many of which contain one or more tone units of tone 4. These are almost all in the unmarked variant of the tone:

// 3. once we've re*/**ceiv**ed it

// 4. I'll make the a/mendments */ **to** it

// 4. ∧ and / then you can / either / come in */ **here** to the / offices and / ∧ em

// 4. ∧ and / sign it */ **here**

*// 4. **or**

// .1. we can / send it / out to you in its / final / form and / you can / ∧ you can / sign it */ **there** //

PLAY Sound 7.7

On one occasion she uses the low variant 4 — in a very characteristic context, namely with a concessive clause:

// 4. ∧ es*/**sen**tially you / ^ em

// <u>4</u> ∧ un/less / ^ un/less you / wanted to / ∧ er / make some par/ticular pro*/**vis**ion

// 1.3 ∧ your ex/ecutor would / have the dis/cretion to / ∧ em */ **sell** the */ **ass**ets //

PLAY ◄ Sound 7.7a

The client on the other hand seems to favour the marked variant:

// ∧ I / just / thought /∧ em / ∧ I mean

// <u>4</u> if my / ∧ em / partner / were / ∧ to */ **die**

// <u>4</u> ∧ I mean we've / talked a/bout the */ **money** / part but the

*// <u>4</u> **ass**ets / er / that would / just be

// 1.3 ∧ my */ **sist**er would / look after */ **that** ..

PLAY ◄ Sound 7.7b

The client is the one who is more personally involved. He may also use this tone for light relief, although this one is perhaps a borderline case:

// <u>4</u> trying to / find it in the */ **house**

// .1. might be a / bit of a */ **job** //

PLAY ◄ Sound 7.7c

All these are non-final, typically dependent, clauses. An example of tone 4. on a final, independent clause, in this case an imperative, is the following, where the lawyer picks up on the previous turn by the client:

// 4. could be */ **diffi**cult so

// 4. ∧ so be / sure that you / do */ **that** //

PLAY ◄ Sound 7.7d

The meaning is 'at least; whatever else you do or don't do' (this is also on the borderline of 4. and <u>4</u>).

A final rise does call for completion, whether it is a question awaiting an answer, as with tone 2, or, with tone 4, a dependency awaiting a termination ('imagine a proposition (fall): now, supposing that (rise)'). With tone 2, the completion is invited from the interlocutor; with tone 4, it is supplied by the original speaker.

(8) Tone 5: secondary system EXCLAMATION KEY

unmarked (high) 5.   strong (low) <u>5</u>

A final fall, on the other hand, is self-sufficient: either uncomplicatedly, as with tone 1, or, with tone 5, a counterexpectancy ('you thought there was doubt (rise)? no way (fall)!'). The low, somewhat breathy variant carries a prosody of 'wow!' (and if *wow* is actually said it is likely to be on this tone); it is the tone that can best be labelled 'exclamatory'.

The restaurant text illustrates tone 5 at use in dialogue. The male interactant says

. // 4. when you come */ **home** to/night you can

// 5. have a */ **look** at it

// 5. ∧ it's */ **great**

// 1. ∧ it's */ **good** //

PLAY ◀ Sound 7.7e

— where the final *it's good* tones down the enthusiasm of the preceding *it's great*, presenting the judgment as more like an objective assessment. Later on, the same male's display is punctured by the female interactant:

// yeah I've got / ∧ em

*// -2. **what's** that one / then

// 1. oh */ **star**struck

// .3 that's */ **it**

*// -2. **was** it / starstruck / ∧

*// 1. **moon**struck //

— // .1. oh */ **puff**

// 5 don't be*/**lieve** you //

PLAY ◀ Sound 7.7f

In adult conversation in general, taking all generic varieties together, tone 5 is almost certainly the least frequent of all the five tones. It is more favoured by children, who value its combination of assertiveness and wonder.

Serious counting on a large enough scale has not yet been undertaken. But on the evidence so far it seems that the order of frequency of the five tones is 1 – 4 – 3 – 2 – 5, with something of a gap between 4 and 3 and another between 3 and 2. Tones 1 and 4 together might turn out to be about one order of magnitude more frequent than tones 2 and 5 together.

What would this suggest about the nature of interactive spoken discourse? It would reflect its character as a mixture of telling and asking, with telling as the predominant motif. In terms of speech function, spoken discourse is largely made up of statements: first and foremost, straightforward statements (tone 1) and next, statements tempered by reservation or doubt, and dependent elements getting their propositional force from others (tone 4). Then come unfinished statements, and those that are given a lower information profile (tone 3). Finally the minor motif of questions: straightforward questions (tone 2), and last of all questions that get overridden, and expressions of wonder or assurance (tone 5). All of these, of course, come in many different varieties;

any attempt to generalize can only be crude and perhaps misleading. But we have found it interesting as a way of contemplating the daily life of homo loquens, as this is reflected in the prosodic flavour of just one of our many spoken languages.

7.8 Secondary tone systems: a summary

We have recognized a total of nineteen secondary tonal categories; these may be summarized as follows:

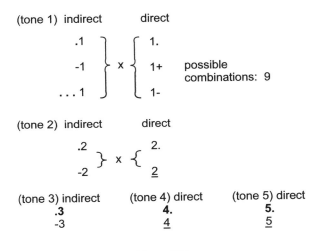

Figure 7.8

Thus, nine for tone 1, four for tone 2, and two each for tones 3, 4 and 5.

We have seen that, in some instances, the secondary variants of one primary tone may enter into systemic contrast with each other; for example, tones 4. and 4 as unmarked versus contrastive options in a system of DEPENDENCY TYPE. It is these systems that we have been describing and illustrating in the course of the present chapter.

But there are also many cases where the systemic contrast is between different primary tones; for example tone 1 and tone 3 as realizing a system within the speech function of command (IMPERATIVE KEY). These were outlined earlier, in Chapter 5. In some of these cases the system appears simply as an opposition between the primary tones, no matter which of the secondary variants is selected. In other cases it is just one of the secondary tones that enters into the opposition.

We have not referred specifically to those in the last category. Where a particular secondary tone is involved, this has been indicated in the analysis guide; and the phonological properties of that secondary tone are as described in the present chapter. For example, in the 'compromising' kind of imperative (IMPERATIVE FORCE), it is typically the low variant of tone 4 (i.e. tone 4) that is found to occur; the phonological nature of this low variant is as set out in section 4.7 above.

Every moment in spoken discourse is the domain of choices in intonation; and each choice is a choice among different possible meanings. It is always a useful strategy, in listening to speech, to observe where a speaker has used a particular tone and then go through the possible alternatives, asking 'suppose the speaker had used this other tone instead; what difference would this have made to the meaning?'. We have taken the analysis up to the point where we feel reasonably confident in recognizing some general pattern; in other words, where the contrast in meaning can be integrated in a general account of English grammar. This is not to say that there are no finer distinctions — there certainly are. But we are not attempting to explore these further, at least for the time being.

Appendix to Part II

Texts analysed for intonation and rhythm, including primary and secondary tones

A.II.1 Australian

A.II.1.1 The Wallace Line PLAY 🔊

[There was this guy called Wallace, spelt W-A-L-L-A-C-E]

S1: // 4. ∧ and / ∧ he dis*/**cov**ered / ∧ that ... that / as you — / as you go — //
// .1. ∧ it's between /Bali and */**Lom**bok //
// 4. ∧ there's this /kind of im/aginary */ **line** //
// 4. ∧ which is — / ∧ re/lates to when / bits broke / off — / bits of / continent
broke */ **off** each / other ... and //
// 4. if you go */ **east** of that / line — //
// .1. ∧ so / Lombok's ... em ... em / flora and / fauna is / very like
Aus*/**tra**lia's it's //
// .1. that kind of */ **scrub**by stuff //
// 4 ∧ whereas */ **Bali** which is / four — //
// 4 four hours a/way on a */ **boat** //
//.1. ∧ is that / lush */ **trop**ical kind of / stuff //
// .1. totally */ **diff**erent yet they're //
// .3 ∧ you */ **know** //
// .1. so */ **close** //
// 4. ∧ and so / when you get — / ∧ go */ **east** //
// .1. ∧ it / just /doesn't */**grow** there's //
// .1+3 just not the / same vege*/**ta**tion << 1+ ∧ at */ **all** >> as there / is
/ west of the */ **Wall**ace /Line //
// .1. nor was — / is there the / same */ **an**imal ... //
// .1. ∧ kind of / popu*/**la**tion //

S2: // .2. does the /Wallace line go /round the whole */**globe** or / is it just .. .//

S1: // .1. ∧ no it / just goes — / ∧ it's / just from / that sort of / south east
*/**as**ia bit //
// .1. ∧ sort of */ **down** //
// 1 like */ **that** //
// 1 ∧ I / think it's when / that — those bits were / breaking */ **off** from the //
// .1. Europe ... em / continent and the ant/arctic and / all of */ **that** about

185

/ which I //
// 4. don't know */ **all** that / much but . . . //
// .1. ∧ it sort of /goes in /one ear and /out the */**oth**er //
// 1 ∧ but it's — / .1 ∧ you can */ **see** it //
*// 1 **real**ly it's //
// .1. so dis*/**tinct**ive //
// 4. ∧ and you know the / major */ **foods** in those / south pacific / islands are //
// . . . 1- things like em / breadfruit / taro / . . . em / ∧ and / those kinds of
<< 4 ∧ in/credibly */ **bor**ing >> horrible */ **things** //
[pineapple, and banana, and watermelon . . .]
// 5.3 ∧ there's */ **none** of those ex/otic */ **fruits** //
// 5. ∧ they don't */ **grow** //

A.II.1.2 Doctor and patient PLAY 🔊

D: // .1. ∧ and / what's the / problem to*/ **day** // -2. ∧ is there /anything
s-spe */**cif**ic //

P: *// .1+3 well / ∧ *// **yes** */ **act**ually I // .1+3 want to know /how ∧ how to
/ cope with */ **stress***/ **real**ly //

D: // .1. ∧ and there've been / quite a few / things going * / **on*** // 2. **have** there //

P: *// 1 **yeah** //

D: // 4. ∧ well per/haps be/fore we / go any */ **fur**ther I / ought to get
// .1. just a / few */ **de**tails // .3 ∧ a/bout your / past */ **hi**story // .1+ ∧ and / any /
major / medical / problems you / may have */ **had** // . 2. ∧ have you / been in */
hospital for / any thing // -3 had any / oper*/**a**tions *// 3 **asth**ma *// 3 **ecz**ema *// 3
hay fever // 2. ∧ anything like */ **that** //

P: *// 2. **ton**sils //

D: *//.3 **ton**sils *// .2. yeah / thats-/ that */ **counts** *// 2 **yeah** // .1. had your
/ tonsils */ **out** // .3 ∧ em / ever been / under */ **stress** or // 1- had any de/pression or
an/xiety in the */**past** //-2 anything like */ **that** //

P: *// 1. no // -3 only the / usual when you / break up with a */ **boy**friend
and . . . . */// 1 **no** //

D: // -3 fair e/**nough** *// 1- **yeah** // .1- ∧ and / any medic/ations that you're */ **tak**ing at
the / moment //

P: *// 1 **no** //

D: *// 1 **no** // -2. nothing at */ **all** //.1. and /any medi/cations that you
*/ **know** you're al/lergic to //

P: // .1. peni*/**cill**in //

D: // .1. peni*/**cill**in */// 1 **fine** *//13 **put** that /right up */ **here** // .2 ∧ what
     / happens when you / take peni*/**cillin** //

P: // 4. ∧ well it's / so long a */ **go** // 4. but . . . em . . . / when I was
     a */ **child** I //.1. broke out in /r-red / ∧ */**r-rash** //

D: *// .1. **ah** // 5.3 fair e*/**nough** *// 1 **yes** //

P: // -3 ∧ it was / very */ **itch**y and ..../ /

D: // 1 **yes** //

P: // .1+ ∧ I / probably / am */ **not** I......// /

D: // 5. well you / often */ **don't** / know but it's // .1. just not / worth
     / ∧ / testing you a */**gain** there's / 5. so many / other medi/cations we can */ **use** //
     13 ∧ and / ∧ po*/**ten**tially you / could have a / major re*/**ac**tion *// 1 **yeah** // em.....// 1
     what about */ **smok**ing //

P: *// 1 **no** //

D: // -3 no */ **good** *// 2. **ever** / smoked //

P: *// 1 **nev**er //

D: // .3 no */ **great** // 1 ∧ and */ **al**cohol // .2. how much /alcohol do you
     / drink ∧ on */ **aver**age in a / week //

P: *// 1 **gosh** //
     [both laugh]

D: // .1+ ∧ it's a /difficult */ **ques**tion *// 5. **isn't** it //

P: // .1. on */ **aver**age // -2. em / probably a/bout ah / ∧ / ∧ / three
     */ **bot**tles *// 2 **may**be //

D: // 2. ∧ of */ **wine** // yeah //

P: *// 1 **yeah** //

D: // .2 so you / drink most */ **nights** do you */ **then** //

P: */ 1 **yeah** //

D: // 4. try and / limit / if you */ **can** // ....-2. ∧ to about / two
     / standard / drinks a */ **night** // -2. ∧ that's your / two / glasses of */**wine** //

P: // -2. ∧ can I /save it /up and /take it /all on */**Sat**urday //
     [both laugh]

D: *// 3 **well** // .1. em .. / two /bottles per */ **week** // .3 ∧ and / that's
     */ **fine** // .1. don't / don't in /crease beyond */ **that** // .1.3 that's /probably a/bout the
     / maximum you / should / ∧ con*/**sume** on a / weekly */ **aver**age //

P: *// 1 **yeah** //

D: // em .... *// 1 **yes** so // 4. ∧ the /problem to*/ **day** / ∧ was ... .//

P: // well it's / just that I've ... // 4. ∧ I / actually */ **feel** like I've
// .1+ got a */ **brick** // .1+ on my */ **chest** //

D: *// 1 **right** //

P: // ∧ that is ... em ... //

D: // -2 ∧ em ...con/stricting your */ **chest** //
— — — —

P: *// 1 **yeah** //

P: *// 1 **yeah** //

D: // .1. when d'that */ **start** // .1. how long a*//**go** //

P: // -2. probably .../ probably a */ **month** //

D: *// 1 **right** and // 5̲ what / happened a */ **month** a*/ go// -2. ∧ was
/that when you / newly moved / into the */ **ar**ea //

A.II.1.3 Lawyer and client PLAY 🔊

L: // .3 ∧ o*/**kay** // 1 ∧ well */**look** ... em // .1.3 ∧ there are */ **no** / difficulties with */
that ... em // 4. ∧ what / what I'll / **do** for / you // ∧ un/less there's /anything /else
which we / haven't / covered which / you —

C: // ∧ I / just thought ... em ... I mean // 4̲ if my ... em .../ partner were ... to */ **die**
I mean we've // 4̲ talked a/bout the */ **mon**ey / part but the *// 4̲ **ass**ets / ah / that
would / just be ... // 1.3 ∧ my */ **sis**ter would / look after */ **that** with the ... *// 1.3
she'd work out / how to ... em / ∧ di*/**vide** that or is // .1. that a / compli/**cation** //

L: // 4. ∧ you named your ... em / sister as the ... [C: second ex] ∧ al/ternate ex*/**ecu**tor
*// 2. **yeah** //

C: *// 1 **yeah** al//.1.ternative ex*/**ecu**tor [L. em ... if] // .1.3 ∧ I'd / leave that to / her .../
∧ dis*/**cre**tion as to / how that ... << .3 ∧ you */ **know** >> / what to / do with those ..
. em .../ household */ **ass**ets of .../ ∧ of mine //

L: *// 1 **yes** *// 1 **yes** // 4. ∧ es*/**sen**tially you'd em / ∧ un//4̲ less/ ∧ un/less you / wanted
to ... er ... make some par/ticular pro*/**vis**ion // .1.3 your ex/ecutor would / have the
dis/cretion to ... em */ **sell** off the */**ass**ets ... er ... //

C: // .3 o*/**kay** //

L: // .1. ∧ oh and and di/vide the / property a/mongst the / ∧ a/mongst the bene/
ficiaries / which you've */ **cho**sen //

C: *// 1 **yeah** // .1. thats.[L: so is that ...] */**fine** //

L: // .3 all*/**right** // [writing] // 3 ∧ all * / **right** // 4. ∧ now / what I / will do */**for** you / ∧ /
is // .3 ∧ I'll / have the / will pre*/**pared** and ... // .3 ∧ in / draft */ **form** [C: okay] // 4.

∧ and I'll / send it / out to you in the */ **mail** . . . em // 4. for you to / have a */ **look** at . . . [C: mhm] // 4. ∧ and . . . er / ∧ as I / said to you be*/**fore** I'll // 4 need the full / names of . . . of [C: sure] / all the bene*/**fi**ciaries so // 4. ∧ I'll / leave / space in the / draft / will for / you to in/sert those */**names** //

C: // .3 o*/**kay** //

L: // .3 once you've / ∧ had a / look at the */ **will** and // .3 made the / changes */ **to** it // .3 send it back */**in** because it // .3 will need a*/**mend**ment // [C: mm] // .3 once we've re*/**ceiv**ed it // 4. I'll make the a/mendments */ **to** it [C: mm] // 4. ∧ and / then you can / either / come in */ **here** to the / office and . . . em // 4. ∧ and / sign it */ **here** *// 4.**or** // 1.1 we can / send it / out to you in its / final / form and / you can / ∧ sign it */ **there** // 4 what */ **we** do / ∧ is // we keep a / copy / ∧ of the . . . // 4 oh / no no / not a*/ **signed** / copy but a / 4. copy */**only** of the / will *// 4 **here** //4 ∧ in our */ **off**ices // .1. ∧ but / you keep the / actual / true copy / ∧ of your / will with / you . . . er << 3 ∧ you */**know** >> in / ∧ in a / place which / ∧ which / you con/sider to be a / safe */ **place** // [C: mm] // 4. ∧ it's im*/**port**ant that you // 4. tell your ex*/**ecu**tor // .1. where you in/tend to / keep that */**will** // .3 otherwise / you could */**die** and the // will would . . . / ∧ would . . . er . . .

C: // 4 trying to / find it in the */ **house** // .1. might be a / bit of a */ **job** //

L: // 4. could be */ **diff**icult // 4. ∧ so . . . / ∧ so be / sure that you / do */ **that** . . . em . . . and // 4. ∧ the . . . */**oth**er thing / ∧ worth / mentioning / is . . . em // 4. ∧ you / don't have a / will at the */**mo**ment / so // 4. ∧ of course / this will / doesn't re/voke any */ **for**mer / wills as there *// 1 **are**n't any / but ∧ you // might em . . . er // 4. ∧ it / might be / prudent to / give / ∧ / thought / every five */ **years** or / so [C: mm] // .3 to . . . er / ∧ the pro/visions that you've / made in your */**will** [C: mm] and // .1.3 give some / thought to / whether you / wish to */**change** the */**will** or // .1. whether you're / happy with the / will in the / way that it */**is** // .3 ∧ at / that */ **time** // 4. ∧ so it's / not / something you / need to / do on a */**dai**ly / basis but // 4. ∧ but / every so */ **of**ten you // .1. might just / want to / think about . . .

C: // .1. that / sounds more / like my */**aunt** //

L: <<[laughter]>>// .1. whether you're */ **hap**py with it //

C: // 1.3 ∧ on a */ **dai**ly *// **ba**sis // [L: yeah] // -2 who's / in / who's */ **out** //

L: *// 1 **yeah** // .1+ but . . . em / otherwise em / ∧ you / know that's / that's really / all that — / all I / need I / think at this */ **stage** so // .3 I'll send that */ **out** to you [C: // 1 o*/**kay**] // -3 ∧ and then / you just / send it / back to me / with the a*/**mend**ments / and . . . em // .1. ∧ and / then you can / sign the / final */ **copy** //

C: // .3 mm that */**sounds** all right *// 1 **yeah** it'll be *//1.3 **good** to / get this . . . / sorted / out at */**last** // 2 **eh** //

L: *// 1 **yes** // [C: yeah] *// 1 **good** // .3 all */ **right** then //

C: // .3 o*/**kay** / ∧ well // .1+ thanks very */ **much** //

L: // 5. no */ **prob**lem //

A.II.1.4 In the restaurant PLAY ◄

M: *// 1 **yeah** and // .1. ∧ 'cause ... and / we were com*/**plain**ing // .1. ∧ 'cause / ... em / ∧ Lor/raine's got *<< 1 **you** know sort of >> */**gin**ger / nuts and so — // .1.3 see / we don't */ **like** the */ **gin**ger / nuts and // .1. we said */ **oh** //

W: // 1+ ∧ you */ **love** / ginger / nuts you / liar //

M: // .1. no I */**don't** they're // .1. too */ **hard** //

W: // .1+ ∧ you're / just i/dentifying with */ **Anne** //

M: *// 1. **no** no they're // .1. // .1. too */ **hard** // ∧ I / don't like / gi — // .1. ∧ I / really */ **don't** like / ginger nuts // 5. ∧ they're / too */ **hard** // .1. crunch your */ **teeth** and / things like / that // 4 when you've got / all the / bridges */ **I've** got I'm *// 1.3 **wor**ried a/bout them */ **then** //

x   x x x x

M: // .1. ∧ did I / tell you I / hired a */ **vid**eo // [W: m-m] *// 1 **yeah** I // .1. hired a */ **vid**eo last / night // .13 ∧ you know / ∧ it / seems */ **eas**ier than / ∧ re/placing */ **mine** // [laughter] // 1. ∧ that's */ **good** // 4. ∧ and / when you come */ **home** to/night you can // 5. have a */ **look** at it // 5. ∧ it's */ **great** // 1.1 ∧ it's / **good** //

W: //.2 did you bring / home some */ **vid**eos / did you //

M: *// 1. **yeah** *//1. **yeah** // yeah I've got ... em — *// -2. **what's** that one / then // .1. oh */ **star**struck // .3 that's */ **it** // -2. was it */**star**struck *// 1. **moon**struck //

W: // 1 oh */ **pfff** // 5 don't be*/**lieve** you //

M: *// 2. **eh** // 4. ∧ well it's / better than / Debbie does */ **Dal**las or // 5. something like */ **that** //

W: [laughter] // -2. deep */ **throat** or ... //

M: // 1+ **mm** ...... // 4. ∧ well I sup/pose if you / had */**ac**cess to // 4. some of */**those** it'd be // -2. good */ **fun** //

A.II.2 British

(For the sounds of the individual tone units, see below Part III.)

A.II.2.1 'You've got to have a system' PLAY ◄

F₁   // .2 d'you / have to have a */ **health** cer/**tif**icate//

F₂   // 1.3 ∧ you get pro*/**vid**ed with */ **that**   // .1. when you go */**in** //

F₁   *// 1 **oh** //

M   // -3 if you can */**walk** / ... // .1. ∧ you're */**healthy** //

F₁   // 5. ∧ oh / isn't that */**nice** of her */// 1. **yes** //

M   *// <u>5</u> **very** / nice //

F₁   // 5.3 ∧ now you */ **were**n't so */ **crowd**ed // .1. on the way */**back** *// 2. **were** you //

M   // .1- ∧ this is a / constant / damn */ **nuis**ance // .1- ∧ that you're / suddenly / called upon for */**pass**ports // .1. ∧ / or / ∧ / called upon for */ **tick**ets // 1. ∧ or */ **land**ing / cards //

F₂   // .1. ∧ well it / isn't / really / when you've got a */ **sys**tem // .1- ∧ you've / got to / have a */ **sys**tem // .1- ∧ and I / think I */ **have** that / system // .1- ∧ from / long ex*/ **per**ience // -3 ∧ you've / got to know / where your */ **pass**ports / are // -3 ∧ you've / got to know / where your */ **tick**ets / are // -3 where your */**board**ing cards / are // ∧ and if you / can't put your / hand . . . // .3 ∧ I like to keep / one side of my */**hand**bag for // .1- only / those*/ **art**icles // . . . so . . . // 4. ∧ and then */**hope**fully if . . . // 4. Wally's got a */ **pock**et // 4. ∧ a / breast */**pock**et // 4. ∧ in his */ **shirt** // 4. ∧ to / slip the */**board**ing cards / into // .1. then they're / easily / pulled */ **out** // .1. otherwise I / just have to / hold them in my */**hand** // .1. ∧ because you / don't want to go / fumbling for */**those** when you're / going / through *// 1. **any**way you'll // .1- find that it's as / easy as */**Pi** // .1- easy as */**Pi** dear //

F₁   // 5. ∧ oh / isn't that */ **nice** of her to // .1. send */ **that** //

A.II.2.2 Pipeline

Scene 13

PLAY ◀ Sound A.II.2.2a

Kay Sanderson: // 4. ∧ the / only thing that / needs to be */ **said** about / this is that // 4. all the in/structions you */ **need** are // .1. on the piece of */ **pa**per / ∧ em // 4. ∧ so you / don't need to re/fer to / any of us */ **lurk**ing // .1. ∧ un/less it's / something you know /urgent / ∧ to do with << .3 ∧ you */ **know** >> you've / broken your */ **ank**le or / something // .3 ∧ but / other*/**wise** // .3 ∧ you're / on your */ **own** and // .1- all the information you / need is */ **here** // .1. ∧ but / we wi-want to have */ **some** responsi/ bility of // .1- telling you / when things */ **fin**ish //

?:   *// 1 **yes** and / there'll be // .1. strict */ **pen**alties . . .

Kay Sanderson: . . . there // .1. ∧ and / these are very /strictly */ **time** limited as // .1. pointed / out be*/**fore**/ ∧ // .3 o*/**kay** so who // -2. ever's going to / take these in*/**struc**tions . . .

[chat]

?:   // .3 . . . / read them out */ **loud** //

Kay Sanderson: // .3 ∧ you're / on your */ **own** //

Laura [reading]:   // 4. your / company is / bid- / bidding to / build a */ **pipe**line con/necting a // 4. recently dis/covered */ **oil** field to // .1. on-shore fa/cilities on the / northeast / coast of */ **Scot**land // .3 ∧ your / team has been in/vited to / take part in the / final / qualifying */ **round** to select // .1. members of the / project */ **team** / ∧ // .1. final selection will be / judged on the de/gree to which / team / working skills are dis/played / during this */ **task** // 4. ∧ the / task is to be es*/**tab**li — // .1. ∧ is to es/tablish a / pipeline to / carry ma/terial between the / recently . . . com/missioned . . .

[chat]

// .1.3 ∧ po/sitioned on */ **one** / side of the . . . */ **room** // .1. ∧ to the / onshore col/lection fa/cilities on the */ **other** / side of the / room //

?:   // .2 ∧ is / that the */ **buck**et //

Laura: // .1. ∧ is / that the */ **buck**et */ // 1 **right** //

Scene 14

PLAY 🔊 Sound A.II.2.2b

Charles: [reading]:   // 4. ∧ the / task will / be com*/**ple**ted when // .3 four / minibarrels con/taining / black */ **gold** have been suc//.3 cessfully */ **trans**ferred // 4. via the */ **pipe**line // .1 into the */ **res**ervoir //.3 ∧ the / gap / marked with */ **tape** / represents the // .3 north */ **sea** and // 4. anything or */ **any**one // .3 touching the */ **ground** // .3 in between the */ **tape** will be // .1. swept a*/**way** // .3 therefore the / pipeline / must remain sus/pended at / all */ **times** and should / have a // .3 minimum of / three human sup*/**port**ers // .1. when com*/**plet**ed //

Scene 24

PLAY 🔊 Sound A.II.2.2c

Lucas: // .1. ∧ so we've / got */ **five** // 4. ∧ so we can have / six */ **pipes** //

Charles: // .3 ∧ we've got /four */ **long** ones and // .1. four */ **small** /ones //

Z: // 4. ∧ so you want the / long one like */ **that** and then // .1. short one then */ **long** one then //

Y: * // 1 **yeah** *// 13 **that** makes */ **sense** //

Charles: // ∧ so you want the / long one . . . */ 1 **yeah** // 4. ∧ the / long ones / straight */ **out** and the // .1. short ones a*/**cross** //

Lucas: //.1. ∧ so we've got to / roll a little */ **thing** down it //.1.∧ so it's / got to go / down */ **hill** //

Y: *// 1 **yeah** so it's got to . . .

Charles: // 4. yeah but you can */ **move** it //

[chat]

Z: *// 1 **yeah** we've // 4. got people */ **hold**ing it //

Y: // 4. ∧ so if somebody can / just sort of / ∧ / whizz down *// **here** and can // 4. just sort of / hold it */ **up** and . . .

Charles: // 4. ∧ if you / have one / person in / each */ **cor**ner // .1. ∧ then you can / move it / down to the */ **next** corner *// 1 **yeah** //

Scene 25

PLAY 🔊 Sound A.II.2.2d

?:   // .<u>2</u> ∧ are — / these are / all the */ **same** //

?:   *// 1 **yeah** //

?:   // <u>4</u> ∧ they're / not at */ **right** angles at *// 1 **all** *// 1 **are** they //

[chat]

?:   // .1. they're the only / people that can / touch the */ **barrels** //

Scene 26

PLAY 🔊 Sound A.II.2.2e

Vince: // .1. ∧ and / what are the */ **mini**barrels //

A: // .<u>2</u> ∧ and then / ∧ / is it the */ **golf ball** //

Vince: // 3 o*/**kay** well . . . // 4. ∧ the / minibarrels can / only be */ **hand**led by // .1. someone / wearing the cor/rect */ **safe**ty gear //

A: // 4 ∧ so / that means / you have to / put it / in the */ **end** I / think and // 4 we / have to like */ **tip** it and // 4 as it's / going */ **down** // 4 you have to be like */ **guid**ed to col//<u>3</u> lect at the / other */ **end** so // 4 we have to like */ **hold** it about // 4 half way a*/**long** so // 4. you can go */ **through** . . . *// 4 **but** // .1. we're / only allowed / one / person on / each of those */ **is**lands so // <u>4</u> you're going to have to / go on */ **one** . . . // <u>4</u> on your */ **own** and // 5. someone's going to / have to / guide you / on it and */ **off** it //

Scene 27

PLAY 🔊 Sound A.II.2.2f

Y: // ∧ so / where are the . . .

John: // .1+ yeah where */ **are** the / barrels //

Laura: // .1. one at / this side / one at the */ **oth**er side to col//.1. lect and / put it */ **in** //

[chat]

Charles: // ∧ so we're going to / have to have / one . . .

?:   */ 1 **yeah** //

Lucas: // .2 so we should / all just / get in a */ **line** and just // .2 push it a*/**long** //

?:   // 5. ∧ un/less you want to / make the / pipeline */ **first** //

?:   // 13 ∧ yeah it'd be */ **good** */ **that** //

Lucas: // .1. yeah / build it / over */ **here** and just // .1. pass it a*/**long** //

John: */ 1 **yeah** and then like // .1.3 put the */ **is**lands out */ **first** //

Z: */ 1 **yeah** // .1.3 get people ′ in po*/**si** tion and */ **then** . . .

Laura: */ 1 **yeah** and // .1. then we can / pass the / pieces a*/**cross** //

?:   */ 1 yeah //

Scene 28

PLAY ◀ Sound A.II.2.2g

Laura: // 4. ∧ well I / take it as / soon as you / get a/cross the */ **sea** you can // .1. stand on / that side with/out the */ **is**lands //

John₂:// .2 ∧ so / would it be a / good i/dea if we / split into / two */ **groups** and then we // .2 build ′ half the / pipework at / each */ **end** and // .2 then just con*/**nect** them //

John₂:// .1. ∧ we can / go a/cross through the */ **is**lands */ 2. **can't** we //

Parul: //.1. ∧ yeah and / one person can / sort of I guess / pick up */ **all** of them //

John₂: // .1. ∧ is that a / good i/dea or */ **not** //

Parul: // .2. ∧ and / are we ′ going to have to / make the / islands in a */ **zig**zag / pattern //

?:   */ 1 **yeah** //

Paul: // .3 ∧ yeah I / think that that's / probably */ **best** if we did / half . . . / one half / . . . // 4. ∧ and then / . . . the other half in the */ **mid**dle //

David: // 4. now we've got an i/dea of like the / zig zag */ **of** it //

Laura: // .2 are we allowed to / move the islands / once we've laid them */ **down** //

David: */ 1 **no** //

?:   // 1 ∧ we're */ **not** //

David: */ 1 **no** // 4 I / don't */ **think** so //

Laura: // 4 ∧ well it / doesn't actually . . .

Paul: // 5 ∧ it / doesn't */ **say** that//

David: ∧ oh it doesn't / say that then */// 53 **I** don't */ **know** //

Laura: // ∧ well it / says that however you can // .1. ∧ you're / fortunate that you can po/
sition ′ these to / suit your ′ favoured */ **route** . . . // 4. ∧ so it / doesn't say you / can't
*/ **change** them it // .1. just says */ **one** on // .1. each */ **is**land so you can . . . yeah //
.3 lie it *// **down** // .3 step on */ **that** one then . . .

Rosani: // .3 lift */ **that** one up and . . .

Scene 29

PLAY ◀ Sound A.II.2.2h

A: *// 1 **see** // .2 ∧ isn't that the */ **is**land that we're *// 2 **gett**ing to / ∧ and then we're //
.1. bringing them / over */ **here** // 4. ∧ 'cause of course we / wouldn't / start on the */
island *// 1 **would** we // 4. ∧ so we / have to / get over */ **there** // .3 get */ **them** / ∧ //
.1. bring them */ **back** // 5 oh */ **blim**ey //

David: // .1. ∧ so we've / had about / ten */ **min**utes //

Scene 63

PLAY ◀ Sound A.II.2.2i

Kay Sanderson: // ∧ em / when I was . . . // 4. ∧ I / didn't come */ **close** up to / your dis/
cussions but // 4. when I / saw you from a */ **dis**tance I // .3 did see that the / four
the / six of you were / facing */ **in**wards and you ap*//4 **peared** to be / kind of *//
1- **list**ening to each / other so // .1. I was im*/**pressed** by / that // 4 ∧ I / thought for
your / first */ **shot** you — you kind of // .3 started to / act as a */ **team** you // .1. didn't
frag/ment im*/**med**iately so th- that was // .1. that was / quite im*/**press**ive . . . em //
4. ∧ in / terms of the / next ac*/**tiv**ity . . . // .2 is there / anything you've / learnt from */
this one / ∧ that you // .2 think you might like to / roll into the */ **next one** //

David: // .1. time */ **man**agement / should be / better //

Laura: *// 1 **yeah** *// 1 **def**initely //

Kay Sanderson: // .1. tell me a bit / more about this / time */ **man**agement //

David: // 4. ∧ well / we didn't */ **real**ize . . . // .1. we didn't / know there was an ex/act */ **time**
limit / well . . .

Laura: // .1. until the / **end** //

David: // 4. ∧ we / knew there was an ex/act */ **time** limit // .1. ∧ but we / didn't know / what
it */ **was** . . . // .1. when we / didn't . . . when we / found out at the */ **end** what it /
was so . . . then we were // .1. ∧ we / just thought */ **ah** // ∧ we'll / take about a / few
minutes . . .

Rosani: // 4 ∧ to */ **read** them //

[chat]

Laura: // .1. ∧ we / weren't a/ware that the / time-limit */ **mat**tered //

Kay Sanderson: // .3 ∧ so if / that . . . / that was at the / bottom of the */ **list** *// 2 **was** it . . . so // .1. what does */ **that** kind of sug/gest to you //

David: // 4. ∧ well it / means the */ **next** time as // <u>4</u> soon as we / get the */ **pap**er we're // .1. going to start */ **tim**ing //

Paul: // .1. check the */ **tim**ing *// 1 **yeah** //

Kay Sanderson: // .1. ∧ so I / act — / ∧ I / actually had / timed you as */ **well** so I *// 1 **stop**ped you but I mean it's // .1. getting / right to the */ **bot**tom *// 1 **isn't** it and // .1. making sure that you / all */ **know** it be/fore you . . . // .1. ∧ be/fore you dash */ **off** // .1. ∧ we / did / notice that / nobody */ **was** in fact / timing you al//.1. though you had / twenty-five */ **min**utes // .1. ∧ so you're / kind of re/lying on the / out */ **side** though it might . . . em . . . // .1. ∧ so / what you'd / like to im/prove is your */ **time** management . . . just // ∧ just / run me / through . . . / how . . . // <u>4</u> a/part from */ **know**ing what the / time is // .1. how would you */ **do** time / management //

Laura: // .1. maybe like / call it */ **out** //

?:   *// 1 **yeah** // .1. call it */ **out** //

Paul: // 5. give */ **warn**ings //

?:   // .1. maybe / like / ten minutes to */ **go** //

Laura: // .3 five */ **min**utes or de//.1. pending on how/ever much / time we're */ **giv**en //

Kay Sanderson: // 4. going / on to the */ **sec**ond / question which is // 4. really a/bout your/ self as a */ **team** as . . . // <u>4</u> ∧ for/getting a/bout the */ **task** which I // .1.3 think you / did very */ **well** */ **act**ually . . . // .1. what kind of . . . / how do you / think you */ **gel** as a / team //

[chat]

Paul: // ∧ we'd / only just / met a/bout like . . .

?:   // .1.3 ∧ that's / probably what / makes it */ **bet**ter */ **act**ually //

?:   // .1.3 ∧ it was / good that / everybody */ **list**ened to each */ **oth**er and like . . . // .1. nobody like / ∧ / started */ **dom**inating // .3 you should / go over */ **there** and // you should / go . . .

Laura: // .1. everybody / made sug*/**ges**tions //

Kay Sanderson: // .1. that's */ **good** // 4. ∧ so . . . in / terms of */ **gen**eral . . . // 4 ∧ i*/**deas** that you might / get about // 4. how teams */ **work** // <u>4</u> ∧ ig/noring / you */ **six** but // <u>4</u> just / thinking in */ **gen**eral // .1. what . . . er / have you / learnt about / teams from / this ac*/**tiv**ity if *// 1 **any**thing //

Paul: // .1.3 ∧ I / think communi*/**ca**tion's / probably the / most im*/**port**ant bit //

Rosani: // 5. ∧ yeah you / need to */ **talk** to each / other //

Laura: // 4. ∧ yeah it's a / lot / easier to */ **solve** a / problem when you can like // .1. bounce
           i*/**deas** off each / other // .1. ∧ than just / stand there and / try to / think it */ **out** //

Paul: // <u>4</u> ∧ 'cause if we / actually */ **did** it like // 4. should we / chuck the */ **is**lands / in and
           just like // 4. try to / make this / pipe straighta*/**way** we // .1. probably would've / just
           com/pletely / messed it */ **up** //

Laura: // .1. ∧ yeah or / broken one of the */ **rules** or / something //

Kay Sanderson: // 4. ∧ so it's / quite im/portant that / members of the / team kind of / take
           a / pause and / think about what / everybody has to / say be*/**fore** they start // .1.
           actually */ **do**ing it // .1. ∧ I / noticed / actually that / some of you were / rather / keen
           to get / ∧ */ **touch**ing the / pipes you know //

Paul: // .1. I was / straight */ **in** there //

Kay Sanderson: // 1 ∧ that's */ **cool** *// 13 **that** works */ **well** *// 1 **too** //

Paul: // 5.3 ∧ we were in/tent on / looking for the */ **gold** */**first** //

Paul: // yeah we were / like that was . . . // .1.3 that was the */ **main** */ **thing** that was / just
           like . . . that was . . .

Kay Sanderson: // <u>4</u> ∧ in / terms of the / whole / ∧ */ **morn**ing // 4. ∧ 'cause you've got a/
           nother / couple of */**ex**ercises / ∧ // .1.3 ∧ be/cause you al/ready work */ **well** as a
           */ **group** I / did — I // .1.3 thought you were / quite im*/**press**ive as a / **group** it //
           4. might be / worth */ **try**ing // .1. different */ **roles** with *// 1 **in** the / group so // .1.
           just have a */ **think** about // .1. what your / role was in */ **this** group // 1 ∧ the — the
           */ **last** ex — // 1 ∧ ac*/**tiv**ity // what . . . it's / something that we . . . // 4. ∧ it's / not on
           this */ **list** but just // .1// .1.3 think about your */ **own** */ **role** // 3 ∧ you*/ **know** // .1.
           how you con*/**trib**uted to it / all — // .1. all */**hap**pening and // .1. maybe / make a /
           couple of / notes to your/self about / what you */ **per**sonally con/tributed // 3 ∧ you
           */ **know** // .3 give yourself a / gold / star for */ **this** or a kind of // .3 trying */ **hard** or
           // .1. something — / some aspects of /team work that you'd like to im*/**prove** and //
           .1. maybe just / make a / quick */ **note** of it on . . . *// 13 **some**where on */**here** // 2. ∧
           o*/**kay** // .3 ∧ I / won't ask you to / tell me what it */ **is** but just / think about . . . the //
           .1+ things that */ **you** contributed *// 1 **per**sonally //

Part III

Analysis guide with detailed commentary

Analysis guide

1 Semantic level, general categories

1.1 Logical metafunction: unit 'sequence'

SEQUENCE TYPE	(a) unrelated
	(b) equal weight
	(c) unequal weight

1.2 Interpersonal metafunction: unit 'move'

| SPEECH FUNCTION | (a) proposition: statement / question |
| | (b) proposal: offer / command |

1.3 Experiential metafunction: unit 'figure'

FIGURE TYPE	(a) doing and happening
	(b) sensing and saying
	(c) being and having

2 Lexicogrammatical level: 'clausal' grammar

Base unit: clause; systems realized structurally

2.1 Logical metafunction: unit 'clause nexus'

INTERDEPENDENCY ('TAXIS')	(a) paratactic
	(b) hypotactic
LOGICAL-SEMANTIC RELATION	(a) expansion: elaborating / extending / enhancing
	(b) projection: locution / idea

NOTE: The elements of structure realizing the systems of the clause nexus are shown by symbols as follows:

INTERDEPENDENCY

| parataxis: | Arabic numerals | 1 2 3 . . . |
| hypotaxis: | Greek letters | α β γ . . . |

LOGICAL-SEMANTIC RELATIONS

elaborating:	'equals' sign	=
extending:	'plus' sign	+
enhancing:	multiplication sign	×
idea:	single quotation mark	'
locution:	double quotation mark	"

These are combined to form complex symbols, e.g.

1=2   paratactic elaborating nexus
α 'β   hypotactic idea nexus

The unit formed by a clause nexus, and by any string of related clause nexuses, is called a 'clause complex'. The symbols combine to show the total structure; e.g. *it grew because we watered it and we fed it*:

either   α ×β1 β+2   or   α ×β(1 +2)

These can, of course, be converted into conventional tree diagrams:

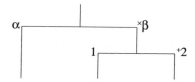

2.2   Interpersonal metafunction: unit 'clause'

MOOD	(a) indicative: declarative / wh- interrogative / polar interrogative (b) imperative (c) exclamative (d) moodless
POLARITY	(a) positive
	(b) negative
MODALITY	(a) modalization: probability / usuality
	(b) modulation: obligation / readiness (inclination / ability)
MOODTAG (declarative or imperative)	(a) polarity reversed
	(b) polarity constant

Elements of structure realizing MOOD systems:

(1) Mood: Subject, Finite, Modal Adjunct
(2) Residue: Predicator, Complement, Circumstantial Adjunct

2.3   Experiential metafunction: unit 'clause'

TRANSITIVITY: PROCESS TYPE	(a) material (b) behavioural (c) mental (d) verbal (e) relational (f) existential

Elements of structure realizing TRANSITIVITY system:

(1) Process

(2) Participants:
[ergative perspective] Medium, Agent, Range, Beneficiary
[transitive perspective]

material:	Actor, Goal, Scope, Recipient, Client
behavioural:	Behaver
mental:	Senser, Phenomenon
verbal:	Sayer, Target, Verbiage, Receiver
relational:	Token, Value; Identified, Identifier; Carrier, Attribute
existential:	Existent

(3) Circumstances
Extent, Duration, Manner, Cause, Contingency, Accompaniment, Matter, Angle, Role

2.4   Textual metafunction: unit 'clause'

THEME	(a) unmarked (b) marked: Adjunct theme / Complement theme / Predicator theme

Elements of structure realizing THEME systems:
(1) Theme: Textual Theme, Interpersonal Theme, Topical Theme
(2) Rheme

3   Lexicogrammatical level: 'informational' grammar

Base unit: information unit; systems realized by intonation

3.1   Logical metafunction: unit 'information unit nexus'

System	terms (features)	realization	associated features in clause grammar	IGBE number
STATUS1	(a) equal	tones 3^1	paratactic 1^2	Systems 3, 5
	(b) unequal	tones 4^1 or 1^4	hypotactic β^α or α^β	
STATUS2	(a) repetitive (b) other	tone concord	elaborating	System 6
RELATIVE CLAUSE TYPE [non-systemic]	(a) descriptive (hypotactic)	tone concord (often with silent Ictus)	hypotactic elaborating α^=β	System 4
	(b) defining (embedded)	[no separate tone unit]		

3.2   Logical and textual metafunctions: units 'clause/information unit'

System	terms (features)	realization	IGBE number
INFORMATION DISTRIBUTION (ɴTONALITY)	(a) unmarked	information unit = clause ('unmarked tonality')	System 1
	(b) marked	information unit not = clause ('marked tonality')	

3.3   Textual metafunction: unit 'information unit'

System	terms (features)	realization	*IGBE* number
INFORMATION POINTING	(a) single focus (major only)	one tonic segment (any tone)	System 19
	(b) dual focus (major + minor)	two tonic segments (tones 13 or 53)	

System	terms (features)	realization	*IGBE* number
INFORMATION FOCUS (↘TONICITY)	(a) unmarked	tonic on final lexical item ('unmarked tonicity')	Systems 8–14
	(b) marked	tonic elsewhere: non-final, or on grammatical item ('marked tonicity')	

Elements of structure realizing INFORMATION systems:
(1) New
(2) Given: Pre-focal, Post-focal

3.4   Interpersonal metafunction: unit 'information unit'

3.4.1   Clause MOOD: declarative

System	terms (features)	realization	*IGBE* number
PROPOSITION TYPE	(a) (neutral) statement	tone 1, Fall	System 18
	(b) querying statement	tone 2, Rise	
DECLARATIVE KEY	(a) neutral	tone 1., mid-Fall	System 22
	(b) strong	tone 1+, high Fall	
	(c) mild	tone 1- low Fall	
DECLARATIVE FORCE	(a) neutral	tone .1, steady Pretonic	System 23
	(b) insistent	tone -1, bouncy Pretonic	
RESERVATION	(a) (neutral) unreserved	tone 1, Fall	System 15
	(b) reserved, contingent	tone 4̲, low Fall-rising	
DECLARATIVE COMMITMENT	(a) neutral	tone 1, Fall	System 16
	(b) uncommitted	tone -3, low Level-rising	
	(c) committed	tone 5, Rise-falling	
AGREEMENT	(a) neutral	tone .1, Fall	System 17
	(b) confirmatory (agreeing, approving)	tone 3, Level-rising	
	(c) contradictory (challenging)	tone 2, Rise	
ENLISTMENT (Logical)	(a) neutral	tone .1, steady Pretonic	System 24
	(b) listing	tone . . . 1, lilting Pretonic	

3.4.2 Clause MOOD: interrogative (polar or lexical)

System	terms (features)	realization	*IGBE* number
SPECIFICATION OF QUERY (Textual)	(a) (neutral) query point unspecified	tone 2., Rise	System 27
	(b) query point specified	tone 2, Fall-Rise	
INVOLVEMENT	(a) neutral	tone .2, high Pretonic	System 29
	(b) involved	tone -2, low Pretonic	

3.4.2.1 Clause MOOD: interrogative: polar

System	terms (features)	realization	*IGBE* number
POLAR INTERROGATIVE KEY	(a) neutral	tone 2, Rise	System 28
	(b) strong, demanding	tone 1, Fall	
INTERROGATIVE COMMITMENT	(a) neutral	tone 2, Rise	System 30
	(b) uncommitted	tone -3, low Pretonic + Level-rising	
	(c) committed, surprised	tone 5, Rise-falling	
MULTIPLE QUESTION TYPE	(a) alternative question	tone 2 $(\ldots^n)$ ^ tone 1	System 32
	(b) listing question	tone 2 $(\ldots^n)$	

3.4.2.2 Clause MOOD: interrogative: lexical

System	terms (features)	realization	IGBE number
LEXICAL INTERROGATIVE KEY	(a) neutral	tone 1, Fall	System 25
	(b) mild	tone 2, Rise	
RELATION TO PREVIOUS DISCOURSE (Textual)	(a) neutral	tone 1, Fall	System 26
	(b) 'echo' question	tone 2, Rise; focus on WH- item	

3.4.3 Clause MOOD: imperative

System	terms (features)	realization	IGBE number
IMPERATIVE KEY (POSITIVE)	(a) (neutral) command	tone 1, Fall	System 33
	(b) mild command, request	tone .3, Level-rising, mid Pretonic	
IMPERATIVE KEY (NEGATIVE)	(a) (neutral) command	tone .3, Level-rising, mid Pretonic	System 34
	(b) strong command, prohibition	tone 1, Fall	
IMPERATIVE FORCE	(a) neutral	tone 1, Fall	System 37
	(b) compromising ('at least ...)	tone 4, low Fall-rising	System 37
	(c) definitive ('... and that's it!')	tone 5, low Rise-falling	System 35
	(d) warning	tone -3, Level-rising, low Pretonic	
PROPOSAL TYPE	(a) (neutral) command	tone 1, Fall or tone 3, Level-rising	System 38
	(b) querying command	tone 2, Rise	

3.4.4 Clause MOOD: *exclamative and moodless*

System	terms (features)	realization	*IGBE* number
EXCLAMATIVE KEY	(a) (neutral) exclamation	tone 5., high Rise-falling	system 39
	(b) strong: contempt, wonder	tone 5, low Rise-falling, breathy voice quality	
VOCATIVE KEY	(a) commanding, summoning	tone 1, Fall	System 40
	(b) querying, inviting	tone 2, Rise	
	(c) warning	tone -3, low to Level-rising	
	(d) requesting, beckoning	tone .3, mid to Level-rising	
	(e) addressing, singling out	tone 4, Fall-rising	
	(f) insisting	tone 5., high Rise-falling	
	(g) reproaching	tone 5, low Rise-falling	

4   Phonological level

TONALITY: distribution of utterance into tone units, with location of boundaries

RHYTHM: distribution of utterance into feet (metric units) with location of boundaries

TONICITY: distribution of utterance into Tonic and Pretonic, with location of tonic foot

TONE, primary:

    1   Fall

    2   Rise or fall-rise

    3   Level-rising

    4   Fall-rising

    5   Rise-falling

   13   Fall plus level-rising

   53   Rise-falling plus level-rising

TONE, secondary:

		Pretonic			Tonic
1	.1	steady (level, falling, rising	x	1+	wide (high fall)
	-1	bouncing		1.	medium (mid fall)
	..1	listing		1-	low (narrow fall)
2	.2	high (level, falling, rising)	x	2.	straight (high rise)
	-2	low (level, falling, rising)		2	broken (high fall-rise)
3	.3	mid (level)			
	-3	low (level)			
4				4.	high fall-rising
4				4	low fall-rising
5				5.	high rise-falling
5				5	low rise-falling

Tones 13 and 53 allow all variants of tones 1 and 5, but only the low variant of tone 3.

Conventional symbols

//	tone unit boundary (always also foot boundary)
/	foot boundary within tone unit (always also syllable boundary)
*/[**bold**]	tonic syllable (in Praat */.CAPS) (*//[**bold**] if initial in tone unit)
^	silent Ictus
..	pause
<< >>	included tone unit

Elements of structure of TONE UNIT
  (optional) Pretonic ^ Tonic

Elements of structure of FOOT
  Ictus ^ (optional) Remiss

The Analysis Guide presents a summary of the principal systems that make up the 'information grammar' of English — that part of the grammar that is realized by intonation; and also of the main systems of 'clause grammar' that provide the environment in which the intonational systems operate to create meaning.

The Analysis Guide can be used as a checklist when investigating spoken discourse. We are not offering a specific protocol for the design of a coding sheet, since discourse analysts will have their own priorities and their own preferred framework and layout. But as a final note we append two short passages from one of the texts in this Appendix II accompanied by annotations based on the categories outlined in the Guide.

For the grammar see Halliday, ed. Matthiessen 2004, or any of a number of other systemic-functional accounts of the grammar of present-day English. These are listed under a separate heading in the Bibliography that follows.

Texts with detailed commentary

1 'You've got to have a system'
[PLAY] Sound A.II.2.1(entire)

F₁ // .2 d'you / have to have a */ **health** cer/**tif**icate // [PLAY]
F₂ // 1.3 ∧ you get pro*/**vid**ed with */ **that** [PLAY]
  // .1. when you go */**in** // [PLAY]
F₁ *// 1 **oh** // [PLAY]
M // -3 if you can */**walk** /. . . // [PLAY]
  // .1. ∧ you're */**healthy** // [PLAY]
F₁ // 5. ∧ oh / isn't that */**nice** of her // [PLAY]
  *// 1. **yes** // [PLAY]
M *// <u>5</u> **very** / nice // [PLAY]
F₁ // 5.3 ∧ now you */ **were**n't so */ **crowd**ed // [PLAY]
  // .1. on the way */**back** */ 2. **were** you // [PLAY]
M // .1- ∧ this is a / constant / damn */ **nuis**ance // [PLAY]
  // .1- ∧ that you're / suddenly / called upon for */**pass**ports // [PLAY]
  // .1. ∧ / or / ∧ / called upon for */ **tick**ets // [PLAY]
  // 1. ∧ or */ **land**ing / cards // [PLAY]
F₂ // .1. ∧ well it / isn't / really / when you've got a */ **sys**tem // [PLAY]
  // .1- ∧ you've / got to / have a */ **sys**tem // [PLAY]
  // .1- ∧ and I / think I */ **have** that / system // [PLAY]
  // .1- ∧ from / long ex*/**per**ience / [PLAY]
  // -3 ∧ you've / got to know / where your */ **pass**ports / are // [PLAY]
  // -3 ∧ you've / got to know / where your */ **tick**ets / are // [PLAY]
  // -3 where your */**board**ing cards / are // [PLAY]
  // ∧ and if you / can't put your / hand . . . [PLAY]
  // .3 ∧ I like to keep / one side of my */**hand**bag for // [PLAY]
  // .1- only / those*/ **art**icles // . . . so . . . // [PLAY]
  // 4. ∧ and then */**hope**fully if . . . [PLAY]
  // 4. Wally's got a */ **pock**et // [PLAY]
  // 4. ∧ a / breast */**pock**et // [PLAY]
  // 4. ∧ in his */ **shirt** // [PLAY]
  // 4. ∧ to / slip the */**board**ing cards / into // [PLAY]
  // .1. then they're / easily / pulled */ **out** // [PLAY]
  // .1. otherwise I / just have to / hold them in my */**hand** // [PLAY]
  // .1. ∧ because you / don't want to go / fumbling for */**those** when you're / going / through // [PLAY]
  *// 1. **any**way you'll // [PLAY]
  // .1- find that it's as / easy as */**Pi** // [PLAY]
  // .1- easy as */**Pi** dear // [PLAY]
F₁ // 5. ∧ oh / isn't that */ **nice** of her to // [PLAY]
  // .1. send */ **that** // [PLAY]

The first speaker (F_1) uses what is for British English the unmarked Pretonic to tone 2 — the high one; and follows it with the 'sharp fall-rise' variant of the Tonic, in which the fall gives prominence to the item that is the object of the query, here the *health certificate*. The tone 2 rise then takes place on the salient syllable of the foot that is New: here *certificate*, which anyway is the only subsequent foot in the tone unit. The choice of a low Pretonic -2 would have been highly marked in this context, and would have meant 'is it possible that . . . ? I find it hard to believe'; while the simple rising Tonic 2. would not have singled out 'health certificate' as distinct from other possible objects of enquiry. The tonality is unmarked — one information unit, one clause.

The second speaker (F_2) responds to the question, putting the anaphoric *that* in characteristic position as minor Tonic, with the major Tonic focusing on the significant element in the answer. The passive allows *you* to remain in thematic position in the clause, as it was in the original question. The hypotactic temporal clause then forms another information unit; it carries another part of the answer to which some weight needs to be given ('provided when you go in' contrasts with 'have [before you go in]'), hence the tone 1. Another tone 3 here, while not impossible, would have suggested that 'when you go in' was of secondary importance; while a tone 4 would have imparted too much contrast, 'as opposed to when you come out'. Both tone 1's are in the neutral variety, not carrying any kind of special emphasis.

The third speaker (M) then comes in with a humorous aside, a hypotactic clause nexus of enhancing: condition, with the conditional clause coming first. The unmarked tone pattern for this would be 4 ^ 1; instead the speaker uses 3 ^ 1 with a low Pretonic, which presents it as a casual, throwaway line because less 'iffy' (3 not 4) and less involved (-3 not .3).

Meanwhile this speaker's quiet intervention is overtalked by F_1 who, apparently, is opening up a gift brought to her by the other two; her appreciative exclamation has the characteristic unmarked (high) falling tone (5.). M then echoes this; but he uses the low variety of the same tone (5̲), which imparts a feature of wonder that, here, is no doubt ironic.

F_1's next turn is obscure; the two authors interpret it differently. The version suggested here is a comment on the travellers' return air journey; the intonation presents *weren't* as the main focus of the question, tone 5 showing the speaker's concern 'I hope!'; there is then a minor focus on *crowded*, as an item which is essential but given, and *on the way back* comes as a separate unit of information in contrast with the implied 'as I know you were on the way out'. There is then an unmarked question tag, unmarked both for polarity (i.e. the polarity is reversed) and for key (tone 2) seeking confirmation.

M then pursues the documentation of the information required. The first two information units are in clear tone concord, the second elaborating the first by spelling out what it is that is 'a constant damn nuisance'. This pattern of tone 1 with a high Pretonic stepping down to a low Tonic is common with expressions of irritation and complaint; it foregrounds the interpersonal Epithet, whereas the Thing (the main noun) has no experiential content and is by then entirely predictable — the whole nominal group carries a prosody of 'I hate it'. The next two information units add further items to the nuisance list; but here the speaker switches to the mid-fall (unmarked) variety of tone 1, which gives them greater presence as items to be accounted for than if he had simply continued with the low (1-) Tonic.

Speaker F$_2$ counters this with another mid-fall (tone 1.) where the high (neutral) Pretonic of Given material, picking up M's motif, leads to a clear focus on the one New item *system*, but without the extra force that she could have given to it by using the high-fall (tone 1+, where the interpersonal key would have intruded — 'see?', which she didn't want). In the next unit, *system* is repeated, but as post-tonic (and therefore Given) following the focus on *have*. The *have* could have been mid-fall (tone 1.), but has been 'lowered' to tone 1- following the Pretonic *(I) think*, which jumps up to mark the beginning of the New. The same pattern is then repeated on / *long ex/perience*, which sounds very much like a true tone concord; that is, it comes over as a restatement of 'I have that system' (elaborating) rather than as an explanation of it (enhancing).

The same speaker continues by enumerating components of her system — knowing where things are, echoing the 'nuisance' items of the previous speaker (except that *boarding cards* replaces *landing cards*). For these she uses the marked low variety of tone 3 (tone -3); a sequence of such information units typically functions in this way, making a 'clause list' analogous to the '(nominal) group list' that makes up the 'listing' Pretonic (…1) to tone 1. She then starts to say what happens if you do not know, but breaks off in the middle of the *if* clause before the Tonic — the Pretonic suggests it would have been tone 4 — and comes back to expounding her system. This is done in one clause with two information units (marked tonality), tone 3 followed by tone 1 — two quanta of information both given equal weight.

The next eight tone units make up a single clause complex, of six clauses. The first four information units form one hypotactic conditional clause; this is followed by a fifth constituting a purpose clause that is hypotactic to (dependent on) the previous one. All have the same high (unmarked) variant of tone 4 which is congruent with their dependent status: the middle three form an elaborating triad (*if Wally's got a pocket, a breast pocket, in his shirt*), which is preceded by a comment Adjunct *hopefully* and followed by the purpose clause. This strongly reinforced condition is resolved, again in typical fashion by a tone 1, unmarked in both Pretonic and Tonic; the Tonic has been in its unmarked location throughout.

This is followed by a paratactic: extending 'or' clause, and this in turn by a hypotactic: enhancing 'because' clause, both on the same tone (.1.) giving each a parallel but informationally independent status. Finally there is a further hypotactic: enhancing 'when' clause which is appended post-tonically, the Tonic being on the anaphoric item *those* which (because this is marked focus) carries a considerable semantic load.

She then rounds off with an evaluation of her plan, introduced by *anyway* as a separate information unit with its characteristic tone 1, and then continued on two units in tone concord, each on a low tone 1-. This is the 'mild key' variant, so giving a sense of 'no more to it — nothing to worry about', while the second is a direct repetition of the first with the addition of the Vocative *dear*.

Speaker F$_1$ takes this as signing off and returns to the contemplation of her gift. She repeats her earlier exclamation on the same tone 5 but adds a 'reprise' on *to send that*, on tone 1, which locates the value in the act of giving rather than in the gift itself. She could have repeated the tone 5, to mark this out as an elaboration of the *that*; the difference is slight, but the choice of tone 1 presents the point as something that is new.

2   Pipeline Scene 29
PLAY

A: *// 1 **see** // .2 ∧ isn't that the */ **is**land that we're *// 2 **gett**ing to / ∧ and then we're //
.1. bringing them / over */ **here** // 4. ∧ 'cause of course we / wouldn't / start on the */
island *// 1 **would** we // 4. ∧ so we / have to / get over */ **there** // .3 get */ **them** / ∧ //
.1. bring them */ **back** // 5 oh */ **blim**ey //

David: // .1. ∧ so we've / had about / ten */ **min**utes //

The interactants are a group of students engaged in a time-limited simulation exercise in which they have to design a project for laying a pipeline from an oilfield in the North Sea to a port on the Scottish mainland. The speaker is one of the group.

*//1 **see** // PLAY

Clause; mental process of perception/cognition, formulaic like *look*, but whereas *look* is more behavioural (answer *I am looking*, not *I look*; cf. *watch!*) *see* is clearly mental (answer *I see*, not *I am seeing*) and means 'observe and understand'.
    Imperative mood, with unmarked falling tone in neutral key. [Where there is no Pretonic to tone 1 we do not usually assign +/./-, since strictly that depends on the relation of the Tonic to the end of the Pretonic — whether upjump, level, or downjump. But we can often recognize a marked choice, and this one is clearly not marked.]

//.2 isn't that the */ **is**land that we're //2 **gett**ing to . . . PLAY

Clause: relational-identifying, with *that* as Token and *the island* as Value; the visible object *that* as topical Theme. The mood is polar (yes/no) interrogative, with primary tone choice unmarked (tone 2) and the Pretonic (high) unmarked for involvement. The Tonic, however, has the marked (fall-rising) variant 2, which picks out *the island* as the particular point of the query.
    This fall-rising Tonic is then repeated on the relative clause *that we're getting to*. Now, if this had been a defining (embedded) relative clause, as the clause grammar suggests, we would have expected it to follow through post-tonically, simply continuing the rise. The tone concord (repeating tone 2) could be explained as just due to the length; but it is not in fact excessively long, and the informational grammar seems to be marking its status as a repetition. If we take it this way, as a non-defining (hypotactic) relative clause, equivalent to 'the island — which is where we're getting to', both tonality and tonicity become unmarked (two ranking clauses — two tone units, each with Tonic on final lexical item). Thus the two grammars are working in tension at this point.

and then we're //.1. bringing them / over */ **here** . . . PLAY

Clause: material, with Actor + Process + Goal + Location, with tonality and tonicity neutral — the focus in its unmarked position at the end. Circumstantial adverbs tend to be treated as lexical items, even if deictic; compare *back* and *there* below, and note how focus on *bringing* would have been clearly marked.

The mood is declarative, neutral in tone (tone 1) and in its unmarked variant for both Tonic (mid fall) and Pretonic. Here there is a total congruence between the informational and the clausal grammar.

// 4. ∧ 'cause of course we / wouldn't / start on the */ **is**land *// 1 **would** we // PLAY◀

Clause, forming a paratactic enhancing nexus with the previous one. The conjunction *because* is regularly hypotactic, with the second syllable salient; but it has now replaced *for* as a paratactic conjunction, in which function it typically has no salience and often loses its first syllable altogether, as here.

The clause is declarative, so the tone 4 is a marked option, giving a prosodic flavour of reservation or contingency — there is a 'but' or an 'if' somewhere around. But we need to make a distinction between global marking and local marking. Globally, the tone 4 is a marked option: the clause is not hypotactic to anything preceding or following. Locally, however, the sense of contrasting with 'bringing them over here' makes the tone 4 entirely predictable; we can think of it as being globally marked but locally unmarked.

The same distinction applies — but the other way round — to the choice of tonicity. The focus is on the final lexical item: globally, in the system of the language, that is the unmarked option. But *island* is clearly given: not merely in that the word has occurred shortly before, but in that the referent is also the same island. Locally, therefore, the focus on *island* is marked; and it could easily have been avoided by putting the focus on *start*. The effect is to reinforce the contrast set up by the tone 4: 'whatever else we might do, we wouldn't . . . '.

This is a tagged declarative: *we wouldn't . . ., would we?*. Such tags are very frequent in informal spontaneous conversation, and there is a complex system operating with a number of options: same or separate tone unit; if separate, rising or falling tone; polarity reversed or constant — these are the main ones. The speaker preserves the finite, *would . . . would*, which is normal (though not exceptionless), and reverses the polarity, which is also the unmarked option. She combines these with tone 1, which — since the tag is grammatically a polar interrogative clause — is in what we have called a 'strong key': she is not opening up her proposition to be questioned (the difference can be heard clearly if it is replaced by a tone 2 *// 2 **would** we //) but rather demanding confirmation and assent — for which in any case she does not wait.

// 4. ∧ so we have to / get over */ **there** //.3 get */ **them** //.1. bring them */ **back** //
PLAY◀

It is helpful to take these three clauses all together, since they form an information unit complex combining two nexuses. Clausally they are all declaratives, the second and third being elliptical: *we have to* is carried over to all of them. This is clearly indicated by the way the speaker has made it proclitic: if she had put an Ictus on *have* — a natural option — this would have located it in the Pretonic segment of the first tone unit, and taken it informationally out of the scope of the other two. As it is, the 'obligation' takes in all three information units.

All three clauses are material processes, the first having Actor as the only participant, the others having Actor and Goal. The first and last end with the locatives *there* and *back*, each carrying unmarked focus and so contrasting both with each other and with the earlier locative *here*. These in combination with the processes of 'fetching' (*get* 'go', *get* 'obtain' and *bring*) make up the main activity and central goal of the project, and the speaker organizes them into a highly structured informational sequence:

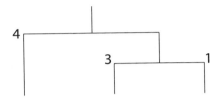

The first quantum of information, 'we go there', is marked by tone 4 as 'unequal status': its significance depends on, and will appear from, what follows. What follows, where the added weight of the tone 1 is reinforced by the presence of the new participant *them*, is a further nexus of two quanta having equal status but with the first being shown as incomplete by the tone 3. The 'housekeeping' of the tone 3, for which the speaker wants the unmarked (mid) Pretonic variant, forces the Tonic focus on to the pronoun *them*; this seems highly marked, since it is a grammatical not a lexical item; but its prominence turns out to be in line with the critical role that 'they' have in the unfolding drama — 'they' being the sections of the pipeline itself.

// 5 oh */ **blimey** // PLAY ◀

– at which point the speaker suddenly confronts the full complexity of what she has been proposing, and rounds off with an evaluative exclamation on its characteristic rise-falling tone.

//.1. ∧ so we've / had about / ten */ **min**utes // PLAY ◀

. . and it is left to David to come back to earth with a matter-or-fact relational process in declarative mood on a single tone unit with an unproblematic tone 1.

Bibliography

The bibliography contains a selection of books and articles that relate to the present volume, providing the context of ideas within which this study can be located. The list includes both key works from leading scholars of an earlier generation and essential writings by specialists of the present day. We have not attempted to give detailed references throughout the text; they would intrude too much, and in any case many of the items cited here have a broad general relevance for our approach rather than relating to particular features of the analysis. Where we have given a reference this indicates a more specific point of connection.

Allen, W. S. (1953, 1961). *Phonetics in Ancient India*. London Oriental Series, 1. London: Oxford University Press.

Banks, D. (2004*a*). 'Degrees of Newness.' In D. Banks (ed.)(2004*b*).

Banks, D. (ed.) (2004*b*). *Text and Texture, Systemic Functional Viewpoints on the Nature and Structure of Text*. Paris: L'Harmattan.

Beckman, M. E., and G. A. Elam (1997). 'Guidelines for ToBI Labelling,' ver. 3. The Ohio State University Research Foundation: http://www.ling.ohio-state.edu/research/phonetics/E_ToBI/.

Bowcher, W. L. (2003). 'Creating Informational Waves: Theme and New Choices in Play-by-Play Radio Sports Commentary.' In Masachiyo Amano (ed.), *Creation and Practical Use of Language Texts (proceedings of the Second International Conference for the Integrated Text Science)*. Nagoya University: Graduate School of Letters.

Bowcher, W. L. (2004). 'Theme and New in Play-by-Play Radio Sports Commentating.' In D. Banks (ed.), (2004*b*).

Brough, John. (1953). 'Some Indian Theories of Meaning.' *Transactions of the Philological Society*

Chun, D. M. (2002). *Discourse Intonation in L2 : from Theory and Research to Practice*. Amsterdam, Philadelphia: John Benjamins. Includes CD-ROM.

Ciompi, L. and J. Panksepp (2005). 'Energetic Effects of Emotions on Cognitions: Complementary Psychobiological and Psychosocial Findings.' In Ellis and Newton (eds).

Clark, J., and C. Yallop (1990, 1995). An Introduction to Phonetics and Phonology. Oxford: Blackwell.

Cléirigh, C. (1998). 'A Selectionist Model of The Genesis of Phonic Texture: systemic phonology and universal Darwinism.' Unpublished Ph.D. Thesis. University of Sydney.

Cummings, M. J. (1998). 'Lexical Repetition and the Given/New Distinction in Written English.' In Sheila Embleton (ed.), The 24th LACUS Forum 1997. Chapel Hill, N.C.: Linguistic Association of Canada and the United States.

Cummings, M. J. (1999). 'Functional sentence perspective, focus of information and semantic relations.' In Shin Ja Hwang and Arle Lommel (eds), *LACUS Forum XXV*. Lake Bluff, Ill.: Linguistic Association of Canada and the United States.

Cummings, M. J. (2000). 'The inference of given information in written text.' In Eija Ventola (ed.), *Discourse and Community: Doing Functional Linguistics*. Tübingen: Gunter Narr Verlag.

Cummings, M. J. (2001). 'Intuitive and Quantitative Analyses of Given/New in Texts.' In Jessica de Villiers and Robert J. Stainton (eds), *Communication in Linguistics: Vol. 1, Papers in Honour of Michael Gregory*. Toronto: GREF Publishers.

Davies, M. J. (1986). 'Literacy and Intonation.' In B. Couture (ed.), *Functional Approaches to Writing: Research Perspectives*. London & New York: Pinter Publishers.

Davies, M. J. (1989). 'Prosodic and Non-prosodic Cohesion in Speech and Writing,' *WORD* (Special Issue), *Systems, Structures and Discourse: selected papers from the fifteenth annual International Systemic Congress*. J.D Benson, P.H. Fries, W.S. Greaves, C. Matthiessen (eds).

Davies, M. J. (1992). 'Prosodic Cohesion in a Systemic Perspective: Philip Larkin reading "Toads Revisited"' In P. Tench (ed.).

Davies, M. J. (1994). 'Intonation IS visible in written English.' In Svetla Cmejrková, František Daneš, Eva Havlová (eds), *Writing vs Speaking: Language, Text, Discourse, Communication* (Proceedings of Conference held at the Czech Language Institute of the Academy of Sciences of the Czech Republic, Prague, 1992). Tübingen: Gunter Narr Verlag.

Deacon, T. (1997). *The Symbolic Species: the co-evolution of language and the human brain*. London: Allen Lane, the Penguin Press.

de Pijper, J. R. (1983). *Modelling British English Intonation*. Dordrecht: Foris Publications.

Donald, M. (1991). *Origins of the Modern Mind*. Boston: Harvard University Press.

Donald, M. (1991, 2001). *A Mind so Rare: the evolution of human consciousness*. New York: W. W. Norton.

Edelman, G. M. (1989). Neural Darwinism: the theory of neuronal group selection. Oxford: Oxford University Press.

Edelman, G. M. (1992). Bright Air, Brilliant Fire: on the matter of the mind. New York: Basic Books.

Edelman, G. M. and G. Tononi (2000). A Universe of Consciousness: how matter becomes imagination. New York: Basic Books.

Ellis, G. F. R. and J. A. Toronchuk (2005). 'Neural Development: affective and immune system influences.' In Ellis and Newton (eds).

Ellis, G. F. R. and N. Newton (eds) (2005). *Consciousness & Emotion: agency, conscious choice, and selective perception*. Amsterdam / Philadelphia: John Benjamins.

El Menoufy, Afaf (1969). *A Study of the Role of Intonation in the Grammar of English*. 2 vols; unpublished PhD thesis. University of London.

El Menoufy, Afaf. (1988). 'Intonation and Meaning in Spontaneous Discourse.' In James D. Benson, M. J. Cummings, and William S. Greaves (eds), 1–26. *Linguistics in a Systemic Perspective.* Amsterdam / Philadelphia: John Benjamins.

Firth, J. R. (1935). 'The Technique of Semantics,' *Transactions of the Philological Society.* Reprinted in Firth, J. R. (1957).

Firth, J. R. (1948). 'Sounds and prosodies,' *Transactions of the Philological Society.* Reprinted in Firth, J. R. (1957).

Firth, J. R. (1957). *Papers in Linguistics 1934 – 1951.* London: Oxford University Press.

Fries, P. H. (2002). 'The Flow of Information in a Written Text.' In Peter H. Fries, Michael Cummings, David Lockwood and William Spruiell (eds), *Relations and Functions within and around Language.* London: Continuum.

Gilbers, D., M. Schreuder and N. Knevel (2004). *On the Boundaries of Phonology and Phonetics.* Groningen: Department of Linguistics, University of Groningen.

Goldsmith, J. A. (1990). *Autosegmental and Metrical Phonology.* Oxford: Blackwell.

Greaves, W. S. (1988). 'An Experimental Validation of M.A.K. Halliday's System of Tone at Primary Delicacy in a Canadian Context' (co-authored with James D. Benson and D. Mendelsohn). In R. Fawcett and D. Young (eds), *New Developments in Systemic Linguistics.* London: Frances Pinter.

Greaves, W. S. (2007). 'Intonation in Systemic Functional Linguistics.' In R. Hasan, C. M. I. M. Matthiessen & J. J. Webster (eds), *Continuing Discourse on Language,* Vol. 2. London & Oakville: Equinox.

Grote, B., E. Hagen, A. Stein, and E. Teich (1996). 'Speech Production in Human-Machine Dialogue: A Natural Language Generation Perspective.' In E. Maier, S. Luperfoy and M. Mast (eds), *Dialogue Processing in Spoken Language Systems.* Berlin/New York: Springer-Verlag.

Halliday, M. A. K. (1963a). 'The Tones of English.' Archivum Linguisticum 15/128. Reprinted in Halliday (2005).

Halliday, M. A. K. (1963b). 'Intonation in English Grammar,' *Transactions of the Philological Society,* 143–169. Reprinted in Halliday (2005).

Halliday, M. A. K. (1967). *Intonation and Grammar in British English.* The Hague: Mouton (Janua Linguarum Series Practica 48).

Halliday, M. A. K. (1970a). *A Course in Spoken English: Intonation.* London: Oxford University Press.

Halliday, M. A. K. (1970b). 'Phonological (Prosodic) Analysis of the New Chinese Syllable (Modern Pekinese).' In Frank R. Palmer (ed.), *Prosodic Analysis.* London: Oxford University Press.

Halliday, M. A. K. (1975). *Learning How to Mean: Explorations in the Development of Language.* London: Edward Arnold (Explorations in Language Study); New York: American Elsevier.

Halliday, M. A. K. (1981). 'The Origin and Early Development of Chinese Phonological Theory' in R. E. Asher & E. J. A. Henderson (eds), *Towards a History of Phonetics.* Edinburgh: Edinburgh University Press.

Halliday, M. A. K. (1985a). 'Dimensions of Discourse Analysis: Grammar.' In Teun A. Van Dijk (ed.), *Handbook of Discourse Analysis.* London: Academic Press.

Halliday, M. A. K. (1985*b*). 'English Intonation as a Resource for Discourse.' In *Beiträge zur Phonetik und Linguistik 48: Festschrift in Honour of Arthur Delbridge*. Reprinted in Halliday (2005).

Halliday, M. A. K. (1985c). *Spoken and Written Language*. Geelong, Australia: Deakin University Press. Republished Oxford: Oxford University Press, 1989.

Halliday, M. A. K. (1985d). 'It's a fixed word order language is English,' *ITL Review of Applied Linguistics* 67–8.

Halliday, M. A. K. (1992). 'How do you mean?' In M. J. Davies and L. Ravelli (eds), *Advances in Systemic Linguistics: recent theory and practice*. London and New York: Pinter.

Halliday, M. A. K. (1993). 'A Systemic Interpretation of Peking Syllable Finals.' In Tench, P.(ed.).

Halliday, M. A. K. (2005). *Studies in English Language (Collected Works*, ed. Jonathan J. Webster, vol. 7). London & New York: Continuum.

Halliday, M.A.K., and R. Hasan. (1976). *Cohesion in English*. London: Longman.

Halliday, M. A. K. and Z. L. James (1993). 'A Quantitative Study of Polarity and Primary Tense in the English Finite Clause.' In J. M. Sinclair, M. Hoey & G. Fox (eds), *Techniques of Description: spoken and written discourse*. London & New York: Routledge.

Halliday, M.A.K, and C.M.I.M. Matthiessen (2004). *An Introduction to Functional Grammar* (3rd edition). London: Arnold.

Hammond, M. 1997. 'Optimality Theory and Prosody.' In D. Archangeli and D. T. Langendoen (eds), *Optimality Theory: an overview*. Cambridge: Blackwell.

Honeybone, P. (2004). 'The Rise of Optimality Theory in Mid-Twentieth Century London.' Paper presented to Edinburgh Linguistic Circle.

Ladd, D. R. (1996). *Intonational Phonology*. Cambridge: Cambridge University Press.

Matthiessen, C.M.I.M. (1992) 'Interpreting the Textual Metafunction.' In M. J. Davies & L. Ravelli (eds), *Advances in Systemic Linguistics: recent theory and practice*. London & New York: Pinter.

Matthiessen, C.M.I.M. (1995). 'Theme as an Enabling Resource in Ideational 'Knowledge' Construction.' *Thematic Development in English Text*. London & New York: Pinter.

Matthiessen, C.M.I.M., A. Lukin, D. Butt, C. Cléirigh, and C. Nesbitt (2005). 'A case study of multistratal analysis.' *Australian Review of Applied Linguistics*.

Ouafeu, Yves Talla Sando (2006). 'Listing intonation in Cameroon English speech' World Englishes, Vol. 25, No. 3/4, pp. 491–500.

Patel, Aniruddh D. (2008) *Music, Language, and the Brain*. Oxford University Press.

Prakasam, V. (1987). 'Aspects of word phonology.' In Halliday, M.A.K. and Robin P. Fawcett (eds), *New Developments in Systemic Linguistics*. London & New York: Pinter.

Prince, A. and P. Smolensky (1993). *Optimality Theory: Constraint Interaction in Generative Grammar*. Rutgers University Center for Cognitive Science Technical Report 2.

Silverman, K., M. Beckman, J. Pitrelli, M. Ostendorf, C. Wightman, P. Price, J. Pierrehumbert, and J. Hirschberg (1992). 'ToBI: A standard for labeling English prosody,' *Proceedings of the 1992 International Conference on Spoken Language Processing.*

Sinclair, J. McH, and M.R. Coulthard (1975). *Towards an Analysis of Discourse.* London: OUP

Stevens, S.S., J. Volkman and E.B. Newman (1937). 'A Scale for the Measurement of the Psychological Magnitude of Pitch.' In *Journal of Acoustical Society of America.*

Teich, E., E. Hagen, B. Grote, and John A. Bateman (1997). 'From Communicative Context to Speech: Integrating Dialogue Processing, Speech Production and Natural Language Generation.' In *Speech Communication,* February 1997.

Teich, E., C. Watson, and C. Pereira (2000). 'Matching a Tone-based and aTune-based approach to English Intonation for Concept-to-speech Generation.' *Proceedings of the 18th International Conference on Computational Linguistics (COLING), August 2000.* Saarbrücken.

Tench, P. (1988*a*). 'The Stylistic Potential of Intonation.' In N.Coupland (ed.), *Styles of Discourse.* London: Croom Helm.

Tench, P. (1988*b*). 'Specification of Intonation for Prototype Generator 2.' *COMMUNAL:* 1–40. Cardiff University: Centre for Language and Communication Research.

Tench, P. (1990). *The Roles of Intonation in English Discourse.* Frankfurt am Main: Peter Lang.

Tench, P. (ed.) (1992). *Studies in Systemic Phonology.* London: Pinter Publishers.

Tench, P. (1994). 'The Boundaries of Intonation Units.' In J.W. Lewis (ed.), *Studies in General and English Phonetics : In Honour of Professor J.D. 0'Connor.* London: Routledge

Tench, P. (1995). 'The Communicative Value of the Tone System of English.' In *Proceedings of the 9th International Symposium on Theoretical and Applied Linguistics.* Thessaloniki: Aristotle University.

Tench, P. (1996*a*). *The Intonation Systems of English.* London: Cassell Academic.

Tench, P. (1996*b*). 'Intonation and the Differentiation of Syntactical Patterns in English and German.' *International Journal of Applied Linguistics,* 6/2

Tench, P. (1997). 'The Fall and Rise of the Level Tone in English.' *Functions of Language,* 4/1: 1–22.

Tench, P. (2003). 'Processes of Semogenesis in English Intonation.' *Functions of Language,* 10/2.

't Hart, J., R. Collier, and A. Cohen (1990). *A Perceptual Study of Intonation: an experimental-phonetic approach to speech melody.* Cambridge: CUP.

Thibault, P.J. (2005). *Brain, Mind, and the Signifying Body: an ecosocial semiotic theory.* London & New York: Continuum.

Thwaite, A. (1997). *Language in Contexts.* Perth: Media Production Unit, Edith Cowan University.

Verdugo, Dolores Ramirez. (2002). 'Non-native interlanguage intonation systems: A study based on a computerized corpus of Spanish learners of English.' In *ICAME Journal* Computers in English Linguistics No. 26.

Wells, J. C. (2006). *English Intonation: an Introduction.* Cambridge: Cambridge University Press.

Some functional descriptions of present day English

Bloor, Thomas & Meriel Bloor (1995). *The Functional Analysis of English: a Hallidayan approach*. London: Edward Arnold.

Butt, David, Rhondda Fahey, Sue Spinks & Colin Yallop. (1995). *Using Functional Grammar: an explorer's guide*. Sydney: Macquarie University, NCELTR (National Centre for English Language Teaching and Research).

Downing, Angela & Philip Locke (1992). *A University Course in English Grammar*. New York: Prentice Hall International English Language Teaching.

Lock, Graham (1996). *Functional English Grammar: an introduction for second language teachers*. Cambridge: Cambridge University Press.

Martin, J. R., Christian Matthiessen & Clare Painter (1996). *Working with Functional Grammar: a workbook*. London, New York, Sydney & Auckland: Arnold.

Matthiessen, Christian (1995). *Lexicogrammatical Cartography: English systems*. Tokyo: International Language Sciences Publishers.

Thompson, Geoff (1996). *Introducing Functional Grammar*. London: Arnold.